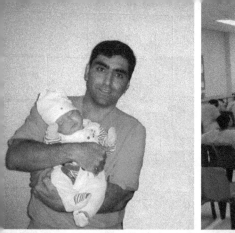
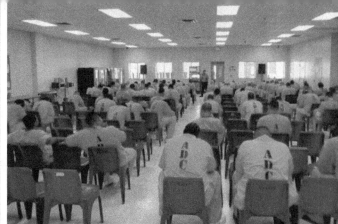

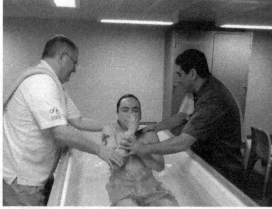

RESCUED
=== NOT ===
ARRESTED

BASED ON THE TRUE STORY OF ROGER MUNCHIAN

H. JOSEPH GAMMAGE

RESCUED
═ NOT ═
ARRESTED

BASED ON THE TRUE STORY OF ROGER MUNCHIAN

H. JOSEPH GAMMAGE

Based on the true story of Roger Munchian—broken through a life of drugs and violence—called, refined, and delivered by the mercy and eternal love of God.

Incidents, characters and timelines have been changed for dramatic purposes and to protect the innocent. Certain characters and events may be composites or entirely fictitious. Any resemblance to real persons, living or dead, is purely coincidental.

SPECIAL ACKNOWLEDGEMENTS

When God decided to build a nation, He called on Abraham. When He wanted to rescue His people from slavery, He called on Moses. When Jesus came to deliver the good news of salvation to the world, He called on 12 misfits. We are not meant to walk this journey alone, and the writing of this book did not come without the prayer and support of many humble warriors in Christ's army. We have so many to thank, yet the list to acknowledge them all would be endless. However, we would like to make special acknowledgements to the following who selflessly offered professional expertise as well as special prayer and support in the successful completion of this book:

Graphics and Design

Bonnie Terk............Book Jacket Design. Website and blog development
Ovadia Milan.........Author photo

Editorial Services

James Veihdeffer........................Manuscript Editing
Nancy Gillespie...........................Manuscript Editing
Pennie Gammage.......................Manuscript Editing
Becky Self...................................Manuscript Editing/Technical Expertise
Sandy Goudzward......................Manuscript Editing

Prayer and Support

Rescued Not Arrested Men's Group
Rescued Not Arrested Women's Group
Rescued Not Arrested Volunteer Team
Stetson Neighborhood Bible Study Group
Tricia Coloma
Rick and Janice Wappel
Laura Domocos
Larrie Fraley

And we would like to give an extra special thanks to all of our incarcerated brothers and sisters whose prayer and support from behind bars goes beyond what any of us will ever know in this lifetime. Thank you! Our hearts and prayers are always with you. May our Lord Jesus Christ continue to bless you and keep you safe in your front-line battle to reach His lost and bring glory to His Kingdom.

MINISTRY INFORMATION

Rescued Not Arrested Prison Ministry is here to reach the incarcerated youth, adults and their loved ones with the gospel, fulfilling Matthew 28:19-20, The Great Commission, in a unique way through ground-breaking methods that have never been used in the past. Additionally, RNA's prayer and desire is to challenge the universal churches on how to effectively embrace the formerly incarcerated including ex-felons and sex offenders, who are referred to as lepers of today's society.

For more information visit our website at www.rescuednotarrested.org or email Roger Munchian at rogermunchian@rescuednotarrested.org or by phone 602-647-8325. You can also reach us through fax at 602-276-0666 or through our mailing address at 500 E. Southern Avenue, Phoenix, AZ 85040.

God Bless.

PART I

God Breaks

PROLOGUE

Thursday, September 25, 1997
Phoenix, Arizona
1:35 a.m.

• •

He heard the faint sound of a phone ringing, the little chirp a cell phone makes. Frantic conversation; mumbled pleas; shuffling footsteps crunching through shattered glass. He couldn't see. Blind. A nylon canvas, slick and full of the stench of blood and vomit, covered his face. From somewhere behind him a beery smell arose, tinged in the stench of excrement released in fear. His weak hands, featherlike, pushed away the airbag, and the world returned as he stared out through the windshield, seeing the desert moon eclipsed in floating black rain clouds. Through the spider-webbed windshield, the world was a misty ruin.

He turned his head, thick in a Novocaine-like haze, and looked around the car, trying to speak, to call out to his passengers, but his words only bubbled on numbed lips. It didn't matter, though. The car was empty.

His dead hand slapped at the door handle, and he heard the door creak open on damaged hinges. He didn't recall unbuckling the seatbelt, but somehow he'd unclasped the latch with numb, nonexistent fingers. His legs were thick, hard to move as he dislodged himself from the crush of the steering column, and he felt his left foot sink into something slick as he stood.

He felt his body swaying, the desert wind toying with him. It all looked calm now. The wreckage in its final resting place; the early-morning air crisp, and quiet. His ears rang, blood pounding thick

1

through his head. His left eye suddenly stung, and a thick film distorted his vision. He wiped it clear and looked at his finger, slick with fresh blood.

A shard of glass dropped from the slivered rear window like a loose tooth falling from a beaten jaw and shattered on the pavement. Roger started staggering away from the wreckage but his left leg collapsed under him. He dropped to his knees and steadied himself on the glass-strewn pavement and looked up.

And that's when he saw her.

Alma, covered in blood, lay face down on the pavement, left arm stretched over the tangle of blood-matted hair as though reaching for him one last time. Her right arm was twisted in a ghastly way behind her back. He stared at the hourglass contour of her waist, hips he'd held on the dance floor only a few short hours ago, hips and legs that moved and gyrated with life, now unmoving, lifeless. He begged, somewhere in the back of his mind, begged for a sign of life. A breath. A slight movement of any sort. Even a moan of agony. He begged … who do you beg to? *Who?*

And God can stand by and watch.

God. Please!

He stood up, legs rubbery, the ground beneath him unsteady. He tried to speak, to call out her name. But his face was numb, dried blood fusing his lips together. A rancid taste erupted from his stomach, and an Absolut-and-orange juice burn seared in his throat. His head pitched forward, a splatter breaking the blood-tight seal of his lips, heaving uncontrollably from his sight-sickened stomach. He continued to heave miserably even after his stomach was empty, visions of her alive, visions of her dead, visions unceasing.

God! Please!

He fell against the crushed fender, pressing his cheek against the cold, mangled metal, eyes shut tight, trying to push away the nightmare, make it go away. A ghastly keening sound of anguish filled the air, and he realized that the ungodly sound was coming from him—uncontrollable sobs torturing the night air.

He opened his eyes and the nightmare worsened. Across the road, another of his three passengers, Marianna, lay amidst the twinkle of shattered glass, as though entombed on a diamond-studded bier along the side of the road. She seemed to be looking at him, an expression of bewilderment asking him *why*? *Why*? It seemed like only moments ago she was a radiant reflection in the rearview mirror, giggly and entangled in carnal backseat bliss with Jaxie Sosa—the deep-dimpled stud she'd snagged at the club tonight. *Why*?

God help me!

He wasn't sure how long he'd stood there. Almost mechanically, his hand dug into his pants pocket, soaked with blood, and pulled out his cell phone. The numbers were a blur when he looked down at the phone's cracked LCD, but they were three simple numbers.

"Nine-one-one," the voice came muffled, the phone engulfed in his bloody, trembling hand. "This is the nine-one-one operator," the voice repeated.

He lifted the phone to his ear. "I ..."

"Nine-one-one, I hear you sir. What's the emergency?"

His lips were thick, tongue swollen. "I was in an ... killed two people. Car accident." His slurred voice, raspy from the bile bubbling in his throat.

"Sir, where is your location?"

He looked around, the world a haze. The road stretched endlessly, north and south. Location. Where is your location?

"Sir?"

He shut his eyes tight, trying to remember, trying to see the road signs, where had he been? He saw the road racing toward him at a hundred-thirty miles per hour; felt Alma's touch; heard her laughter. Electrically alive only moments ago.

God help me!

"...you said there were fatalities?"

He nodded at the phone.

"Sir?'

"Help. Send help."

"Are you injured sir?"

He hung up. *Are you hurt? Why are you not hurt? You should be dead ... deserve to be dead...*

His eyes focused on the wreckage. Funny. Sitting there, a crumpled heap, slightly askew in its lane, but he noticed that it was pointed in the right direction, sitting in the northbound lane, heading due north. Had it not been crippled by the flattened tires and garroted undercarriage, he'd be driving now. He'd be driving home.

And he started to laugh. Not a giddy laugh, but a hopeless cackle; the kind of despondent snort that echoes off of the emptiness of forlorn toil, the mind's last tranquilizing defense against the onset of insanity. Home was only a few miles away. A few more miles and sweet Alma would be surrounded in downy luxury, trundled away and giggling in a king-sized playground, sparkling with life and surrounded in the zest of frivolity and carnal adventure.

Life.

Instead, she lay in a forever sleep on a cold, shard-covered asphalt slab, drenched in the violent butchering and harsh elements of a nightmare—mercifully at an end for her—the beginning of a nightmare for him.

And then he felt the tears begin to brim over his lower eyelids, cleansing them of the blood that had pooled from the unseen gash in his forehead. His body trembled, muscles tightening, squeezing broken and bruised appendages. Pain. A sign of life. A life he no longer deserved. At first they started as shuttering sobs, heavy with grief. Soon, his primal cries of anguish filled the air, billowing toward the heavens, and he dove back into the wreckage.

He saw his hands, running over the plush floorboards, the slice of glass shredding skin as he frantically searched under the seat. It was here somewhere. It was always there. The .9mm was a comfort he was never without. He kept it holstered. Extra magazine nearby. Always tucked under his front seat. Normally, for safety, to save his life.

Tonight, it would take his life.

A desperate pant filled the car. He couldn't find it. *Where did it go? There!* Something, in his hand. He pulled it out, and through a tear-filled glaze he recognized the signature green of a Heineken bottle.

Jaxie!

His third passenger.

Where's Jaxie?

The image of the last moment he'd seen Jaxie came to him, seeing the slack-jawed horror of his face in the rearview mirror, paste-white and turned toward the window, Heineken neck still touching his lips—watching in disbelief as the cement barrier wall stormed toward them.

He continued his frantic search, looking around the wreckage, seeing only hair, blood, and powdered carnage. Recessed in a fold of the passenger airbag, he saw the black handle of his briefcase. He grabbed it. The clasp had broken in its tumble from the back seat. He opened it. No gun. Insurance papers, contracts, a pen, legal pad, a wad of $100 bills from a recent drug transaction.

He looked at the legal pad and saw his bloody fingertips tear a piece of paper free. A note. Suicides always leave a note, right?

He staggered toward the front of the car, his stomach still wanting to vomit, life passing by in a blur. He spread the piece of paper on the crumpled hood, and stared at it, pen poised, ready to write … but write what? What should he say?

He'd be blowing his brains out. They'd need to identify him … identify the body. He began to scrawl …. HRACH MUNCHIAN …

Now what? There needs to be more to it than that. . He added his address. *Okay, so they know where you live … what? Something … say something …* His hand trembled as he wrote the only final thought that came to mind, the last words he'd leave this world with: *GOD HELP ME!*

He tucked the note under the damaged windshield wiper and looked up the road. There was no time to find the gun. Somewhere up there, halfway home, he knew there was a bridge, an overpass. If he could make it to the bridge, it would be over. The nightmare would be over.

He started to trot, his left leg searing, the rush of adrenaline and his destiny with death pushing him on.

1:48 a.m.
. . . .

High above, rays of moonlight penetrated the dissipating dark clouds, and Roger looked down through blood-tinged tears—tears searing his eyes like hot coals—and stared at his blood-speckled hands. Anguish overwhelmed him again, stopping his faltering gait as he dropped to the roadside, pebbles and rock sinking deep into the rotten plum-like flesh of his shattered knee. He felt his mummified lips break the blood-seal that had fused them as a tortured cry escaped from deep within him, filling the air with an inhuman wailing that could only have come from the deepest pit of Hell. Reliving the murder scene again—seeing his hands gripping the murder weapon—the car wheel—he felt the helplessness, a sense of toppling from a window and falling endlessly, never hitting the ground, swirling in his own eternal cries of desolation. In the torrent of cries, he recognized only one phrase, the same words he'd scrawled on his suicide note and left pinned to the mangled wreckage of the death scene:

God help me!

He couldn't erase the images from his mind, endlessly tormented by visions of the life he'd taken in a single, drunken moment. He could see it clearly now, as though watching as a voyeur, the very moment the screeching impact with the barrier wall turned the precision machinery that encapsulated the pride of his unquenchable thirst for wealth and power into a murder weapon—and erased two beautiful lives that had been knit together by God's own hands.

God help me!

The pavement around him suddenly came alive with the dance of blue and red strobes. Far behind him, he heard the garbled voices, orders and commands barked through intercoms and police mics. Looking back, his stomach sank at the sight of silhouettes exiting police cruisers and fanning out around the wreckage, assessing the scene. He got to his feet, pushing harder now, needing to get to the overpass before they discovered that the murderer was less than a mile away fleeing—not for his life—but for his certain death.

The blinding spotlight from above lit his path. He'd been in the spots of a police helicopter before and he'd given flight—wanting to survive. This time the lights were an aid to death, lighting the way through the tangle and rock of the desert floor as he clawed his way uphill to the overpass. He could feel the warm, desert air swirl around him, the chopper blades beating loose the desert floor, dust sticking to blood and sweat, blinding him in mud-caked tears. He felt his feet hit solid pavement. Wiping the muddy tears from his eyes, he saw the rail on the other side of the four lanes of the overpass. He was almost there. In moments, the nightmare would be over.

Garbled commands barked from a megaphone from above, commands to halt, arms above your head, on your knees sir, commands he knew too well. Orders to surrender. Not this time. This time, he would only surrender to death.

He pushed on, breaking into a gimping run, the searing pain from his pulverized knee forcing a ghastly cry that rose above the roar of chopper blades. To his left and right he heard screeching car tires, red and blue strobes of police lights animating the overpass, confusion swirling in more barking commands:

"Stay where you are!"

The overpass rail rushed toward him, blurred in a flood of fresh tears. He was almost there. Heart racing, breath coming in choking spasms—he heard the thud of an army of rushing feet pounding the pavement, charging toward him—but he knew they could not reach him in time.

"K-9 released!"

He heard the snarl of the beast behind him as he reached for the rail, his hands getting a firm grip as he readied himself to dive over. Razor-sharp pain shot through his leg as the canine sunk its fangs into his right calf. He felt his scream come from deep within his lungs, first a cry of pain, then a cry of desperation as the beast thrashed its head and pulled him free from his grip on the rail. In the blinding glare of spotlights and strobes, he saw the silhouettes rushing toward him. Dancing on his bad leg, pain bringing him to the brink of unconsciousness, his desperation to break free from the clench of the beast grew fierce. He reached for the rail and caught a firm grip and pulled, dragging the snarling beast along. He'd take the mutt over with him if that's what it took.

"Stay where you are!"

"Freeze!"

They were within reach now. He could hear the clank of their buckles, the rattle of their cuffs and could smell their BO—ripened in the stress of the day's shift—mixing in the swirl from the chopper hovering above. He yanked his foot hard, leaving a chunk of his own flesh dripping from the snarling jowls of the K-9—but he was free. He heard the desperate cry of the hunters about to lose their quarry as he felt his legs fly into the air. The sharp rocks, dotted in the dried sage and spiked foliage of the desert floor below, glowed in the police chopper's spotlights and rushed toward him as he went over the rail.

It was all over.

God help me! God help me!

CHAPTER ONE

Saturday, June 3, 1989
Los Angeles
6:25 a.m.

· ·

Hrach "Roger" Munchian was getting ready to work his Saturday morning shift at Security Pacific Bank when he heard his pager go off. With the insane demand for quality weed, hot bumps, and jacked rides, a buzzing pager was better than a ringing cash register. Roger could get anything, really fast, and at a good price. And he had all the right connections: Crips, Bloods, Armenian Power, Mexican Mafia. They all had his digits. They all knew he was a guy who could get them what they wanted. He was well connected to top L.A. area dope suppliers like Chico Martinez who normally wouldn't give a young punk like him the time of day but saw something in him that told him the kid had a future.

Roger hadn't been scheduled to work this morning, but one of his fellow tellers had called in, and he grabbed the shift because he needed the money. He was still in hock twenty-two hundred bucks to his parents for the bail money they'd recently thrown to spring him from the L.A. County lock up. He did have a serious wad of cash in his sock drawer, most of it coming courtesy of the owners of one Jag and one Audie who'd been kind enough to make a roadside donation to him off Sunset Boulevard the other night, but he didn't feel right paying his parents back with money he'd gotten from the point of his Bulldog .38 and his charming smile. He'd gotten $500 a pop for each of the luxury vehicles he'd driven straight from the Boulevard to his favorite chop shop. All in a day's pay.

The arrest happened up in Burbank. He was a straight A student, sitting on an academic scholarship to Cal State, L.A., and it all went down on April 24th, just a month before high school graduation. It was his first beef, and he had no idea that it was just the beginning of an eight-year journey that would end at the door of Death Row.

He'd had a perfect two-year stretch before the misstep in disconnecting a car alarm drew him his first sheet and revealed a hidden life beneath the "model student" veneer. Along with his stellar academic record, he was also a varsity jock and a second-chair violinist with the John Marshall High School orchestra. Fast on his feet as a running back, he'd made the first string by his sophomore year. But that was also the year that his teammate, Ernesto Sanchez, a third-stringer with lungs baked from his two pack-a-day Newport habit, introduced him to his first toke of weed. Man, it felt good. One toke restored a self-esteem that had been shattered by the injustice of growing up as an inner-city Armenian immigrant. His Dad, Andranik, had learned the survival virtues of vodka in the Siberian gulags, the bottle now his only version of the American Dream. His mother picked up work here and there, keeping minimal food on the table for Roger and his sister. But things got really good when Roger learned the rewards of moving hot goods and brokering dope. He hooked up with the right people and learned the value of packing armor and being effective with the hardware. With the snub nose Bulldog or his Smithie .357, he could jack a car in seconds for a quick $500 turn. For night shift duty, he always kept a couple of screwdrivers handy and a pocket full of sparkplugs. Spot a car loaded with nice bumps, shatter a spark plug on the pavement and chuck a shard of the ceramic casing at the car window, and the window implodes. With a reliable partner standing at the front bumper, he could reach in, pop the hood, and get the alarm wires snipped before the first chirp and have the stereo out in seconds.

Two years without arrest. Down the toilet now because he'd gotten careless and let that idiot Ernesto jack up his deal. The idiot, standing there in front of the hood, too jagged on weed to figure out which end of the wire snips to use, let the car alarm sound too long as Roger worked the stereo from the dash. The stone-headed carelessness drew heat, and now he was a straight-A student, varsity football player with a full-ride scholarship to Cal State—with a record.

He walked over to the marred nightstand next to his unmade bed and looked at the number on the pager. It wasn't one he recognized. Always a good sign. It usually meant a new customer.

Wearing his slacks and white undershirt, he walked into the kitchen and dialed the number.

"We got unfinished business, onion."

Roger recognized the voice immediately. He went by the street name of Hondo—a rogue member of the Armenian Power street gang. Although Hondo ran with an Armenian gang, he wasn't one of them. He shared their gang colors—not their ethnicity. He was a Euro white trash punk who didn't fit in anywhere else. AP was an emerging L.A. gang, not quite with the rep of the Crips or Bloods, but their current leader, Boxer, was determined to get them into the major leagues fast. Roger had grown up with most of them, the guys immigrating at the same time Roger's family had come over, the experiences of poverty and broken homes pushing them into the acceptance of the gangster world. The more lethal ones, like Boxer, had come over later, the scars of war-torn ugliness intensifying their ruthlessness. Boxer allowed hybrids like Hondo in to add to the AP numbers. Hondo figured his affiliation with the AP gave him license to use the racial barb for Armenian immigrant, 'onion' whenever he wanted.

The "unfinished business" that Hondo spoke of was the fact that Roger had dropped him hard a week before graduation. It went down on the last day of school, Hondo and his AP flunkies sitting in their usual spot outside school grounds, Hondo entertaining his homies by picking on a squat kid, a fellow Armenian named Ara. Roger felt compelled to step into the gap, standing in for Ara, and it was over in two hits. Roger hitting Hondo, Hondo hitting the pavement. Roger ended his high school career a hero, standing up for a fellow Armenian and dropping a gangland punk with barely an effort.

Now Hondo wanted to even the score.

"Hondo! You never call. You never write. It feels like it's been simply forever! So, tell me, how's the wife and kids? You get that halitosis under control yet?"

"Halitosis?"

"Bad breath, moron. Do I constantly have to explain these jokes to you Hond'?"

"You got a lucky shot in, onion. That don't sit so good with me."

"You know, I only let my friends call me onion. And even then I ain't so sure I like it."

"You wanna do something about it? You know where we hang. Tonight, onion. Don't bring no homies. You and me. No blades. No irons. Skin on skin, hom'. You got it?"

"Name the time."

"Eight o'clock. Sharp."

"Sounds good. I have an eight-fifteen appointment. Five minutes to finish you off and ten to get to where I need to be."

"You know what I hate about you, onion? You got one eyebrow. Stretches across your whole forehead. I'm gonna separate that for you."

Hondo hung up.

Hollywood Boulevard
7:50 p.m.
· ·

The giant hot dog, loaded up with oversized faux cubes representing onions, rested on top of Red's Hot Dogs, a shack-like drive-in on the corner of Hollywood and Western. A graffiti-etched, bulletproof Plexiglas wall surrounded the drive-in's patio with a sign that said, "Parking in Rear," which Roger did. Across the street was the Texaco gas station the AP had claimed as its turf.

You know where we hang.

Roger stared at the Bulldog .38 resting on the passenger seat of his Camaro. *No blades. No irons. Just skin on skin.* But instinct told him to pack. He was heading straight for AP territory. But there was honor at stake. His word was his bond and he'd agreed to no irons.

He slid the Bulldog under the front seat and got out. A warm June breeze blew in and swirled a crumpled section of newspaper and a discarded paper cup around his feet. Tucking his thumbs into his jeans' pockets, he walked to the corner. The Texaco gas station was aglow in harsh red and white neon. Around the corner of the building, Roger could see the shadows of AP milling around. He couldn't pick Hondo out from the group, but he did spot the Low Rider, the one Hondo always got chauffeured around in by a flunky named Detox, parked in its usual spot. Detox, the ride's owner, was leaning against the hood, sucking from a bottle wrapped in a crumpled paper sack.

Roger looked at his watch. Straight up 8 o'clock.

Detox was the first to spot him. Leaving his wrapped bottle on the hood, he pushed away from the car, brushing imaginary crumbs from his hands, then held them out, giving Roger an inviting come-on-in sign with a smile on his face that told Roger he shouldn't have left the Bulldog behind.

"Hey Boxer!" Detox shouted. "We got company!"

The AP's attention turned to Roger as he crossed the street, and they moved in unison, forming a horseshoe around him as he walked into the parking lot. At the tip of the horseshoe stood Boxer, meaty arms folded, gothic-lettered AP tattoos covering arms thick as tree trunks.

"You packin', little man?" Boxer said.

"I'm here to see Hondo."

"Hondo?" Roger felt his heart sink as he watched Boxer looked around in mock curiosity. "I don't see no Hondo around here. You got an appointment?"

Roger felt the horseshoe tightening and he knew he was in trouble. The first blows came from behind, a steely array of knuckles into the lower ribs, propelling him into the oncoming kick that indented a Nike swoosh into his forehead. He felt his heart race, his adrenaline surge, standing his ground as they closed in fast, Roger desperately swinging, blocking, crouching, protecting vital organs as they converged on him like a rabid pack of jackals tearing at prey. He heard jaws crack, teeth gnash, ribs pop, and bellies heave as he swung hard and fast at anything that came close. But his efforts only intensified their savage attack.

Exhausted, unable to lift his arms, he dropped first to his knees, then several blows to the head and chest dropped him into a fetal position. The blows came endlessly, the frenzy pulverizing bone, tearing skin, crushing internal organs. Roger felt the world around him fading.

Then it stopped abruptly.

He sensed someone kneel down next to him, grabbing a fist full of his hair and yanking his head back, getting his full attention. Through the one eye not yet swollen shut, Roger looked through a stringy web of blood and pus and recognized the blurred apparition of Hondo, staring down at him with a yellow, Cheshire grin. He heard a familiar click and saw the bright parking lot lights glint off the blade, followed by the feeble plea of his own voice saying 'no' as the razor edge started down toward his face.

"I'm gonna separate that one eyebrow for you now, onion. Just like I promised."

"Slice him head to groin, Hondo!" Boxer's voice came from the distance, booming like the voice of God.

The blade came down slowly, and he felt the tip pierce his forehead, right between the eyes, as Hondo promised.

In the distance, police sirens grew louder, approaching fast.

"Drop it Hondo—let's move out!" Boxer's order becoming a voice of salvation.

In the distance, the blue and red flash of police strobes danced off the buildings, and he heard Hondo's blade click shut.

"You got lucky this time, onion." Hondo bending down close to Roger's ear, his fermented breath ripe and combustible.

The AP scattered. Roger got to his feet and staggered toward his car. His legs buckled and he collapsed in the middle of Hollywood Boulevard, cars careening around the bloody mess lying in the street. Horns blaring, tires screeching, headlights blinding, he crawled the rest of the way to his car, leaving streaks of blood that looked like crimson highway lines painted by a drunken road crew. He managed to yank his car door open, pulling himself behind the wheel as a black-and-white's tires screeched by, turning into the Texaco station, siren whaling and lights spinning. Roger pulled the Camaro into gear and wheeled it into the street, turning left at the light and driving away as another black-and-white passed him coming from the opposite direction. Through his one good eye, Roger watched the police cruiser fade in the rearview mirror.

He was only a few miles from home. Sitting in a deepening pool of his own blood, he was sure he wouldn't make it.

CHAPTER TWO

He could not quench his thirst for revenge—and it only intensified with time. Roger's hatred festered as he spent the rest of the summer healing from the stripes Hondo and his band of flunkies had inflicted. It had taken well over a month before the pulpy veil over his left eye receded, and his chest, back, and arms remained a blistered indigo mass for several weeks. Three broken ribs forced choked agony with every breath.

Despite making necessary preparations to start his first semester at Cal State in September, revenge absorbed his every thought for the rest of the summer. He registered for his classes, bought his books, organized his supplies—and loaded his Uzi. Keeping the automatic weapon tucked under the front seat of his car, he'd detour by the Texaco station nightly after classes, Uzi in his lap, ready to fill Hondo full of .9 mm holes, but he could never zero in on Hondo in the group.

On a crisp October evening, the full moon high over Hollywood Hills, he was sitting with Ernesto in the bed of Ernesto's pickup truck. Roger's ribs had healed enough so that he could get a decent toke on the thick joint Ernesto had rolled.

"Your offer still good?" he asked, passing the joint back to Ernesto.

"What's that?" Ernesto's drug-addled mind had already forgotten the conversation they'd had less than ten minutes ago. "What offer?"

Roger pulled a toke slowly into his lungs and let the smoke absorb, the dope going to his head real nice. Offering the joint back to Ernesto and said, "Like I was just telling you, moron. I need some guys. You know, to back me."

Ernesto took the joint, shaking his head. "Oh. The Hondo thing. Wow, man."

"Yeah, wow, man."

"Dude, like, wow man."

"Wow man what? Spit it out, moron."

"Wow, man. Don't you, like, think it's over now?"

"Hondo and me, we ain't square yet. I just need some guys behind me so I can get close enough to him to put one between his eyes." He watched Ernesto's bloodshot eyes focus on the healing slit where Hondo had planted the tip of the switchblade.

"You look like an Indian," Ernesto said. "You know. The dot on their forehead. Spots for dots."

"You gonna back me on this, or do I gotta go somewhere else?"

Ernesto nodded his head and said, "Okay. Yeah. Don't worry. Ernesto's got your back on this one. I'll get some guys."

Saturday, October 21, 1989

• •

Ernesto got some guys, rounding up six members of The White Fence, an L.A Chicano gang run by a hulking gold-toothed Mexican named Oso. They were tipping bottles and blowing smoke outside Ernesto's truck as Roger pulled up in his Camaro.

"We can get 'em all, man!" A banger named Loco shouted, the guy all jagged up on blow tonight, the white powder snorting out of his nostrils like smoke from a crazed dragon. He was trouble, and Roger didn't want him along, but he had no choice. He needed the numbers.

Loco pulled a .22-caliber pistol from his jacket. "I can pop them easy, man. We blaze through and cut 'em down."

"That's not the way it's gonna happen," Roger said. "I just need some iron backing me so I can pop Hondo. But no one gets capped till Hondo hits the pavement, understood?"

Loco said, "No, man! AP goes down tonight! All of them! Down, man!"

He got in Loco's face. "You pop off one round, and I sink you in the pavement next. We clear on this?"

Oso's second lieutenant, El Lagarto, The Lizard, stepped forward. His narrow head sat perched on top of a thin, vein-striped neck and his eyes popped out of deep sockets, neither one looking directly at you. "Don't worry about it, onion. Like you said, it's your gig. It's all understood. But you own it, holmes. Anything goes wrong, I hold you accountable."

They loaded up. He got into his Camaro, and The White Fence loaded into the bed of Ernesto's truck.

Ahead, he saw the glow of the Texaco sign as he turned onto Hollywood Boulevard. Adrenaline surged. Wearing his floor-length trench coat, his Savage .12 gauge shotgun, sawed off at a manageable 18 inches, made him feel invincible the way it rested within reach inside the flap, five deer slugs in the pipe. Rage consumed him to the point of irrationality when he spotted the Low Rider. The sound of his squealing tires and the smell of burning rubber turned his rage lethal as he roared into the parking lot. The AP reacted fast, taking position as he jumped from the Camaro. Their eyes suddenly squinted, Ernesto's high-beams throwing a high-noon blaze as his truck careened into the lot and screeched to a halt. The White Fence poured from the truck bed. Roger took the point, The White Fence falling in behind him, fanning out, making their numbers look greater. Hearing Loco's high-pitched, nervous giggles behind him, he got a sick feeling in his stomach, sensing that the amateur hour was about to get him killed.

Blowing the feeling off, he shouted, "Where's Hondo?"

Keeping both hands at his sides, flap of his overcoat open, he knew he'd have less than a second to pull the trigger before an armory of AP lead blazed his way.

Boxer wasn't there, which was a good thing. This kept the AP drunk and in disarray.

"Right here, onion!"

AP colors separated in a wake of confusion as Hondo pushed his way through. Their eyes locked, Roger's hand moving as deft as a trained gunfighter, and a moment of understanding reflected in the nut-ball's eyes, realizing that he was about to have his head separated from his shoulders. Primed and ready when Hondo reached for the gun tucked behind his back, Roger pulled the Savage, pointing it skyward as he pumped it ready for action before the moonlight made its first glint off Hondo's steel.

Roger still had the barrel pointing high, not yet aimed at Hondo when it happened. From behind, Loco's hiccupping giggle went insane, and out of the corner of his eye, Loco was a blur, charging for the AP, gun blazing.

In a roar of gunfire and the stinging stench of cordite, Roger froze, gun barrel still pointing heavenward. He watched stunned as Hondo's body twitched and convulsed in the rip of lead before going down.

Gunfire roared from behind, orange muzzle flashes animating the graffiti painted on the side of the Texaco building. With gunfire now coming from both directions, Roger dove over the hood of his car, hearing screams and war cries rise over the roar of gunplay.

Looking over the hood, Roger watched a spray of lead stop Loco in his tracks, and he stood there, his giggle turning into a high-pitched squeal as bullets ripped his body apart, reminding Roger of that scene from *Scarface*, Tony Montana standing on top of the world, bullets shredding him, refusing to go down.

The shooting stopped, scrambling bodies mere silhouettes in the red haze of smoke and neon, fleeing in every direction. From somewhere behind the cordite mist, he heard shouting, authoritative voices barking commands, but they were distorted by the metallic ring roaring in his ears.

A bloody apparition emerged through the haze, arms outstretched, staggering disjointedly toward him. Loco's eyes, glazed and dead-white, pleaded for help as a red gore bubbled past his lips, his white T-shirt slick with blood. Collapsing, he threw his arms over Roger's shoulders, the dying kid's dead weight nearly pulling him to the pavement.

Car tires squealed. Out of the corner of his eye, he caught the tail end of Ernesto's pickup disappearing from the parking lot, followed by a chorus of squealing tires and confused shouts. As the smell of melting rubber overpowered the stench of cordite, chrome raced past him and the flash of headlights painted Hollywood Boulevard, racing engines converging in a full-throttled roar off surrounding buildings and concrete.

Dragging Loco to the Camaro, he tumbled him into the passenger seat and tossed the Savage into the back seat. Sliding behind the wheel, he punched the accelerator and got out of there.

He sped three blocks at 80 mph before slowing down. The ringing in his ears cleared, and for the first time he heard the choked gurgle coming from Loco, the kid's chest heaving, his lungs fighting for breath, his mouth working up and down with every labored gasp, his eyes pleading, but fading.

"You stupid, stupid—*stupid hack!*" Roger slapped at the steering wheel, looking ahead at the road. Somewhere there was a hospital. A hospital nearby. Where? He knew … think clearly. *Think!* "You *hack!* What were you *thinking!* Look at you. Just *look* at you!"

He wasn't sure how he'd gotten there, but up ahead he saw the sign aglow in the words "EMERGENCY." He pulled into the half-circle drive in front of the Emergency Room doors and hopped out. The triage nurse's eyes widened as he came barreling through the door. She picked up a phone and called for help, then her eyes went from shock to confusion as Roger sat the bloody patient in a seat and ran back out the door.

"You're on your own, you dumb, stupid, crazy plebe!" Roger said into the rearview mirror as the hospital faded away in the distance.

The hours passed slowly. He'd gone to a self-serve car wash and cleaned Loco's blood off of the passenger seat. His pager had gone off several times, each call from Ernesto, with the tag 9-1-1. Their signal: stay away. Stay away as long as you can.

He finally arrived home just before midnight. Turning onto his street, a flash of headlights in his review mirror caused him to squint. As he rolled to a stop in front of his apartment, the vehicle pulled in behind him. He reached back and grabbed the Savage, pointed it at the door, finger on the trigger, until he recognized the approaching silhouette as Ernesto.

"Man, you gotta get out. You gotta go now, Rog'!"

"What happened?"

"Word from the hospital. Loco is dead. *Dead*, man! Word got to Oso. The White Fence. They're holding *you* responsible!"

But you own it, holmes.

Ernesto said, "Loco took a bullet meant for you. El Lagarto told Oso the gig was yours. They've been on me all night, asking me where you lay your head. They're everywhere tonight, looking for your car. And the

AP—man, Hondo, he'll hunt down your crib. It's only a matter of time before they find you!"

"I saw Hondo go down."

"Man, it's all a mess! We don't know who went down. Just that Loco's gone, man. And now you got Oso and Boxer tagging a price on your bean. Man, Rog', what are you gonna *do*?!"

There was shock on their faces, but no surprise. Things added up quickly for his parents. His Dad sobered up quickly as Roger gave them a story he thought they'd believe, and that there was no time for debate. He had to go. He had to go tonight. If he stayed, if he didn't leave now— he would be dead.

"I'm going with you." The sober words from his father shocked him.

"Dad, no."

"I'm going, Hrach. In Armenia, it's tradition. The father follows the son. Hrach, we do this together." In the spirit of Armenian tradition. Like vodka. Always with tradition.

"Where?" His mother's voice cracked with tears. "Where you go?"

"I don't know, Mama. All I know is we can't stay here. We can't stay."

They loaded his Dad's car with what they could and took the Camaro to his cousin's and hid it in the garage. He was always careful to never let any of the homies know where he laid his head, but they knew the black Camaro. They'd be looking for it, and he knew that he'd have to hock it as soon as possible. He could no longer have anything to do with his ride. He could no longer have anything to do with his life in L.A.

They were soon heading eastbound on the I-10 in his father's car. As they hit the peak of a hill, he looked up in the rearview mirror, saw the last twinkle of L.A. lights vanish in a black void. He was still pumped and full of adrenaline. He wasn't sure how far it would carry him. Long enough, he hoped, to get far away from that place.

Far away.

CHAPTER THREE

Phoenix
May 1990

• •

Claudia Reynolds' neck was basically a windpipe sheathed in a wrinkled, leathery swatch of skin so thin that he could practically see the smoke from the Virginia Slim flow down into her lungs as she sucked away at the cancer stick, leaving chunky lipstick on the butt. Her straw-like hair, streaked silvery-gray, was pulled into a bun so tight her thin eyebrows stretched halfway up her wrinkled forehead. The doily fringed blouse she wore was cut too low, dipping deep into her sunken cleavage, giving her chest the look of spoiled cottage cheese. She was not the woman Roger imagined when he'd first seen the sign tacked to a telephone pole saying: "Business For Sale. Easy Entry—Great Potential. Call Claudia Reynolds at 602…"

Phoenix was as far as he and his father had made it after fleeing L.A. His father had been sound asleep in the passenger seat when the early dawn light appeared over the Phoenix Valley mountain ranges. Roger pulled off the I-10 for gas and nearly fell asleep filling the tank. Spotting a Motel 6 across the street, he decided that this was as far as he could go.

He made friends fast, finding his type of peeps again: the party crowd, the gang bangers, fast chicks, hot cars. With plenty of chrome, trim, dope and suds available along the cruise on Central Avenue, his weekend social calendar was always booked with carnal delight. Despite the temptation around him to start dealing again, he played it straight. The criminal life had nearly gotten him killed. The closest he'd come to jumping back into the game was when a guy named Frankie Richmond, a member of a gang of homies calling themselves Dog Town, approached him one night at a desert party, sensing Roger was a guy who could get things. Frankie got right to it, letting him know that he was in the market for a five-kilo load of weed to mix into Primo—weed laced with coke. Roger knew he could pull that kind of weight together fast, and with high quality dope. But he turned Frankie down, souring his relationship with him in a way that would come back to bite him soon enough.

His mother had moved out from L.A. and they'd settled into a house in the West Valley. Roger had gotten himself into a new set of wheels, a Mustang convertible. After getting it insured, he was pulling out of the parking lot of the small, unimpressive building that housed West Side Insurance and that's when he saw Claudia's sign, tacked to the telephone pole, advertising a business for sale.

He figured getting his family into this "easy entry, great potential" gig, would make him a businessman again—a legitimate one this time. And he knew he needed something legit—especially with guys like Frankie Richmond around, guys with money and always in the need for the kind of score that could easily suck him back into a business that left him with a hefty price on his bean back in L.A.

So he dialed Miss Claudia Reynolds' digits.

The Frankie Richmond thing would play out in due time, he sensed it, but was not going to worry about it tonight. Tonight was the night to finally get legit. He could feel goose-bumps rise up and down his back as they sat there at the kitchen table, Claudia Reynolds shuffling the paperwork around, real business papers, the kind written and reviewed by lawyers and such. Virginia Slim stuck to her upper lip in thick, caked lipstick, she gave each important document her squinty-eyed review through the chained specs teetering on the end of her nose before sliding it over for her new buyers to review.

Claudia Reynolds' nail-polish-chipped fingers picked up another piece of paper from the stack in front of her. She examined it for a moment, stream of smoke seeping from her narrow lips and said,

"Now this is a stand'ud agreement on the payoff of the land contract."
She spoke with a heavy New York accent, and her voice sounded like
someone had turned her larynx into a Pez dispenser and loaded it with
pebbles. "The payment is three th-aw-sand a month, as we discussed,
you see, and I deduct what's left after interest from the principal …
uh … you following this, dearie?" She looked over at his mother, who sat
staring blankly at the papers, wringing her hands. His father, Andranik,
had the same uncertain look in his eyes.

Roger excused himself to Claudia and spoke to his parents in
Armenian, embarrassed at their misunderstanding. "It's called a land
contract. We can't qualify for a business loan, so she is going to be our
bank."

His mother said, "But Hrach, the monthly payment, it's so much."

He showed her the balance sheets and pointed to the revenue
number. "Mama, look. Choo-Choo's Deli is nicely located right in the
middle of an office complex. Like Miss Reynolds said, it attracts a great
breakfast and lunch crowd since there's not much else around there.
Now, I can work mornings there to keep the cost of hiring anyone down.
And look at the revenue number … it's bringing in almost twice the cost
of our payment. We'll have plenty left over. We can even make extra
payments to pay off the balance."

He could sense Claudia was getting impatient. "I'll need you to sign
and initial that, please."

She was pushy and excessively eager to take her check and get the
deal closed. He tried to review all of her paperwork, but she would
quickly jump in at each page he turned to and explain what it meant.
Then again, Roger wasn't in the mood for fine print. He wanted this
done. Owning a business would make them a fortune. He was tired of
scraping by. He knew they could do better.

He grabbed the paper work and eagerly signed and initialed.
Reluctantly, his mother and father followed suit, and he slid the certified
check for twenty grand, his parents' life savings, over to Claudia's eagerly
awaiting claw.

Her lips parted into a yellow-toothed smile and she held out her
bony hand for anyone to take. Roger reached out and she grabbed his
hand in a clammy grip. It was like shaking hands with a corpse.

"Let me be the first to congratulate," she rasped, "the new owners of Choo-Choo's Deli. Payment is due the first of every month, and I charge a ten percent late fee for every five days past due."

He was averaging three hours of sleep a night. The numbers at the Deli for the first month looked horrible. After operating expenses, Choo-Choo's fell over two grand short, and Roger had to pick up extra hours at his night job at UPS to make up for the shortfall. The numbers got even worse the following month, and he ended up borrowing on his parents' credit cards to make the payment.

The little chime on the deli's door rang and Fernando Nunez pushed his way through, wearing his flannel shirt, buttoned up out-of-line, shirttails hanging out and uneven, the uniform of his homies, the Hollywood 39. He moved with that crooked saunter that he thought made him look tougher than he was. He was straw-thin, topping six-two in his soiled Converse high-tops. He fancied himself a master at hoops and hung heavy with the brothers, earning him the nickname "*Negra Nunez*".

Roger was assembling a pastrami sandwich and was in a foul mood.

"Man, this place is a morgue," Fernando said, plopping down at a table nearest the counter. Fernando pulled a pack of Marlboros from where he had them rolled in the cut sleeve and blazed up, saying, "Where you keep the bodies? Freezer in the back?"

"Not in the mood, Fernando."

He sacked the sandwich with a bag of chips and tossed it on the counter.

"I was talkin' to my boy 'Nulfo. Man, he thinks you been had on this place."

Arnulfo DeGarcia. They called him Nulfo. Some hotshot who started hanging around a lot lately down on the Central Avenue cruise strip. A guy thinking he's something else because he had a few featherweight boxing titles behind him. The guy had an angle, the overly nice-nice way he treated Roger, asking questions all the time—too many questions. Roger didn't trust him. But he knew the guy was smart, and somehow, in the back of his mind, he knew he could use him someday.

"What does 'Nulfo know about running a business?"

Fernando took a long hit off of his cigarette. "All I'm sayin' is he figures this old bat sees a family of onions fresh off the boat who don't know no better, you sell 'em a lemon. Happens all the time."

"Armenians don't come across on boats, moron. Last boat in Armenia was Noah's oversized ark." Then he said, "'Nulfo's trouble and you know it."

"Hey, he'll hook you up real nice, you wanna get back in the game. The guy can read a bail of weed, that's for sure. A quick look and whiff, and he can tell you what's in the middle."

The door chimed and a portly man in a business suit, sweating from the Arizona heat and his own bulk, walked in. He paid for his carryout and left.

"There's your lunch rush," Fernando said.

"Shut up."

Fernando stood up and re-rolled his cigarettes back into his sleeve. "I gotta bolt." He looked around the empty deli, shaking his head. "You oughta get a lawyer to check the chick out who sold you this joint. Man, I think she saw you comin'."

Roger suddenly realized rent was almost past due, and if he was late, Miss Reynolds was going to hit them with a ten percent late fee. He started thinking about Frankie Richmond, wondering what kind of deal Frankie was open for this month. Roger knew that in just a few quick pops, he could get his family out of this hole. Just a couple of quick deals, that's all he needed.

He thought of Arnulfo. Yeah, Arnulfo was smart. He was a guy to watch. He was the kind of guy who could get him back in the game.

Saturday, November 17, 1990
7:25 a.m.

• •

His working hours were exhausting. He needed sleep. He needed it bad.

His eyes drooped heavy as he drove northbound on I-17 on his way home from his graveyard shift at UPS, driving another new vehicle, this one a gray Nissan pickup that he'd bought after flipping his Mustang ragtop in the desert just outside Quartzite back in April.

The accident with the Mustang happened during one of his weekly early morning runs back to L.A. with a buddy. Despite the price on his head, he continued his studies at Cal State, driving back to L.A. every week, sticking close to campus to avoid the threat of the 22-caliber headache that awaited him in his old neighborhood. Because of the fatigue from his insane hours working graveyard at UPS, keeping up with business at Choo Choo's, and his studies, he let the dude drive while he caught some shuteye in the passenger seat. But the idiot had dozed off and ran the Mustang up the highway embankment. After cutting them loose with the Jaws of Life, rescuers couldn't figure out how they'd possibly survived, telling them they should have been decapitated, rolling over a ragtop like that and skidding upside down nearly fifty yards across the harsh desert ground.

Now he looked up at the exit sign, and could barely make out "Exit 204." The speedometer was a blur, the fuzzy needle bouncing along a tick past 80. When his burning eyes turned back to the road, the Ford F-150 in the middle lane came at him fast. He twisted the wheel, but not in time. His head slammed into the steering wheel on impact with the Ford, and he felt his truck leave the road as he watched the F-150 spin 180 degrees and slide into a hard skid, watching blue smoke pour from its undercarriage as it careened across two lanes of traffic, coming to a rocking halt in the left emergency lane. Roger felt his truck twist in the air. He looked out the windshield and saw the wall coming at him fast and squeezed his eyes shut tight, bracing for the impact, thinking it would be a miracle for a guy to survive two such deadly crashes in a row.

Wesley, driving along the I-17 in his newly detailed Ford F-150, felt that inevitable sense of helplessness as he looked up in his rearview mirror and saw the grill of a gray Nissan pickup roaring up on him real fast. His mind told him to speed up, get out of the way, but his brain shut down the second his head slammed hard into the headrest, the Nissan barreling hard into his rear. His head rattled off the driver's side window, the truck spinning, hearing his tires screech across two lanes of traffic, horns blowing, traffic weaving. Next thing he knew, he was staring out the windshield watching the whole show, hearing himself say, "Whoa!", as he watched the way that the Nissan left the road, spinning in the air, crashing through the thick wire fence atop the barrier. Blue smoke from his shredded tires obscured his view momentarily, but not before he saw the body fly through the windshield as the Nissan skidded across the service drive on the other side of the barrier wall, and he remembered thinking, 'That dude is dead. How am I going to collect insurance from a dead guy?'

CHAPTER FOUR

Jim McFadden, owner of Westside Insurance, was sitting at his desk rereading the accident report. He looked up at the guy who'd offered to help his customer. The customer, Pablo Cabrera, had come in really ticked off about some small item in his policy, and he didn't speak English. McFadden's bilingual agent was out sick today and this guy, Roger, all banged up and cut from the accident, offered to step in and explain things. Roger spoke Spanish fluently and had a way about him that put Pablo at ease. Roger and Pablo were sitting at the small, cluttered table in his office, Roger going through the policy, answering his questions like a pro.

In the meantime, as Jim read through the accident report again, he couldn't believe this Roger guy had survived and was sitting here in his office now, making a claim as though he'd been bumped by someone's Aunt Tilly in a grocery store parking lot. Accompanying the report were pictures of the scene, the gray Nissan a mangled mass of metal, wheels turned heavenward, lying in the middle of the I-17 service road. Debris that had flown from the truck as it had spun in the air lay scattered all over the road: papers, a duffle bag, crumpled fast-food sacks, a security guard uniform.

And guns. Lots of guns.

There was the hole in the windshield through which Roger had been ejected. A clean hole. Unlike he'd ever seen—at least, unlike he'd ever seen anyone survive.

There was laughter over at the table now and Jim looked up and saw Roger and Pablo shaking hands. Pablo stood and gave Jim a gold-banded, toothy smile, bowing gratefully and saying, *"Gracias, gracias."*

Roger slowly got up from the table and limped over, dropping himself into the creaking wooden chair in front of the desk.

"Well, you certainly totaled it," McFadden told Roger after Pablo left.

McFadden looked at the pictures again. The truck had bounced up the slope of the barrier wall, pivoted into the air, and crashed through the mesh fencing on top of the highway wall. The fencing was only about twenty-five yards in length. After that, the barrier was solid concrete, rising high in the slope of the exit ramp.

He said to Roger, "You got guardian angels watching over you or something?" He pointed at the picture. "You went through this fencing. Had you hit that vehicle a split second sooner, you woulda hit solid wall and we'd still be peeling what was left of you out of nothin' more than a crushed tin can."

Roger was silent while McFadden finished figuring the claim. It wasn't good news. He could see Roger starting to tremble, visibly becoming enraged. McFadden didn't know how this was going to play out. This was a guy who packed serious armor and didn't look like the kind of guy you wanted to deal with when things weren't going his way. Then he got an idea.

"Roger," he said, thinking of the way he handled Pablo. "Listen. I want to expand my business. I only have this one office, but because of this location, most of my clients here are Hispanic. I got a guy who's usually here to help with customers like Pablo, the ones who don't speak English. But he's unreliable. Look, maybe I can offset some things in your claim if you come and work for me here in this office." He grinned and chuckled to lighten the mood a bit. "Hey, the way you drive, maybe the insurance business is for you."

CHAPTER FIVE

Thursday, December 20, 1990
Phoenix

• •

Roger was amazed by the way the lawyer's bulging neck swallowed his shirt collar whole—necktie and all. Looking through spectacles resting on the tip of his rosacea-splotched nose, the high-priced ambulance chaser stared down at the papers he'd brought, grunting as he flipped through them, his thick, meaty fingers tapping the surface of the mahogany desk. Through the gold-tinted windows behind the desk, a mid-December haze hung over downtown Phoenix, the busy streets of Phoenix twenty-three stories below.

The lawyer grunted one last time as he finished the stack of financials and agreements, shaking his head and removing his spectacles. The hankie he pulled from his top pocket to wipe the lenses of his specs matched the tie resting between the mounds of his chest.

"Immigrants," he said. "They always target immigrants."

"I didn't exactly land in this country yesterday," Roger said.

The lawyer tucked his hankie back into his top pocket. The name plate on his desk, all golden lettering, said "Sidney A. Lieberman." Lieberman had been recommended to him by McFadden. He was a high-priced lawyer in a swank, high-rise office downtown. But he'd agreed to consult with Roger's problem as a favor to McFadden. McFadden had taken him under his wing and had spent the last few weeks teaching him the ropes in the insurance business. He worked hard, coming in every day, bags under his eyes, McFadden always asking him if he ever slept. Finally, he felt comfortable enough to share with him what was going on with the business. Choo-Choo's continued losing money and he was aging fast trying to keep up. McFadden recommended he go see Lieberman.

Lieberman said, "Your parents speak English?"

"No. Not much."

"Then they're immigrants. Prey for people like Miss Claudia Reynolds."

"*Pray* for her?"

"No, not *pray*, as in have Jesus save her soul. I mean *prey*—as in an animal pouncing on its food. Come to America. Pursue the American dream. Scabs like Claudia, they watch and wait. She hangs out a sign as bait. Usually, she snags beaners, but this time, a couple onions come in, only one who can speak for them is their eighteen year old son…"

"Nineteen. I'll be twenty in a couple of weeks."

"…okay, nineteen, going on twenty in a couple of weeks. Kid looks sharp enough, but he's still young. Big words and numbers, maybe he can figure them out. I can tell you're smart. I can see it."

"Yeah. I'm pretty smart for an onion."

"How the hell did 'onion' get hitched to the Armenians? 'Beaner' for the taco jockeys I get. But onion for the bushy-brows? I don't get it.

He continued on. "Anyway, this Claudia bimbo, she plays on your young-and-eager side. You wanna do better. Risk is no problem for this young onion, all eager and ready to go. Make the numbers look good, collect the check, congratulations, you're a businessman, young stud. You done good for your parents, see?"

Lieberman tapped the signature line of one of the forms, dotting Roger's scrawled name with the grease from whatever he had for lunch. Something with onions and sauerkraut, he figured, based on the ripeness of his breath spewing across the desktop. "Sign here and here. Boom. It's done. See, the thing is, what you normally should do is have the books audited by an independent. A CPA."

Lieberman pointed to a line item on the paperwork. "Sure, look here, you've got the signature of her accountant. That's why you thought this was legit. Independent audit would have shown those gross numbers get chomped way below your payment by operating costs. That's how she does it. You can't keep up with the payments, and according to the contract, she gets the property back. Then she goes after the next victim. Collecting a twenty percent down payment, she probably turns that property two, three times a year."

Lieberman slid the paperwork across the desk and leaned his heft back in the huge wingback chair. "Contract's solid, son. You could spend a fortune in legal fees, maybe try and get her on fraud. But to do that, we gotta prove intent. She blames the bad numbers on her accountant, claims she fired him, and in the end, you'd still own a losing business and be in hock up to that one single eyebrow of yours in legal fees. Sorry, son. I wish there was more I could do for you. Hey, take it as a life lesson? Right?"

Friday, January 4, 1991
10:25 p.m.

His buzz felt nice and mellowed him just enough to take the edge off of his anger, but he stayed sharp enough to be ready for what was about to go down tonight.

This week's girlfriend, a nice piece of trim named Angie, had done things up real nice for his twentieth birthday. Her parents' house overflowed with the gang from the Central Avenue cruise and the neighborhood homies, the bash swelling the house's walls and spilling out into the front yard. Kegs had been tapped, and hip-hop bumps boomed from the DJ she'd hired for the gig, a first-rate jock named Sallie Tunes who had set up his jams out at the backyard pool.

Roger's anger had run deep since that lawyer had given it to him straight, telling him that he'd been jacked by some Virginia Slim-sucking old bag with cottage cheese cleavage and a class A real estate scam that any idiot should have seen coming. But he realized that he'd been too eager. He loved money and he'd always wanted it fast and always wanted it large. It had come both ways through the route he'd chosen before, but the only problem was that route had nearly left him full of gangbanger lead on Hollywood Boulevard and had gotten him a heavy price on his bean. He'd played it straight for just over a year now, playing by the rules, keeping his nose clean, walking a fine line, but always staying on what he thought was the right side of the law. And where did it get him? He got jacked by an old bag and lost big.

He wasn't about to let that happen again, and it was going to start tonight. It was going to start with that guy Arnulfo, the guy getting ready to make his move. The guy about two steps away from being on the wrong side of Roger's gun.

He felt that Arnulfo had been watching him just a bit too closely all night, sensing that he'd been counting how many times Roger had visited the keg and how many tokes he'd been taking on the Primo tonight. To throw him off, Roger had made a few extra trips to the trough, dumping his refilled cup in the nearest planter, hitting the doobie line but faking the toke. As the night wore on, he observed Arnulfo slip out the back door of the house when he thought Roger was distracted.

He followed at a distance, watching Arnulfo start up the street toward where Roger had parked his new truck. Perhaps sensing he was being watched or just being cautious, Arnulfo angled off the sidewalk in a direction opposite the truck, and disappeared through a row of hedges.

Arnulfo wasn't sure if he was being watched or not, but he veered off the sidewalk and went around the block, approaching his target from another angle just to be safe. For the last six months he'd been watching this Roger Munchian guy real close, the guy they'd started calling Roger Rabbit once he'd put the decal of that Rabbit who'd gotten framed on the bumper of his new wheels. The guy was cool, always aloof and out of the game, but Arnulfo knew he was a guy who'd been a player before. Arnulfo thought that if he could just figure out where the guy laid his head, where he made his moves, he could get the right angle on him. He especially liked the way the guy had tweaked out his new ride. Oh, yeah, and there it was up ahead there, sitting under the streetlight, the maroon Nissan pick-em-up truck, Roger Rabbit, looking like it should be in a showroom somewhere, the way the light glinted off the chrome.

Arnulfo knew that Roger was a man of class and that he'd sunk serious coin into his truck after rolling it off the lot: trimming out the rubber in chrome deep-dish Dayton wheels. Inside the bumps thundered nice through an Alpine stereo system, and the entire truck showed really dime in its custom stripes. What gave it its personality was the decal of Roger Rabbit on the rear bumper, and when the homies spotted that ride on the Central Avenue cruise, bumps jamming, chrome glistening, babes crawling in the back for a ride, they cheered Roger Rabbit on. Roger Rabbit was a hit. And what was really *muy loco* was what Roger had done with the tailgate, the custom paint job where he added the letters I in front of the word NISSAN and an E at the end, turning NISSAN into INISSANE—insane.

Roger was one insane homie.

Arnulfo slid the slim jim down the gully between the door and the passenger side window and had the door unlocked in a second, not chipping an inch of paint. He slipped inside quickly, making sure the dome light was a mere flash and started working in the dark, feeling around under the dash. He knew that Roger had installed a secret compartment where he would have either stuffed some cash, his dope, or some of his armor.

He worked slowly and without concern, figuring Roger was passed out by now or in the sack with his new squeeze, Angie, the way the guy was hitting the smoke tonight. The guy had been off his game lately, all bent out of shape for what that bimbo did to him, jacking him serious on that Choo Choo's Deli thing. Man, that whole thing made ol' Roger look bad, making him look like just another dumb immigrant.

His hands stopped probing when the dome light suddenly popped on. When he looked up from his work, he was staring down the business end of a .357 Magnum, Roger's single eyebrow furled and looking serious as he stared down the sight, trying to figure out the best spot on his forehead to put the bullet.

It really didn't matter. The .357 Mag was going to remove his head completely anyway.

CHAPTER SIX

There was silence in the cab, the guy finally shutting up as Roger drove along, one hand at twelve o'clock on the steering wheel, the other resting in his lap, pointing the cannon straight at Arnulfo's chest, finger on the trigger. He had told him to get up from under the dash, pointing with the gun barrel to the passenger seat, telling him to sit down, buckle up for safety, we're going for a ride. And that's when Arnulfo's brown features turned dead white and he started whimpering, "Oh, man! Is that how you roll? You gonna take me out in the desert somewhere, put a bullet in the back of my head, leave me lying face down in the dirt? Man, just do me here, okay? Put me down in my own neighb', not out in the scrub where I'm gonna end up coyote crap!" And he went on and on like that for nearly a half hour, Roger driving, not saying a word. Eventually, he shut up and sat in silence, staring out the windshield, Roger knowing that the guy was sitting there ready to mess his pants, wondering how far out in the desert he was going to take him before putting a slug in his head.

He spotted a McDonald's golden arches up the road and said, "You hungry?" and turned into the parking lot, heading for the drive-thru.

"What, you gonna buy me a last meal? Shouldn't it be a steak or somethin'?"

"Best I can do is a Quarter Pounder with Cheese."

"I'd rather have a Big Mac."

They were parked in the half-empty lot, Arnulfo inhaling the last quarter of his Big Mac, fingers glistening in french fry grease, feeling the color returning to his face, realizing that perhaps this was not going to be his last meal.

"I tried to play it straight, over a year now I tried," Roger was telling him, eating his Quarter Pounder with one hand, still holding the pistol with the other. "I mean, where was the criminal life leading me, huh? I saw a guy go down from a bullet meant for me and I still got a serious price on my bean. Now I gotta watch my step certain places I go so I don't end up getting put down for a permanent nap."

"Yeah? Where'd this go down?" He asked, knowing that Roger could see his face grow hopeful in the dashboard lights.

"It doesn't matter, and don't get cute."

"Sorry. Habit."

"You're a guy who knows how to work all his angles, I can say that for you. And you look like a guy who can hold his own. I seen you dance the ring. Featherweight?"

"Yeah. But I'm lookin' for a new gym. All I get around where I train is a bunch of flat-footed pugs. I've been trying to get where my little brother trains, but I ain't got the clout he's got." He was proud of his brother, Geronimo DeGarcia, a featherweight Olympic contender.

Needing a hit to calm his nerves, he cautiously pulled a joint from his top pocket, not wanting to make any sudden moves, knowing the gun was still pointed straight at his heart. He blazed it up with his Bic disposable and offered up a toke, but Roger waved it away.

"So what happens next? You always take guys who try and jack your ride out to dinner? Kind of a ritual before you cap them?"

"I got a proposition for you."

"Yeah? You catch me tryin' to steal your stuff, you drive me out here at the point of a gun, and now you wanna cut a deal with me? Sounds pretty insane to me. Guess that's why you got that word stamped to the back of this truck."

He could tell that Roger was ready to go insane—ready to go all out nuts rebuilding his network. After getting screwed by Claudia Reynolds, he knew that Roger decided never again. No one was going to put that onion down again. Roger would show them. He'd show them what he could do—what insane Roger Rabbit could do. Yeah. That was him now. *Insane!*

Roger said, "First, let's get something straight between me and you, okay."

"Okay?"

"No one messes with me, 'Nulfo. You got that? No one messes with me. No one messes with my truck. No one messes with my stuff. You've been working an angle, trying to get in close to me, trying to find out where I lay my head, lookin' to pick your moment to jack my stuff. You made your play this evening, and it could'a gone way different for you. You get that, don't you? I want to make sure you are really solid with that. No one messes with me. I've seen the act before, 'Nulf. It ain't new to me, okay? You play the act real good, 'Nulf', better than most. But you ain't good enough. Not good enough to get to me, okay? So let's cut it now, and we can do business."

"Hey, Rog', man, I don't know where…"

"You're smart, 'Nulfo. You're good. But you're not as good as me. It's kinda like you in the ring. I know you move and jab real good. You know your stuff in there. But on the street, one-on-one, me and you, I'd bury you."

He looked over at Roger, feeling the flair in his jaundiced eyes, knowing that Roger sensed he was about ready to make his move right there from the passenger seat and prove him wrong. In the silent understanding between them, he thought twice about it, sizing this insane onion up, thinking about the gun. He took a deep hit on the joint and exhaled out the open window.

"Yeah," he said. "Yeah, I bet you would. So what do you have in mind?"

"I understand you're a guy who knows how to pick out quality weed."

"Yeah, I know my *ganj*. I also know my Yayo and Glass."

"I don't mess with coke or meth."

"Good profit in both. Especially the G."

"Meth rots your face away and I saw a guy die taking in a lung full of coke. No thanks. A little coke for the Primo, and that's the extent of it."

Roger explained to him that he needed to start putting a supply base together for marijuana. He told him that he wanted to stay clear of his old L.A. connections and build a good base out here. He said he wanted to keep his rep of supplying good stuff fast, and that he needed a good quality manager to pull it off.

Then Roger asked, "What about goods? What do you move?"

"VCRs, stereos, wheels. Sometimes jewelry, but not always. I don't like doing jewelry stores so much. Cops respond faster to an alarm at a jewelry store. Blockbusters, they're my best target. In and out in fifteen minutes. Cops get there in twenty."

"How many times a week you pullin' jobs?"

"Oh, I don't know. Varies, I guess. Few times a month I s'pose. You know. Whenever I need the dough."

"I can pull us together a customer base that will have you hoppin' every night if you want."

"Every *night*?"

"It's a worthy goal to shoot for. You gotta have a goal, 'Nulfo. You can't randomly do this stuff just 'cause you need the dough. You gotta have something to shoot for, otherwise you just blow it all, wasting away on your own stash, and eventually end up like all the other brain-dead homies around here."

'Nulfo sucked the rest of the joint into his lungs and flicked the roach out the window, holding the toke deep, thinking about it. *Oh, wow—every night!*

He heard Roger saying, "Okay, so here's how we do it. We set up a pager system, a numbering code. Say I end a call in something like '9-5'; that means I got an order for five VCRs, okay? A nine means VCRs, and five is the quantity. I start with an eight, it means car stereo. Six, mag wheels. Five, an Eldorado…"

"*Eldorado*? What, you want me to break into a Cadillac dealer? Drive the car through the showroom window?"

"You never jacked a car? Like, roadside, taken it at gunpoint, not hot-wiring it from some parking lot at night?"

"No. Never took a car that way."

"It's a good trade to learn. How you handle a gun?"

"I'm better with my fists."

"You're gonna have to learn to handle armor. Even if you ain't a good shot, at least look like you can give someone a serious case of lead poisoning. What do you think? You on board for all this?"

He wadded up his Big Mac wrapper and chucked it out the window and held out greasy his hand. "When do we begin?"

"School's in session."

"Thanks for dinner."

May 19, 1991
10:22 p.m.

• •

Undercover unit number 223 cruised eastbound on I-10. Officer Mike Miller, sitting in the passenger seat, comfortable in his jeans and T-shirt, was getting tired of listening to the lieutenant ramble on and on in the back. Miller, a twenty-three-year veteran of the Arizona DPS, had spent the last twelve years with the Narcotics unit. His partner, Keith Arnett, was driving as they worked a special detail along the Phoenix highway system. There had been a lot of gang-related shootings along interstates running through South Phoenix lately. The detail had staged unmarked units to patrol the area.

From the back seat, Lieutenant Lee Glassy's ripe breath stunk up the vehicle with every inane syllable that came from his mouth, the guy regaling swashbuckling tales of his days on the DEA Task Force. His breath was ripe with the stink of Dunkin Donuts coffee and rotting cigarette tar that passed from his singed lungs. As he rattled on, rancid breath curling around in the front seat, a maroon Nissan pickup roared by in the far left lane. Arnett hit the accelerator and changed lanes, catching up to the truck, following without the flashers. The tailgate read INISSANE, with a decal of the cartoon character of Roger Rabbit stuck to the bumper. Miller looked over at the speedometer. Eighty miles per hour.

They pursued Roger Rabbit quietly for several miles, Miller trying to run a make on the car, frustrated that the computers apparently were down. Roger Rabbit exited the I-10 and merged onto southbound I-17, still topping 80 mph. At mile marker 199A, Grant Street, Arnett hit the lights and Roger Rabbit's taillights lit up. He slid over into the right lane and a-half mile later exited at Durango Street and pulled to the side of the road.

While Arnett called in the stop, Miller hit the spot light, lighting the truck up. The rear split window suddenly slid open, and Miller knew what it was about. Either booze or dope. Either way, the suspect was trying to air the cab out real quick before the officers got there.

Arnett approached on the left, Miller on the right, his badge clipped to his left hip, his hand resting on the holstered gun, the strap unclipped. Lieutenant Glassy stayed behind, leaning against the hood of the police vehicle, dipping a cigarette into the lighted match cupped in his hand. Miller heard Arnett bark a command, standing just behind the open driver's side window, and the door slowly popped open. The dome light illuminated the interior, and Miller could see that the driver was the vehicle's only occupant. He sniffed, and a strong smell of marijuana wafted from the split cab window.

Miller opened the passenger door as Arnett led the subject, a Hispanic-looking guy, approximately nineteen, long, curly, shoulder-length hair, to the rear of the truck. Miller pulled his Mag light from where it was tucked between his belt and the small of his back and flashed it around the cab. Various papers lay scattered across the passenger seat and a black gym bag sat on the floor. The name tag on the gym bag read, "Roger Munchian."

Miller walked back to the rear of the truck where the subject squinted in the bright spot lights, answering Arnett's questions, telling Arnett he was an insurance agent and a student at Phoenix Community College.

Miller asked, "What's the rush tonight, Roger Rabbit?"

"He said he's rushing to pick up his mother and sister from Sky Harbor. They're apparently coming in on an eleven forty-five flight from L.A."

Miller looked at his watch:10:40.

"You've got over an hour," Miller said. "There's a black gym bag in the front seat. Says 'Roger Munchian.' That you?"

"Yes." The guy saying as little as possible. Miller looked over at Glassy, still leaning against the police unit, smoking his cigarette. "You run a make on this guy yet?"

Glassy blew a stream of smoke and said, "Computers are still down."

"You wanna try again. Maybe they came back up on your smoke break." Miller looked at Munchian, the guy squinting back at him in the bright spots, trying to look cool although the lights were obviously cooking his retinas. He said, "Mr. Munchian, I smelled marijuana emitting from the vehicle. You want to tell me why that would be?"

The guy shrugged, looking indifferent. "Dunno. Desert's full of exotic plant life. Maybe some's growing on the side of the road and my exhaust is blazing it up."

"My guess is it's coming from that black gym bag of yours. You mind if I search it?"

"I'd rather you not."

"Why not?"

"I'd be embarrassed. There're toys in there … you know … things my girlfriend and I use."

"You mean like things that vibrate and twirl?"

Arnett chuckled, "or inflate."

"Something like that."

Miller wanted to whack that smile of the punk's face with the butt of his Mag. "Okay. I'm going to remove the gym bag from the vehicle now while we wait for the dog to arrive."

"Fine with me."

As Miller lifted the bag from the floor, he saw the stock of a gun wedged between the driver's seat and floorboard, strategically located for easy access by the driver. He retrieved it, a 12-gauge sawed-off shotgun and specially fitted with a pistol grip. He broke it open and saw it was loaded, brass heads rimming both pipes.

He carried the gun and bag to the rear of the truck where Arnett was still questioning the subject Munchian. "Mr. Munchian, you are under arrest for possession of a deadly weapon, concealed within immediate control."

He watched as Arnett spun Roger Rabbit around and forced him spread eagled against the truck bed. Upon frisking him, he pulled two digital pagers out of his front jeans pocket, both buzzing, and set them on the bumper. As Glassy got back on the radio and called for a uniform to come and transport him to the Highway Patrol zone, Miller set the bag on the ledge of the truck bed and unzipped it. He reached in and pulled out miscellaneous paperwork, school papers, a notebook, calculator, insurance papers, and two plastic Ziplock bags filled with what he estimated to be somewhere in the neighborhood of a half-pound of marijuana. "Add possession of marijuana to the charges. Not your night, is it Munchian?"

"That's not my gym bag. Someone left it in my truck."

Miller showed him the name tag. "Okay, so this one belongs to the *other* Roger Munchian?"

As Arnett put the subject in cuffs, Miller went back to inventory the vehicle before the tow arrived to haul INISANE off to impound. He popped open the glove box. A wallet sat on top of a green box of LifeStyles condoms, ribbed, 40-count pack. Inside the wallet he found $375 and a valid driver's license for Hrach Roger Munchian. Inside the glove box he also found a loaded .44-caliber blue steel, snub nose revolver and a holstered .25 semi-automatic handgun with a box of ammunition. He dug around and came out with a red plastic container containing two white rocky substances, one large and one small, and another Ziplock sandwich bag, this one filled with white powder. He took the container and bag to Arnett.

"You wanna run a quick field test on these?"

Miller went back and continued searching the vehicle. Under the driver's seat he found a loaded stainless steel .357 revolver, unholstered. Under the seat he also found an open box of Ziplock sandwich bags, and yet another sealed bag containing a leafy substance. He opened the bag and smelled marijuana.

"Initial tests are positive for cocaine. Two rocks of crack and a bag of blow," Arnett told him when he returned to the back of the truck.

The blue and red flashers glowed off the roadside as the DPS patrol car pulled up. As the uniformed officer stepped from the unit, Miller said to the subject, "Here's what we're looking at, Mr. Roger Rabbit. We've got possession of a narcotic drug for sale. Possession of marijuana for sale. With the weapons, we can add a charge of narcotics trafficking while in possession of a deadly weapon. Possession of a prohibited weapon. And carrying a deadly weapon within immediate control." The tow truck arrived next, McClure Towing, to take the truck to impound. The uniformed officer started escorting Roger to the cruiser, and Miller said, "Mr. Munchian, if you give me the flight number, I'll be sure and let your mother know that you're going to be a bit late. I'd say about ten to fifteen years."

CHAPTER SEVEN

Salvador Hernandez, aka Sally Tunes, aka Sal-EG—Educated Genius—
sat deep in the beanbag chair, his lap bright orange in Cheetos crumbs,
staring at the TV, toes sunk in the puke green shag carpeting. The new
bong had a great draw and the thick smoke he exhaled from his last hit
curled in front of the TV screen where Devo did their crack-that-whip
number on MTV. He shoved another handful of Cheetos into his mouth,
and coughed out a cloud of orange as he watched the routine, *yeah, crack
that whip*, the thin guy all dressed in black, wearing that plastic red hat
on his head, the rednecks sitting on the rail fence, drinking Budweiser,
watching him cracking the whip. *Ooh, yeah, break your mamma's back!*

"So, who was this dude, man? Why we doing the gig?" PIG said
breathlessly, taking an extra toke on the bong before passing it back.
PIG: Puerto Insane Genius. It's how his homies in the Hispanic cartel
called each other. Insane Genius. Educated Genius.

Sal-EG reached for the bong, took a hit and held it. "You know him.
That guy Roger. You know. The one owns the sub shop. Choo-Choo's.
We did his birthday bash back in Jan-u-ary."

"Yeah, I know that dude. Man, I wouldn't mess with him. He's
always packed, and he ain't from around here."

"I think he's from L.A or something."

"No, I mean, not from around *here*, you know. Someplace else. He
talks the language real good, you know, mixes with the homies just fine,
but then sometimes you hear him speaking that other language. One of
those languages makes you sound like you got a loogie caught in your
throat all the time."

"Armenia."

"What?"

"That's where he's from, I think."

"Where's that?"

Sal said, "I don't know. Near Las Vegas I think. Anyway, this dude, Roger, they call him Roger Rabbit 'cause of his truck, he gets this idea he's gonna open his sub shop as some kind of a place to party and jam. You know, after-hours stuff. He wants to charge top dollar to get in, so, you want a real bash, you want good tunes, and who do you go to for the bumps around here other than ol' Sally Tunes, right? So, he's in my studio, tellin' me he wants me exclusively, Friday through Sunday nights."

"Geez, Sal. That dude's dangerous. I mean, you want quality weed, he's the guy. But, man, he belongs to no one. The dude's a no-man's land. He's tight with all the bangers. Man, he opens that place up, he gonna have the Brown Pride, VTC, Westside Chicanos, Vista Bloods, Dog Town, Hollywood Thirty-Nine, man, all of them bangers in the same place at the same time. That's a blood bath waiting to happen."

"Yeah. That's why I told him I was all booked up. And he asked me for how long, and I told him for the rest of my life. He didn't like that, me getting' smart with him that way, so he said maybe I ought to recheck my schedule. I pretended to look, saying, no, I'm booked."

"Then why we doin' the gig?"

"Because he came out fast with a nickel-plated revolver and put a dimple in my forehead, saying, 'Look again.'"

"Wow. Yeah. I see the red dot's still there on your forehead. You look like you converted to Hindu. What'd you do?"

"I looked again. This time, I found an opening."

September 24, 1991
7:00 p.m.
• •

"You gotta be kiddin' me," Fernando Nunez said. "Just dropped it, huh?"

"They used the word 'scratched'," Roger said. "I guess it means they dropped all the charges."

He was sitting behind the wheel of Roger Rabbit, Nunez in the passenger seat, parked on the corner of 73rd Drive and Comet, a chain-link fence and block wall-lined subdivision, houses topped with rusty swamp coolers, the kind of 'hood carved up into ridged gang turf boundaries. Looking out the windshield, he was watching his latest girlfriend, Jenny, getting the information from the Dog Town homies. Frankie Richmond had called, inviting him on up to his crib, telling him he knew where he could get an order for some quality weed, serious weight. He wasn't buying his line. Frankie was up to something, he knew it.

He really wanted to be at Choo-Choo's tonight, making sure Sal-EG kept the bumps going, making sure things stayed calm between the *Varrio* Tolleson Chicano—VTC—boys and the Westies. Things started heating up earlier tonight when that little VTC punk, Solo, wanted to go in packing, ticked that the black dudes from the Westies were out there on the dance floor mixing it up with Chicano trim. Roger had gotten in his face more than once, telling him it was always ladies' night at Choo-Choo's, there was plenty to go around. Cool off. It's a party. Then he got the call from Richmond and left Arnulfo in charge and took Nunez along for the extra muscle. Dog Town and the Hollywood 39 didn't mix well. Jenny was along as a neutral party to get things going.

Moving the weed and rock brought in enough cash to stay current with the monthly payments to that leach Claudia Reynolds, but he decided that he didn't want to be lining her accounts with the proceeds from his enterprise. Things were going good and he wanted to keep his own winnings. So he got the idea of opening Choo-Choo's as an after-hours hot spot. Do it up right. Bring in a class A jock to blast out the bumps. Pay up, four-at-the-door, and you drink all night. Line it nice with hot babes, all trimmed out and looking really dime, and the dudes would pay prime to get in.

He'd "persuaded" this guy, Sally Tunes, one of the hottest DJs in town, to jam exclusively for his parties, and Sal brought in the crowds. Sal was happy to do it, especially after getting a nice new dimple in his forehead from some nickel-plating. Word spread fast and every weekend they spilled into the parking lot and Choo-Choo's after-hours brought in the profits—enough to keep Claudia sweating it out and enough left over for him to pocket.

While waiting for Jenny, he was telling Nunez about his arrest a few months ago. They'd booked him down at that rat hole, Madison

Street jail and he'd spent all night moving from one tank to another through the intake area they called the Horseshoe. He told Nunez that it had taken over a week to wash the stench of stale urine and BO off him once he got out. He finally got in front of the judge and was now in twenty-two hundred to a place called AZ Bail Bonds after putting up Choo-Choo's as collateral.

A few weeks later as he was waiting on his court date he got notice that the case was "scratched." There'd be no court date.

"So by 'scratched,' you mean the State just dissed your case? They ain't comin' after you?"

"That's the way it appears."

"Man, that's just messed up."

Speaking of messed up, Roger looked out the windshield and saw Frankie out there in front of his Low Rider with four of his homies, starting to make his dippy, gang-like gestures at Jenny, getting in her face about something. Roger reached over and popped open the glove box and pulled a .25-caliber Beretta from its holster and handed it to Nunez. "Keep that handy," he'd told him.

Nunez took the gun and said, "Scratched, huh? Yeah, I just ain't buyin' it." Nunez checked the Beretta's clip. "And you got pulled over by a couple unmarked narcs? For speeding? See, those guys, man, the guys ridin' unmarked, they don't do traffic stops. No. Somethin' ain't right. They's on to you. If I was you, I'd lay low, you know? Cut it for a while. No. Somethin' ain't right."

"Somethin' ain't right out there, either," he said, nodding his head out the windshield. Frankie was really irate, ranting and flashing his gang signs, animating his homies now. They couldn't hear what he was saying over the hip-hop bumps thundering from the speakers in the open trunk of the Low Rider, but whatever he'd said sent Jenny running for the truck. He reached under the front seat and grabbed his Uzi and jammed in a 45-round magazine. "Let's do this."

They both stepped from the cab, Roger shielding himself behind the open door as Jenny let out a girlish squeal and crawled into the cab.

Moving this way now, Frankie squared off and shouted, "Hey, Roger Rabbit—nice truck! What 'chew doing bringing a Thirty-Niner across the Dog Town set?"

He slid the Uzi from under his shirt, keeping it hidden behind the truck door saying to Nunez, "I guess he don't like your colors, *Negra*. Maybe you oughta button that shirt straight."

"He's all jacked up on something, man," *Negra* Nunez said. "Hollywood Thirty-Nine don't change colors for no one."

Roger shouted over the thudding hip-hop, "Frankie, *you're* the one who dialed *my* digits. You got something happenin', okay. If not, we're leaving."

Frankie moved to the center of the road. Two of his homies followed, making a staggered human roadblock.

Behind him, the road ended in a cul-de-sac. The only way out was through the Dog Town boys. Someone had turned down the bumps in the Low Rider, and Frankie said, "Yeah, you can get out of here all right. Yeah, no problem. On foot. You leave the truck. I'll take it as toll for bringin' the spade Thirty-Nineer across my set."

"No one messes with my truck, Frankie. You know that."

"Not your truck no more, holmes," Jo-Jo G, Frankie's second lieutenant, said. "Wheels belong to Frankie now."

They started moving forward in unison. Nunez stepped from the shelter of the passenger door and stared walking toward them, left shoulder dipped in traditional Hollywood 39 battle stance, pistol down low, hidden behind his thigh.

"Stand down, Thirty-Nine," Jo-Jo said.

When Nunez reached the front of the truck, he raised the Beretta and fired three blasts into the air. The Dog Town boys stopped briefly, laughed, and continued their advance, more determined this time.

"Man, Nunez!" Roger shouted, stepping from behind the door and leveling the Uzi. "*Never* pull a heater," squeezing off a blast, meaning to kill. "Unless you mean business!" And he laid out another spray, blue smoke and the scent of cordite filling the air. The Dog Town boys scattered, ducking and dropping to the ground. Sparks flew, car windows shattered and the hip-hop bumps died in a shower of .9-millimeter slugs.

When an evening breeze whisked the smoked away, the road was clear.

"*Get in!*" he shouted and hopped into the driver's seat and cranked the ignition.

"Man!" Nunez shouted at him as he blew the stop sign at 75th Avenue, turning north and getting it up to 80 mph in no time. "I just wanted to scatter them!"

"My way was more effective. I told you, no one messes with my truck." He snapped the magazine from its breech and did a quick count. "See that. Thirty-three shots. I could have got them all."

The red and blue flashers of the Peoria police cruiser hit the rearview mirror and he pushed the accelerator to the floor. He lost the cop, temporarily he knew, and careened into a strip mall anchored by a Safeway grocery store. He pulled down a narrow alley and screeched to a stop next to an overflowing trash bin.

"Roger, honey, what are you *doing*?" Jenny said. "Let's go … let's get out of here!"

"Man, Roger, they're gonna find us here for sure!"

He popped open the door. Faint in the distance, but approaching fast, he could hear the sirens of multiple cruisers responding to the chase.

"Both of you—get out!"

He grabbed the guns and kicked them under the trash dumpster.

"What are you doing, man?"

"Roger—come on! You're scaring me!"

"Nunez, your apartment is two blocks from here. I'll meet up with you both there. Stick to the back way. Do not hit the streets."

He hopped back in the truck. As soon as he careened from the alley, two police cruisers were on him. He knew he would never out run them. He just wanted to get as far away from the guns as possible.

By the time he blew through his third red light, there were four police cruisers on him, and a Phoenix police helicopter dropping down from the sky. Blinded by the chopper's spot lights, he lost control of the vehicle and hopped a curb, skidding to a stop in the middle of a Circle K parking lot. Tires squealed around him, the cab suddenly ablaze in the flood of headlights and spotlights. Overhead, the thud of the helicopter's blades whipped the night air, reverberating through the cab.

Armed officers scrambled for position, their forms mere silhouettes in the blinding glare of the lights. He sensed their guns drawn on him from behind open car doors and over the roofs and hoods of the surrounding police cruisers, feeling their restrained instinct to shoot. Fear paralyzed him when he looked up and caught the glint of a sniper rifle's blue steel boring down from the open door of the helicopter.

"Throw out your weapons and step from the vehicle with your hands on your head!" The voice came through the intercom.

He rolled down the window, the whirl of the chopper blades above blasting him in a vortex of desert air and sand. He held his arms out, feeling the tension, realizing the intensity of the situation could mean a bullet to the forehead at any second.

He shouted, "I'm unarmed!" trying to be heard over the thud of the chopper blades. "Don't shoot! *Don't shoot!*"

"Mr. Munchian, this is your final warning! Throw your weapons out immediately and exit the vehicle!"

"*Please!*" He waved his arms frantically now, feeling the trembling intensity of the sniper barrel overhead, ready for the bullet at any moment. "I don't have any weapons! I'm *unarmed!*"

"Now, Mr. Munchian!"

He popped the door open and fell to the ground, hands on his head, fingers interlocked. Bodies converged on him, his face slammed into the pavement, the grind of pebbles and rocks slicing his cheeks. He cried in anguish as they yanked his arms hard behind him, and then felt the cold steel clasp of cuffs clamping over his wrists.

"I'm unarmed!"

They yanked him to his feet and thrust him into the back seat of a patrol car. As the door slammed shut, he looked through the wire mesh and watched a convergence of officers on Roger Rabbit. His attempt to dump all his weapons had been hurried and frantic. As the patrol car pulled away with him in it, he hoped he'd dumped them all.

CHAPTER EIGHT

Sunday, January 4, 1992
Choo-Choo's Deli
Appx 10:45 p.m.

The hip-hop roar of Sally D's tunes filtered from the stage and poured into the rear parking lot as Roger watched Arnulfo push through the back door of the restaurant, carrying two froth-brimmed Styrofoam cups of beer. The smoked-glass door eased shut on its hydraulic hinge, silencing Sal's tunes to a murmuring thud.

He was leaning against the bed of Roger Rabbit, pinching a joint, packing it tight. He was dressed comfortable tonight, chilling it back wearing a baseball cap and a black pair of sweats with "Raiders" in gray lettering embroidered on the pant leg, his high school football jersey pulled over a hooded sweatshirt. Casual tonight, celebrating his 21st birthday.

Arnulfo handed him a beer. "Happy birthday, inmate number three-eight-oh-six-two-six."

He grabbed the beer, saying, "Not funny, 'Nulfo."

The incident with Frankie Richmond had gone down over three months ago and Roger was still ticked with Nunez for blowing the whole thing. After getting booked down at Madison Street, sitting in the zoo as booking number 380-626, he was confident he'd soon be walking free. Without the weapons they couldn't nail him. But while he was sitting in the tank, waiting his turn before the judge, the cops had gotten a line on Nunez and Jenny and came knocking at Nunuz's apartment door, freaking both of them out. Crapping his pants, Nunez spilled his guts, leading them to the guns. By the time he'd gotten before the judge, the existence of the guns had been added to the case, linking him to a 9 mm automatic that had been fired into a crowd of boys standing in front of their residence in Peoria that evening. Pinning a charge of aggravated assault with a deadly weapon to his jacket, he was on his way from the judge's bench upstairs, spending the night in the Madison Street zoo with a cellie named Ajax. In the morning he got hold of his bail bondsman and again put up Choo-Choo's as collateral. By five o'clock, that evening he was standing on the corner of Madison and 4th Ave., waiting for Jenny to come pick him up.

'Nulfo said, "You get a trial date set?"

"Heard nothin' so far."

"Hey, maybe they scratched this one, too. Man, Rog' sometimes I think you got some major weight in heaven—you got guardian angels with serious clout watching over you."

He sipped his beer, thinking about it. No indictments had come down yet, but the state was looking to go after him on five counts of aggravated assault, ten years a pop. That would mean he was looking to spend the next fifty years living the ADOC jumpsuit—the "peels" as they called the garb up on the big boy yard—maybe more if the drug charges came up again. He decided to change the subject. He noticed that Sally D's tunes had stopped, Sal taking a break between sets. "Things still looking rough in there?" he said, nodding at Choo-Choo's.

"Yeah. The West Side Chicano boys have been lookin' for trouble all night. They got those two black dudes running with them, you know, Louie Warner and that big, dumb-looking ape with the weird name, Bosco Bokowski. Gilly already tossed Louie out three times so far tonight, Louie always trying to get in packing his twenty-two. Then some of the Tolleson VC boys showed up a while ago, and he and Bosco have been talkin' trash to them."

"Solo Chavez in the mix?"

"He ain't here yet. The only Tolleson boys here so far are Gonzo and one of the Reyes brothers, the youngest one, Poncho. Gilly's been tryin' to keep a buffer between Louie and the Tolleson boys. But yeah, things are getting hot in there."

"That's why I think I'm gonna let the party wind down." He took a toke on a fresh joint and handed it over to Arnulfo. "How's the kegger?"

"About half full. You really got a bad feelin' about tonight?"

Sally D's tunes came back to life. He said, "Once the kegger is gone, we pull the plug on Sally D and get everybody out."

11:45 p.m.
• •

In the parking lot outside the Red Lobster restaurant, Ricky "Coco" Coca sat in the passenger seat of Dario's white Impala, getting annoyed at the way Dario was tapping his fingers nervously on the steering wheel. He got that way before going banging, trying to look cool about it, pursing his lips and nodding his head to the rhythm of the hip-hop thudding through the speakers. But he tapped that hand out of sync with the music, a nervous twitch he couldn't hide. The other guys in the car were ready. Silvio "Mad Man" Montalvo and Freddy Reyes sat in the back, sharing a joint, Silvio talking Freddy's ear off, going on with another story about his gang-banging days with the Happy Homies, a real tough group of bangers that got too weird when they started cutting the hands off their victims; so he left them.

Coco reached under the seat and felt for the .357 Magnum, assuring himself that it was still there. It was a nice piece. Blue steel revolver manufactured by Taurus. He always packed heavy armor, especially for occasions like tonight, occasions that made Ricky tap his fingers all nervous like that on the steering wheel. The whole gang had been at Mad Man's house earlier, getting mellow with a few chicks when Freddy's brother, Poncho Reyes, and a bunch of others decided to go to the blowout over at Choo Choo's. Couple of hours later Poncho calls and tells Mad Man there's trouble. The two spooks from the WSC were messing with him, namely a smoke named Louie Warner and the ape they called Bosco and he was gonna need help. Mad Man told him they had to pick up Solo from work, but they'd be on their way, packed and ready. The spooks running with the West Side Chicanos were going down tonight.

Coco wished they would have decided to ditch Solo, but here he came now, Solo walking out from the kitchen entrance of the Red Lobster, doing his swagger across the parking lot. He was out of his dishwasher whites, wearing bib overalls and a white T-shirt, the short sleeves rolled up on his skinny arms. Like the other dudes in the car with him, Solo was wearing his black baseball cap, the one with the Varrio Tolleson Chicanos insignia scrawled under the bill.

He knew they were in trouble the way Solo got in the car all wide-eyed and ready for blood. As Dario punched the accelerator to the floor, Coco reached under the front seat and grabbed the .357 and showed it off, trying to play it cool, not wanting his homies to think he was punking out. He looked over and saw Freddie lift his sweat shirt and reveal the butt of the .25-caliber tucked away in his waistband, nestled in belly hair, and he wondered if Freddie felt it too. Solo was trouble tonight, and if he couldn't be dialed down, he was going to get them all killed.

By the time they pulled into the Choo-Choo's parking lot, he could see Solo drooling vengeance. Coco knew that the divot-like scar punctured just under Solo's left eye in the shape of the high school insignia was courtesy of the big class ring Louie Warner wore the night he and three other WSCers beat him and left him for dead. This was the night he'd "accidentally" crossed their set wearing his colors. That was over a year ago and he was only fifteen back then. Now that he was sixteen he figured Solo considered himself one of the big boys—and that it was finally his turn to even the score.

His heart began to race when Dario killed the engine and he heard Sally D's tunes thudding from inside. He watched Solo pop the rear door open and hop out first, flashing his gang signs at a group waiting in line to get in, signaling that the Tolleson boys were here, trouble was on its way.

He jumped out of the car next and grabbed Solo by the arm. "Dial it back, Solo!" Shoving him against the rear bumper, he said, "Let's figure this thing out first, okay?"

"Figure what out, Coco?" Solo getting in his face. "Man, all we gotta do is go in there and pop a couple spooks and split. No one messes with

Tolleson. No one, man." He watched as Solo subconsciously rubbed the school-ring shaped scar under his eye.

Freddy said, "Let's go check it out, Coco."

"Solo stays here."

Still gripping the .357 tight as a security blanket, he heard Freddy say, "Hey, Coco, Gilly's workin' the door. Man, you better leave the cannon out here."

He tucked the .357 back under the front seat and told Freddie, "You hang here with Solo. If there's trouble, you know where things are. In the meantime, help Solo get his head on straight."

"I wanna go!"

"Shut up, Solo."

Roger recognized the Tolleson boys as they came through the front door, getting a heavy pat down by Gilly. They were looking all steely-eyed at the four West Side Chicanos making their moves on a pack of babes on the dance floor—Louie Warner, in that stupid-looking flowered shirt, Bosco Bokowski, Arch Flowers, and Rudy Enriquez. He saw it coming, but it happened too quickly; the banger he knew as Coco pushing his way across the dance floor and plowing hard into Warner. Warner hit the dance floor and came back up swinging.

Sally D's tunes stopped. The mix-up on the floor lasted ten seconds before the shooting started, the shots coming from the parking lot.

Coco was the first to run out into the parking lot and saw Solo hunched behind the rear quarter panel of the Impala, the .357 aimed toward the street, squeezing off rounds, firing at a fleeing white Grand Prix. From inside the deli, he heard Roger's voice over the DJ mic announcing the party was over, clear out.

He turned and saw Louie Warner pushing his way through the door, the .22 in his hand, and watched him crouch behind the rear bumper of a Mitsubishi, leveling the gun at Solo.

"Solo, get down! *Down!*" Coco made a move toward Warner, running full tilt, ready to dive over the hood and knock him off his game, but was stopped when he took a knee in the rib cage and heard his own breath spew from him in a heave as he toppled hard to the asphalt.

He looked up into the thick, black-gummed grin of Bosco Bokowski, and then saw the worn treads of Bosco's tennis shoe coming down on him. He squeezed his eyes shut tight and felt the gravel slice into his cheeks, tasting blood and the rubber of the soiled tennis shoe, Bosco dancing ceremoniously on his head, howling a savage jungle cry. Over the ringing in his ears and the big dumb ape's tribal roar, he could hear shots being fired from all directions now, the sound of his .357 rising distinct over the tradeoff of gunfire, Solo emptying the magazine.

Then he heard Bosco's war cry turn into a primal scream. He looked up and saw the big black ape scurrying away, a fast, fleeing limp toward the shelter of the building. Through eyes slowly swelling shut, he saw the blood seeping between Bosco's thick, black fingers, pouring from the fresh wound just below his right butt cheek. He watched Arch Flowers come rushing to Bosco's aid, easing the big, dumb spook down to the sidewalk, hearing the ape crying, "I've been shot! I've been shot!"

Staggering to his feet, he figured Solo had reloaded three times by now, trading off shots between Warner behind the Mitsubishi and Rudy behind a black Ford Escort on the other side of the lot, Rudy blowing the air away with a sawed-off shotgun. Then he saw Freddie Reyes sprinting across the lot and diving into the rear of the Impala. Feeling the blood pouring down his face, he started toward Solo, hearing Warner's little pop from his tiny .22, and looked up in time to see Solo's head snap sideways, his black hat fly free as he dropped out of sight behind the car.

Oh, God—no!

"Freddie! Freddie! Solo's been shot! *Solo's been shot!*" He heard his own cries fill the air as he continued sprinting toward the car.

He slid over the hood and saw the .357 lying on the curb where Solo had dropped it. He snatched it up and leveled it over the car roof, but Warner was gone. He rushed over to Solo, lying in the grassy median between the street and the parking lot, a dot of blood in the middle of his forehead streaming down and pooling in the high-school insignia ring indentation under his eye.

"Get him in the car! *Get him in!*" he shouted as Freddy wormed his way out of the back seat. He tucked the .357 under his belt as Freddy helped him load Solo's limp body into the back while Mad Man hopped into the driver's seat and cranked the ignition.

He felt the warmth of Solo's blood pouring over his hands as the shooting started outside again, the rest of the Varrios piling into the car. He heard Mad Man's cry of rage as he punched the accelerator to the floor, the Impala hopping the curb, tearing up the median grass and laying a meandering patch of rubber on the street as he raced out of there. He didn't want to let go of Solo, but he heard the bullets pelting the car. Intoxicated by a rush of adrenaline, he yanked the .357 from his belt and, holding it tight in his bloody grip, and slid out the rear window, firing away as they raced up 33rd Avenue.

"Man, is he breathin'? I don't think he's breathin'!" he heard Dario say as he slid back into the car, seeing Solo now lying across the laps of Dario and Freddy.

"This ain't happenin', man," he heard himself say. "This ain't happenin'! Man, he's only sixteen! He's only *sixteen!*"

Saint Joseph's Medical Center
Phoenix
5:10 a.m.

Officer Silvia Reeves returned to St. Joseph's Hospital and went to the examination room where she was told they had taken the boy. It didn't seem like five hours had gone by since she'd been here before. After responding to a shooting reported at an establishment called Choo-Choo's Subs, Reeves and her partner were passed by a speeding white Impala coming from the direction of the call. They'd whirled their patrol car around and pulled the vehicle over, finding it occupied by six Hispanic males, one of whom had suffered a gunshot wound to the head. They pulled him from the car and administered CPR on him until the ambulance arrived. Reeves had followed and remained at the hospital until the boy was wheeled into surgery. She was told the prospects did not look good. She also learned that another victim of the shooting had just arrived, a black male, gunshot wound to the right buttock, serious, bullet lodged in the abdomen.

The boy's name was Edward Chavez, and there he was, lying naked on the gurney they'd used to wheel him out from the CAT room. His wound had been sutured. The same doctor entered the room, shaking his head. He handed her a vial containing the bullet that had been removed from young Edward's head. It was a .22- caliber slug.

"For all intents and purposes, he's dead," the doctor said. "Bullet went in and rattled around in there long enough to erase all of who little Edward here was. We've got some more tests to run. I should be able to make a formal pronouncement of death within the hour."

The doctor left and Reeves stayed for a moment, looking at what used to be a young boy named Edward Chavez. As they had been performing CPR on him, she remembered hearing one of his homies shouting, "Please save Solo! You gotta help Solo!" She knew that she had to leave. She had evidence to get to Ballistics and reports to write. But it was tough to leave this boy here alone. It was painful knowing that she'd be leaving Solo here in this cold room to die solo.

Wednesday, January 7, 1992
9:20 a.m.

Roger hated wearing a shirt and tie to work but he had an appointment at police headquarters downtown this morning for more questioning about the shooting. He looked over at the newspaper on his desk, *The Arizona Republic*, still folded to the headline that had come out two days after the sixteen-year-old kid had gotten himself shot in the parking lot of his parents' sub shop.

1 Killed, 1 Hurt in Gang Fight

Phoenix, Jan. 6 — A fistfight that escalated into a shooting spree between two gangs left a 16-year-old dead and a man critically wounded early Sunday in west Phoenix, authorities said.

Edward Chavez, 16, believed to have been from the Tolleson area, was killed in a flurry of shots fired about 12:15 a.m. outside Choo-Choo's Subs, said Sgt. Chester Robertson, a Phoenix police spokesman.

Robertson said people were attending a dance party inside the shop when a fight outside turned into a gun battle. Several types of weapons were used, including a .357-caliber handgun and a shotgun, Robertson said.

Leon Bokowski, 20, also was shot and was listed in critical condition late Sunday at St. Joseph's Medical Center.

The gangs, which police declined to identify, have been feuding for about a year, Robertson said. No arrests had been made as of late Sunday.

Choo-Choo's was still roped off in yellow police tape, and he was irritated that police investigators were taking their own sweet time getting the investigation done. It didn't really matter now when they told them it was okay to reopen. The closure and the ceasing of Choo-Choo's late night blowouts already put his family in default with Claudia Reynolds. Solo lost his life. Roger's parents lost their business.

He looked at his watch. Almost nine-thirty. Time to head downtown. He was unaware how busy downtown would be today. In addition to the questioning of dozens of Choo-Choo's guests that night and a flurry of other related investigation activity, a Superior Court judge was finally getting around to signing an arrest warrant from a grand jury indictment that had hit his desk two months ago:

Warrant for Arrest: Hrach Roger Munchian

To all peace officers of the state of Arizona:

An indictment has been filed in this court against above-named defendant charging that on or about the 24th day of Sept. 1991, the crimes of counts 1 through 5 Aggravated Assault, a class 3 felony, have been committed.

The court has found reasonable cause to believe that such offenses were committed and that the defendant will not appear in response to summons, or that a warrant is otherwise appropriate.

You are therefore commanded to arrest the defendant and bring said defendant before this court to answer for the charges.

CHAPTER NINE

Tuesday, March 24, 1992
Phoenix Sky Harbor Airport, Terminal 2
8:00 a.m.

• •

Whenever DEA Agent Rod Wesley got that feeling in his gut, he was rarely wrong. He looked across the terminal and saw the two guys struggling with large suitcases near the USAir ticket counter—a tall, thin white guy and a short, stubby pipsqueak of a Hispanic. The way they moved, the way they handled themselves, looking around nervous, told his gut that something was going down.

He watched as Tall Whitey went up to the ticket counter and paid cash for a couple of tickets while Pipsqueak nervously slithered out of the terminal. After pocketing the tickets, Whitey followed, leaving the terminal, nearly self-inflicting himself with whiplash the way he whipped his head back and forth, looking around all paranoid. As the baggage handler moved the suitcases to the baggage area, he went up to the counter and asked the clerk for the flight information and learned that the suspects would be boarding Flight 223 to Washington DC, set to depart in about an hour. He saw his buddy, officer Kevin Deacon of the Phoenix Police Department, down near the TWA gate, walking the baggage area with "Crackers," the 2-year-old Labrador Retriever. Catching his attention, he motioned for him to bring Crackers down here.

He told Deacon about the suspects and walked along as Deacon led Crackers up and down the baggage carts, presenting the search to her. The suspects' suitcases were on the third cart, and, sure enough, as they passed by the third cart, Crackers stopped, giving the indication that she detected a scent, eager to get off the leash and go after it.

He watched Deacon cut her loose, and she did her thing, running up and down the cart, nosing along until she stopped and started pawing at one of the large Samsonite suitcases that the suspects had been carrying. He walked over and pulled it off the cart and set it aside while Crackers went back to work, sniffing and scurrying, excited about the scent she'd picked up and stopped and started pawing and biting at the other suitcase.

After thanking Deacon for his assistance, he picked up both bags, set them next to a pillar and advised the baggage clerks they were not to be moved. He checked the tags on the bags. Both contained the name "Anthony Rizzo," city of address: Menifee, CA. He accompanied Deacon to his car where they secured Crackers in her kennel and proceeded up to gate A to have a chat with the two passengers awaiting takeoff on Flight 223.

The little beaner sitting next to him staring out the window watching the baggage ride up the conveyor belt into the belly of the plane grossed him out, the way he kept digging away at the wax in his ear with that unfolded paperclip. Tony Rizzo didn't want to do this gig. It was his first time running something like this. Man, twenty pounds of marijuana sitting in two suitcases, deliver it to the ear-picker's connection in DC. The ear-picker, named Miguel but with traveling papers by the name Bobby Cruz, was no good, man. Rizzo had just hooked up with him, but he knew the guy was out on bond from Maryland on two counts of grand theft.

He didn't want to get hooked up this way. At least get him hooked up with someone semi-clean, older, someone who knew the ropes more, and certainly not an ear picking beaner like Miguel.

Things had been tough since the divorce. He was unemployed and his last bout with a Schick Super-2 marked his third attempted suicide. With that thought he subconsciously looked down at his left wrist, the vertical incision all pink now but healing fine. After his wrists had healed, his girlfriend Paulette insisted he check into that mental hospital, the expensive place, not the one covered by insurance. Then she dumped him. Then told him she'd take him back, but he had to start helping out paying the bills. Yeah, right. How was he going to do that? No job. Crappy economy. And all these hospital bills now from the suicide attempt.

He'd driven out from California to see Uncle Vinnie down in Tucson. Uncle Vinnie, with that big ranch and all those acres, was always well-connected. He owned a used auto parts shop outside Tucson and hopefully he'd give him a job working there delivering parts or something, but he knew that auto parts wasn't where the big money came from. Vinnie had connections in Mexico and had a solid network running weed up from the border. At least he *thought* Uncle Vinnie's network was good. Vinnie didn't talk about it much, but he remembered one time seeing bundles of the stuff stacked like hay bales in the barn.

Uncle Vinnie had given him a job delivering parts but never said anything about cutting him in on the dope business. He played it subtle, dropping hints, but Vinnie just wasn't getting it. Or maybe he was out of the business.

Then one night Uncle Vinnie took him to a swank night club in downtown Tucson and got him introduced to a guy all iced out in gold chains and draped with chicks, a real hotshot named Carlos Martinez. All night Uncle Vinnie kept telling Martinez about poor Tony, down on his luck and all, lots of bills to pay, saying he couldn't pay him enough, maybe Carlos had some work for him. Carlos asked Tony do you have a pager and he said yeah. Carlos handed him his card with a phone and a pager number and told him if something came up, he'd page him to that number. Give him ten minutes after paging before calling because it was a pay phone he had to get to and usually no one was on it, but sometimes he had to wait.

Four weeks later, his pager went off and he recognized the number. Carlos had a job for him.

The way it worked, he was supposed to foot the bill for two nice-sized suitcases and two one-way airline tickets from Phoenix to Washington DC. He picked up the suitcases from a luggage shop called Zarfas Luggage and Gifts in downtown Tucson, paying cash. He then picked up Miguel as instructed at a restaurant in Tucson called The Solarium. They hooked up with Carlos and Carlos gave them $1,000 spending cash, saying that once they got to DC, Miguel would recognize the connections they were supposed to meet and they'd take the luggage and give them their tickets back to Phoenix. Real simple. Get it loaded and delivered, easy cash. Do this job right, there'll be more.

He and Miguel loaded the bags into his Nissan pickup and drove it up to Phoenix where they'd stayed at the Residence Hotel near the airport, room 229, and got up early to catch the flight to DC.

Now that they were on the plane he started to relax a bit. He'd be even more relaxed once they started pulling away from the gate, and really relaxed once they were in the air and he had a good, stiff gin and tonic in his hand. He looked out past the ear-picker's narrow head and saw that the luggage was all loaded. The baggage crew was clear. The cabin doors were closed. Everyone was seated.

Why weren't they pulling away?

"Will passenger Anthony Rizzo please report to the front of the plane?" The silky voice of the flight attendant came over the intercom. Miguel turned from the window for the first time since they'd sat down, his jaundiced eyes wide. "Passenger Anthony Rizzo, please report to the front of the plane."

As he walked up the aisle, he saw a sliver of light fill the galley area as the cabin door popped open. His heart sank when he saw two cops step into the aisle, looking really serious, as he approached.

CHAPTER TEN

Tent City, Maricopa County Jail
Saturday, September 11, 1993
8:00 a.m.

He was lucky enough to have figured out the trick, the thing you do with your bedding so you don't get your face chewed by the rats during the night. His first night in Tent City Jail, Roger had observed the veteran inmates rolling their wafer-thin mattresses up at the head of the bed and securing the roll with the loose end of the pink sheet. Not only did this provide a makeshift pillow, but also it kept the sheet from falling to the ground, which was how the rats climbed into bed with you.

The first thing they went for was your face.

Unfortunately, his former cellie over at Estrella Jail, Martin Hernandez, had learned the trick the hard way. On their third night after being transferred here from Estrella, Martin's horrific screams had woken the entire barracks as a cat-sized rat gnawed chunks of meat away from his face, starting at his jaw and chewing up just below his left eye. As Martin screamed, writhing in agony and bleeding all over his bunk, the rest of the barracks erupted in a cacophony of whoops and hollers, insanity breaking out as the inmates went after the rat. They'd gotten the rodent. Martin got three days in the infirmary.

A muffled voice came over the speakers swaying from the sun-bleached tent pole in the middle of the compound, waking him up. He sat up in his bunk and slipped his shoes on, wearing his prison-striped bottoms and his pink flannel undershirt. His striped top hung from the bunk. He grabbed it and slipped it on. A cool breeze blew in from the west, carrying the stench of horse crap and stale garbage. The temperatures were finally cooling down from the scorch of the Phoenix summer, but the stink was still just as rancid. He was thankful he only had to endure one summer in this stench as he was approaching the last month of his one-year stretch in County.

They'd nailed him on a traffic stop on January 14, almost two weeks after the shooting at Choo-Choo's. That night he'd picked up his new girl, Corina, and took her out cruising. He had Roger Rabbit southbound on Grand Ave about 10:30, Corina draped all over him, distracting him, causing him to weave around the road going 30 in a 45 mph zone. This caught the attention of a passing DPS cruiser, and after pulling him over and running his plates, the cop came back to the car and informed him that there was a warrant out for his arrest. Aggravated assault. Step out of the car, please.

As he was being cuffed, a Phoenix police cruiser came out to take Corina home. He watched them inventory his truck, confiscating his Chinese-made Norinco .9mm with all nine rounds, including one racked in the chamber, and his Davis .38-caliber. They then tucked him into the back of the DPS cruiser and he was soon back downtown, going through the booking process at Madison. Good ol' Choo-Choo's, still worked as sufficient collateral for bond.

That was when the court fight had begun. Nunez was right. His cases were never "scratched" as in wiped off the books. They had been more or less preserved, set aside like savings bonds becoming more valuable to the D.A. as more charges racked up. They pulled the assault and marijuana charges together, telling him he was looking at a couple of dimes worth of time—twenty years—as a personal guest of the State. Hope you like orange.

After eight months of court battle, he'd pled *nolo contendere* to all counts, accepting a plea of twelve months' county jail time and four years' probation. Pooling his charges made the State's case stronger, his attorney letting him know that he stood little chance in front of a jury.

"This is the way the State plays ball with guys like you, Rog'" his public defender had said. "Stick your charges in a little savings account, so to speak, dump it all on you later. Get you to plea so you don't gotta do the full time. That way they don't overload the courts and don't run out of beds at ADOC. In the meantime they make sure the real hell you go through is dealing with your case in court, the way they hang that serious time over your head. You're one of the few lucky ones. Most can't come up with bond, so they end up fighting their case from the cage."

It was either take the plea, or face the full rap through jury trial, and jury trial would give him max. Yeah, it had been hell all right, the long months thinking he'd be old and withered by the time he got out of the ADOC peels.

His sentence started October 16, 1992, the one-year stretch beginning at Estrella County Jail. His cell mate was a guy named Martin Hernandez doing county time for moving serious weight in marijuana up from Mexico. Arguing that he had a business to run, Roger qualified for work furlough. Just under a year into his stretch, Tent City was opened, built from a bundle of Korean War surplus tents that Sheriff Joe had obtained and enshrouded in a razor-ribbon campground behind the Estrella Jail. As a joke, a sign reading "VACANCY" glowed from the guard tower, setting the compound aglow in red neon every night. He and his pod over at Estrella were among the first of Joe's happy campers.

The tall, thin guy occupying the bunk next to him was still asleep. He'd been transferred from the Durango jail to Tents about a month ago, a fresh fish who'd introduced himself only once as Tony Rizzo and didn't say much after that. Although he was tall and had a ruddy toughness about him, he carried himself with a girlish timidity that made him an easy target. He'd seen Tony beat down at least twice in the last week, and Roger didn't care much for him. But after Martin lost work furlough and got sent to the Madison Street jail for fighting, he started getting to know Tony Rizzo a little bit better.

2:20 p.m.

• •

The tent flaps hung open and there wasn't much to do except watch the afternoon sun bake the desert floor, dryer and dryer by the minute. They were on lockdown, confined to their bunks, Roger flipping through a game of Solitaire, Tony stretched out on his bunk, hands interlocked behind his head, staring up at the bunk overhead.

Rizzo got right down to it, telling him all about himself. The guy didn't hold back much, flapping his gums, and he knew that this was a guy who'd turn on you real fast out in the streets. He blamed his partner for the whole thing, a guy named Miguel, the guy getting by on an aka of "Bobby Cruz."

"See, Bobby … Miguel … he was the one responsible for packing up the suitcases. I was just supposed to help carry them and buy the tickets. Miguel picked the stuff up and packed it. Man, wasn't smart enough to at least line the suitcases with something, you know, to throw the dogs off? I thought he'd be smart enough to do that."

"Would you have been?"

Tony was silent a minute, and he could see that he was thinking about it, trying to figure out what you'd line a suitcase with to throw the dogs off. Then Rizzo said, "No. I guess not. Anyway, they booked me in at Durango Jail, leaving me sitting in that stink hole, Building One, A Pod, till I could get my Uncle Vinnie to put up thirty-five hun'red for bail. Then I started playin' their court games the next two months. Man, I'm glad I made bail. I don't think I could'a stayed in that hole, goin' to court in stripes like those other guys."

"Where's Miguel now?"

"Over in Towers Jail. Man, he's sitting somewhere that's at least cool. Not like sitting out in this sweat. Anyway, Miguel's got priors. He's looking at doing some time up at ADOC. Me, I got six months here, work release, and then one year probation. I gotta do my probation here in Arizona, man. I can't leave the state. Can't go back to Cali. Man, if it wasn't for my girl Paulette I'd be sitting back in that hole in Durango. She's the one picks me up from here and takes me to my pool cleaning job. Without her, I'd violate, you know, not be able to get to my job, and they'd toss me back in Durango. There's some guys up there didn't like me real good." Which didn't surprise Roger. "Politics up there is real bad, man. I just couldn't play, you know?"

He lost his hand of Solitaire and started reshuffling the deck. "You really need to start getting a clue, Tony. You gotta start walking around here like you know what you're doing, otherwise you'll never see California soil again."

"That why you walk around here always lookin' so sure of yourself?"

He re-dealt his cards. "No one scares me around here because I don't let them."

"Man, I'm not sure what I'm gonna do, though. They're gonna give me this job full time when I'm done with my stretch in here. A permanent job, you know. But the cops took my truck, impounded it 'cause we used it to transport the weed up from Tucson. But Paulette, like I said, she's my ride, and now she says she's gotta go back to California. Her daughter is staying with her grandmom, and Paulette doesn't feel she's being such a good mom, being down here and all, helping me out. Says no way can she stay a whole year, driving me to work every day so I don't violate my probation. You know? 'Cause I gotta have a job, you know, to pay the probate fees and stuff. I mean, Roger, she's serious. She's talkin' about going back to Cali next week, man! Then I ain't got no ride and I'm going back to Durango for sure. I can't go back there, man. Not even for a day."

"So, buy yourself a junker, something that will get you back and forth to work."

"Got no money, man."

"You know, you find an awful lot of excuses for making life tough on yourself, don't you?"

Well that's when the dude really opened up, telling him all about his sad past. He told him about his recent problems in California with the divorce and how that was impacting his two young children.

Then he got into his childhood, telling Roger how his mother started abusing him at age five, two times so severely he was hospitalized. He said he'd attempted suicide three times after that, the last time was when he got himself admitted into a crisis hospital, and yeah, it got him feeling better, but the bills really sunk him. So, he thought, one or two runs for his uncle and he'd be in good shape.

And now here he was. The guy was a perpetual loser and Roger knew it.

Wednesday, September 15
• •

The only good thing about work furlough was he had nothing else to concentrate on other than his job, which allowed him to build a solid book of business. Every morning, Old Man McFadden would smile at him, pleased with the way his jail bird employee was producing. But he sensed a growing anxiousness about him. His hair thinning daily, worry turned McFadden's clayish pallor a deep gray under unshaven, prickly white beard stubble. He was gone a lot, out pushing hard to start up new branches throughout the Valley. When McFadden returned to the office late at night, he could smell the mint-masked stench of stale booze on his breath. He frequently asked how he was feeling, McFadden forcing a yellow-toothed smile, saying, "We're expanding, boy. Expanding." And then he'd lock himself in his office and he wouldn't see him the rest of the day.

One night he returned to the jail at 8, his curfew time, his new girl, Annette, dropping him off at the gate. As he joined the line of Joe's happy campers waiting outside to get processed back in, he saw Rizzo pushing his way through the crowd toward him.

"You look like death warmed over," he said to Rizzo. Worry lines creased Rizzo's face, and he looked like he hadn't slept in a month.

"I'm going back into the hole, man," Rizzo said. The line moved forward slowly. Ahead, a line of inmates, dressed in civilian clothes, stood spread-eagled, hands gripping the chain link fence, getting the usual rough pat down by the DOs working the gate tonight. "Durango. Man, they're sending me back to that stink hole Durango."

"What happened?"

"Paulette. Man, she's leaving on Friday. Back to Cali. Like I said she was gonna do."

The line inched forward again, he and Rizzo next to hit the fence.

"You're getting out in a month. It's not like you're gonna be sittin' in the hole for a full stretch. May do you some good. Quiet time to yourself."

"Roger, didn't you hear what I said the other day? I can't go back there. I got problems with people there. I won't last, Roger. I won't make it a week."

He was relieved when the DO cut their conversation short, ordering them to spread eagle on the fence. He was hoping that the interruption ended the conversation permanently, but no such luck. Walking in the sodium glow of the compound lights, Rizzo caught back up with him.

He said, "The only solution is if I could buy that heap I was telling you about. You know, the pickup I found for five hun'red? But, man, I ain't got the dough."

They entered their tent, walking to their bunks.

"Another solution would be to ask for PC. Make sure they don't stick you out on Main Street."

"Protective custody means I'm on twenty-three hour lockdown. Man, I can't handle that. No way."

"Then you got real problems, Tony."

He grabbed a paperback from his drawer and crawled into his bunk, shutting Rizzo off by sticking his nose in his book. Rizzo sat on the edge of his own bunk, staring down at the floor. "Man, if I could just come up with the five hun'red for that heap."

Getting tired of Rizzo's game, he closed his book, popped up on his elbow and said, "Why don't you just get to it and ask me, Tony?"

"Uh…you got five hun'red bucks you could float me, you know, until I can pay you back?"

"I ain't exactly got it on me, Tony."

"Yeah, but, you know, you work at some insurance agency, right? Me and Paulette, we could be there tomorrow morning, you tell me where it is."

The last thing he wanted was for Tony Rizzo to be able to connect with him on the outside. But the guy looked pathetic, genuinely terrified about going back to Durango. Even if he was able to get himself locked away in PC, he knew that he'd snap in lockdown, and they'd find him one morning in the showers dangling at the end of his towel wrapped around the showerhead. No one survives four attempts at suicide. He knew he'd regret it, but he heard himself saying, "Okay, Tony. You show up tomorrow and I'll float you the loan."

The next morning, he was at his desk when he looked up and saw a rusted-out maroon Impala pull into the parking lot. They got out of the car, Tony and a girl, the girl the one who was doing the driving, and came in, Tony with a big smile on his face.

After a few brief pleasantries, Tony said, "Hey, you never formally met Paulette."

She was a rail-thin, high-haired brunette with big brown eyes that could suck you right in. She had a straight-toothed smile and a voice of silk, and she gripped his hand with a subtle message that told him next time Tony ain't around, give me a lookup.

He gave Rizzo $500 in cash and they left, Paulette looking back and throwing him a wink and a pouty-lipped air kiss as Rizzo pushed his way through the door, eager to go pick up his new heap.

Roger figured he'd never see that money again.

As it turned out, it would have been better if he hadn't.

CHAPTER ELEVEN

Tucson, Arizona
February, 1996
• •

"See, but the way it turns out, you cost me over a hun'red grand."

Tony Rizzo, trying to talk tough into his drink. They were sitting at an open-air bar looking out at the crazy pastel-colored stucco buildings of downtown Tucson. Rizzo had a tall draft beer in front of him and was working on an oversized, rare-cooked burger and heaping plate of fries.

Tony did eventually return to repay the five hundred bucks he'd borrowed. He came back a year later, showing up looking really dime, all studded out in gold and driving new wheels. Turned out, while Roger had spent the previous year keeping straight, sticking to his probation, Tony started expanding. Tony spilled it all, as usual, telling Roger how he'd started running loads of weed to his uncle's customers all over the country, on the road all the time, moving major weight and collecting ten large per load. Then he'd picked up some customers on his own, his best guy a Yid up in Detroit they called Robbie the Jew.

Tony was an idiot, telling him how he almost didn't live past his first load up to Robbie, how he'd pulled the whole thing together by securing a bundle of high-quality hemp from Carlos, his connection in Mexico. He had driven the whole load up to Detroit himself in February, coming up from Arizona not dressed right for the freezing slop and slush of downtown Detroit in the middle of winter. Tony said he was supposed to meet Robbie at a place called the Omni Hotel, but when he got there, one of Robbie's flunkies, a big black guy named Juan White, met him in the bar. Tony said that he had left the load in the car, the car parked

72

down the street, and Juan seemed overly eager to get the car keys and go check out the load before paying him. Tony said he thought he was playing it right, insisting they go check out the load together, but he only ended up ticking Juan off. Juan came back and said the stuff wasn't quality, offering him half of what they'd agreed to. Tony said he had no other connections in Detroit and didn't want to get stuck taking the load back, so he called Carlos and got Carlos to agree to Juan's offer.

When Tony got back to his uncle's ranch in Tucson, Carlos was there, standing outside his uncle's barn, leaning against the pickup, sipping a longneck Bud. Tony handed him the cash, expecting Carlos to peel off the ten K payment and give him his split as he usually did. Instead, Carlos pocketed everything, telling Tony that he owed him over fifty grand, to make up the difference. Tony said he didn't understand. Carlos had agreed to the deal when he'd called him from Detroit. But Carlos explained in his nutty way that he expected a certain margin out of every deal, and he expected his guys to make up the difference whenever a load fell short. Tony said he'd gotten two words out in protest before a set of brass knuckles shut his mouth for a month.

Tony also explained that he'd stopped running loads for Uncle Vinnie, Vinnie owing him money. It was okay, though. It made him focus on getting customers, which Tony said he was good at. The only thing Tony seemed good at, he figured, was getting ripped off.

Tony paid him back the five hundred, peeling it off a wad of bills he wanted him to see.

But he knew that Tony had an ulterior motive in showing up to pay back the money. Tony, working an angle, wanted in on the insurance business and asked if McFadden had franchising opportunities, asking if he could set it up so he could open a branch down in Tucson. Tony claimed he wanted to start something legit. He knew that Rizzo needed a way to launder his dope money.

McFadden wanted a hundred grand to start the franchise. Tony plopped it down in cash, and McFadden assigned Roger to oversee the new Tucson operation, keeping him tied closer to Tony Rizzo than he wanted to be.

Tony never made a dime on his investment, never taking the thing seriously. Paulette mainly ran the operation. Roger made regular trips down there, trying to get the thing solvent, trying to show Paulette how to make it work. But the branch kept sinking, Paulette becoming a basket case, Tony always too doped up on his own supply to notice that his business was heading for the sewer.

And then McFadden announced he was bankrupt. That's when it all came together—McFadden's battle with the bottle; his constant meetings with bankers; his crazy, around-the-clock schedule.

He had expanded faster than his dough could keep up.

The Tucson operations were liquidated with everything else. When Roger showed up to put the "Out of Business" sign on Tucson's doors, Tony started talking trash, grabbing his phone and letting Roger know that he was making a call right now, going to have some of his "people" drive up to Phoenix and pop McFadden. As Tony pounded the dial pad, Roger walked out to his car and grabbed his holstered .9mm. It had been the first time since the start of his probation that his finger curled around the trigger of a gun and the rush of power felt good. He walked back in, Tony on the phone, and walked up to him and dotted his forehead with the barrel of the gun, saying, "Lighten up, Tony."

Tony put the phone down, not even bothering to say goodbye. When Paulette came in the office, all wrapped snug in a thigh-length Halston dress, Tony tried to act tough, his voice squeaking as he said, "Get out. You and me, we're done."

He walked out, holding the gun at his side, feeling it again—that power surge that came from pinning a guy down at the gun point, the feeling of control over life and death—more powerful than any drug. Once again, he'd tried to play it straight, the life of crime costing him a year's freedom. He had been certain that his one-year stretch in the Tents was enough to keep him straight. Certain, until the power surge that came from dotting Rizzo's head with a gun barrel got him rethinking things.

He missed the godlike feeling of complete control. The kind of control you only got from power—the kind of power that only came from handling the business end of a gun.

Roger kept his clients and talked his parents into using the West Side location to open their own insurance outfit, still feeling guilty about what happened to them with Choo-Choo's. They renamed the establishment "Diamondback Insurance." His probation continued keeping him focused and out of trouble until six months later when he'd received another call from Tony, wanting him to drive down to Tucson and have a meeting. He made sure he was packing his .9mm when he drove down to meet him, re-igniting the power surge, giving Roger that sense of invulnerability that he'd started craving again.

So now here he was, Tony getting right to it, reminding him again how much he'd lost.

"Tony, it was an investment, okay? Sometimes you win, sometimes you lose. You take a risk."

"You mean to say you didn't know the old man was having financial problems? Man, you could'a just told me. I would'a backed out, man."

"No, Tony, I didn't know."

Tony shook his head, taking a sip of beer. "Wish I could believe you, man. A hun'red grand."

"So what do you want me to do about it, Tony? What?"

Tony sat there, staring out at the pastel-colored buildings, mouth of the beer mug resting on his chin, making it look like he was giving it some thought. He'd plumped up over the year, and if Carlos didn't eventually kill him, his grease-polluted arteries would.

It was just a matter of time for either one.

Rizzo sat there a long time, pretending to think about things. But Roger knew different. The guy had this all planned out.

"I got some drivers running product for me. I'm trying to send them on a couple new routes, helping me set up some new customers. But I gotta make sure I take good care of the Jew up in Detroit. He's a guy you don't wanna tick off, and he's gonna get ticked if I don't keep his product flowin'."

The bartender set another Absolut and orange juice in front of Roger. "What kind of product and weight are we talking about?"

Tony cocked an eyebrow at him, pleased that he was showing an interest. "Between four and five hun'red pounds per load. Weed. All wrapped for you and loaded in duffel bags. All you do is slip behind the wheel of my Jeep, drive to Detroit and make the drop. Make sure

Robbie the Jew don't try and stiff you like he done my first trip up there. Juan White's the guy you gotta watch out for. Don't trust him. Outside a that, it's simple. I usually pay anywhere from ten to fifteen grand to my drivers for making the Detroit run. You do five straight for me and I'll call the debt even."

He felt a rush that he hadn't felt in a long time. This was beyond the rush he'd felt in moving the small weight of product that cost him one year down in the Tents. First, the gun in his hand the day he dotted Rizzo's forehead. Now this. It all felt good. Real good. Money and power were once again within his grasp.

He knew he owed Tony nothing. The guy made an investment and handled it like a moron. Tony was dumb and lazy, two of the most dangerous traits in a criminal. Yeah, maybe times were good for Tony for now, running dope around the country, but Roger knew he wasn't going to last. He was riding lucky, but when luck runs out, it's the ones with brains, instinct, and the ability to use the irons who survive.

Tony had none of that going for him. He was a moron. Worse, he was a moron who thought he was good—making him a dangerous moron.

However, Roger's instinct told him this lucky wave may last just long enough for him to get in on something.

"So, what do you say, Rog'?"

He gulped down the rest of his drink, feeling compelled to set Tony straight. "You run your dope business the way you ran your insurance business, you and I are gonna have serious problems down the road, you got that? I only warn you once. I'll go check this thing out. I sense anything wrong, anything out of line, I come back with the product, pop a cap right dead center in the middle of that high forehead of yours and I find my own customer — we understand each other?"

Tony turned on his seat and looked at Roger, trying to look him straight in the eye. "You threatening me?"

"No. I'm promising you."

"Don't screw with Carlos' stuff, I need to warn you about that."

"I don't sweat Carlos."

"You should."

"No one messes with me. No one messes with my stuff. I'm just laying it out straight, Tony. I'll do this for you. But you try and screw me, you're a carcass."

He held out his hand, and Tony took it. Tony's hand was cold and clammy, but the deal was sealed.

Hrach, "Roger Rabbit" Munchian, feeling the rush of power, was back in business.

CHAPTER TWELVE

Detroit, February 1996

• •

The guy on the radio, Detroit 760, WJR, was saying that with the wind-chill, the temperature outside was ten below. Roger knew that it would be even colder downtown, with the wind blowing off the ice-covered Detroit River and howling between the stone and granite buildings of downtown. And that nut-job Robbie the Jew wanted him to park the damn Jeep at some meter five blocks away, thinking he was idiot enough to hoof it through the winter slop.

No way.

He pulled right into the parking garage of the Omni. In the back of the Jeep, hidden amongst other bags of luggage, was a duffel bag full of tightly-wrapped bails of marijuana. Two hundred pounds. He pulled into the closest parking slot to the elevator.

He looked at his watch as he entered the posh hotel lobby. Fifteen minutes late. Perfect. You arrive late to these things, give yourself a chance to scope out trouble. He stopped near the front desk, giving himself a view of the lounge, noticing that the bar was populated mostly by slump-shouldered business men and tired-looking women, but no one matching Robbie's description. But there was a beefy black dude there, fat-lipping a Bud, obsessing with his cell phone, anxiously watching the entrance to the lounge. He let him stew another five minutes before walking in.

The guy watched him enter the bar, no reaction at first until he realized that this was the guy he was waiting for. He saw the anger flush across his face as he stood up from the barstool.

"You Munchian?" He asked.

"Who wants to know?"

"Don't play cute. I ain't in the mood."

"You don't match the description of the guy I'm lookin' for."

"Yeah? What's he supposed to look like?"

"Who's askin'?"

"Boy, you don't know who you's messin' with."

"I have a pretty good idea."

They stood there, staring each other down, Roger knowing that the guy was thinking about his next move, sizing up this newbie. He shook his head and let out a laugh, slipping back onto his barstool. "Okay, man. Name's Juan. Juan White. You's lookin' for a guy named Robbie, right?"

"That's who I set the appointment with. Why ain't he here?"

"He's the boss. Boss ain't gotta do nothin' he don't wanna do. He sent me. You wanna tell me where the Jeep is? You was supposed to park it up the street."

"How do you know it's not there? You got somebody watchin'?"

"We gotta make sure you followin' the plan. Which you ain't so far."

"Or maybe you're just looking to jack my product."

"Where's the vehicle?"

"It's around. Where's the money?"

"It's around. Robbie tell you how this works?"

"He made some suggestions."

"*Suggestions*?! Man, who you think you talkin' to?" The guy made a move with his hand, pushing his jacket up so he could see the butt of the gun tucked in the waistband of his jeans. He looked Juan firm in the eye and gave the right pocket of his jacket a little pat, making sure they understood each other. Juan swallowed hard then said, "The way it works is you give me the keys to the vehicle and wait here while I go get the product checked out. That's the gig, holmes."

"Not this time."

"How 'm I supposed to make sure the product is good?"

He stepped in closer to Juan and pulled a sandwich bag of weed from his pocket, tucked it in his hand. "Get this checked out. If Jew-boy likes it, I take you where the rest of it is, we make the exchange."

Juan stared at him, then let out a laugh and tucked the bag of weed in his jacket pocket. He slugged down the rest of his beer and said, "You're one crazy onion, but I like your style. Your guy, Tony, he's an idiot, and he hires idiots to run for him. Not you, though." Juan stuck his hand out and he accepted it. "Yeah, I think we can do good work together. Sometimes I hear things, you know, people who appreciate a good delivery guy. I'll let you know."

Just outside Detroit
April 1996

Roger finally met Robbie the Jew on his third load up to Detroit and had a bad feeling about him right away. He stood at five-nine, about 190 pounds and a graying goatee despite the fact that he was in his mid-thirties. Engine oil-blackened fingers and calloused hands told him that the guy was a gear head who probably spent most of his days bent over the hoods of old heaps that had seen better days since rolling off the Detroit assembly lines.

They met at a small greasy-spoon diner called "Walt's Coney Island," a rickety dive with a wooden sun-glassed hot dog hanging over the front door. Robbie pulled a Coney dog from its puddle of grease and chomped half of it down with one bite, licking the grease from his oil-blackened fingers.

Roger had a Coke.

"You don't know what you're missin' man," Robbie said, chunky hot dog juice pushing past his lips and vanishing into the silvery curl of his goatee. "Detroit, man, nowhere but Detroit do you get Coney dogs like this."

"So, go on, you tellin' me how this works," Roger said, wanting to get this meeting over with.

"Yeah. Well, okay, so, let me get this straight. Rizzo's got you running his loads for free?"

"I agreed to clear a debt for him."

Robby shook his head and finished the rest of the dog in one bite and went for the second one. "You're a natural at this. Juan says you're smart.

You could easily set up your own gig. Sniff out a few good customers. I can set you up with a couple suppliers. Boom. You're in. Stay away from that crazy Carlos, though. Too volatile. Rizzo, he's heading for trouble with that one. One, he ain't smart enough to see it. Two, he's too dumb to know how to get out of it once Carlos's gears pop loose."

"So what are you saying?"

"Untie yourself from Rizzo as soon as you can. First impression we got of the guy, the first load he delivered to us, he showed up here middle of winter in a windbreaker and tennis shoes and lets Juan take him, getting him to agree to take half on the load. Shows us right away he's a guy who can get rolled. Got clocked good by Carlos when he got back, brass knuckle indentation in his face. Dumb. And he's getting slow and fat. I gotta pinch him soon for screwing up a load last month."

"You'd planned on pinching him big *my* first time, didn't you? Juan had someone ready to jack the vehicle as soon as I parked it, do I read that right?"

Robby dug into his second dog. "What's past is past, you know. Yeah, cars get stolen in downtown Detroit all the time. Place is worse than Beirut, you know? Only difference is we got that big glass stack of poker chips down on the River they call the Renaissance Center and an oversized welcome sign in the shape of Joe Louis's fist shouting racial harmony.

"You know, one time I drove a load up to Fargo and I drove through Brainerd. *They* got a big blue ox up there. *We* got a spade fist. Sometimes I think they oughta just put a big switchblade in that fist and tell folks what to really expect here. Welcome to Detroit. But, yeah, hey, I'll admit it. Tony tells me out of the blue he's got a new guy coming up my way. I ain't too pleased with his usual guy, the dude who always looks like he smoked half the stash on the way, so I don't have real high expectations, you know. But then a guy like you shows up, Juan telling me I gotta meet this guy, a smart onion runs circles around him. Made me rethink things, you know? Takes a lot for Juan to admit to something like that."

"Thanks for the vote of confidence. So, again, how do things work around here?"

Robby inhaled the rest of his Coney and shoved the plate away. "The way you differentiate yourself is by proving you can move good product and get it fast. You deliver it good and you deliver it quick, and you're dime. Tony's got a pretty good supplier. But the way Tony runs things..." Robby shook his head. "Sloppy. I handle mostly west side. Farmington Hills, Southfield area. Some blacks, but a lot of affluent whites. You know. Auto execs and such. My east side guy is Simon. I ain't gonna tell you his last name, but he deals with the east side blacks real good. He's had a tough time penetrating the Chaldean community though. The guy known there, ironically, is another guy named Simon, but spells it with an 'e'. Chaldean guy named Simen Semma." Robbie chuckled. "Typical rag head. Goes by other names like Hundred-Percent, Yo, and Teflon Simen. Anyway, I been trying to tap his network over there in the southeast suburbs. Big camel jockey community over there, but they're tight, you know. Thing is, Roger, you get a rep delivering it good and delivering it fast, you'll do good. Shootings, jackings, not at our level. Let the Neanderthals below us kill each other off. We just buy it and distribute it, you know. You ready to make some serious coin now, Roger? I mean *really* serious?"

"You said no jackings, yet you were going to jack my first load up here."

"Just to pinch Tony a little." Robby stood up and dropped a few bills on the table. On the way out he grabbed a toothpick from the dispenser at the counter and picked his teeth all the way out to the Maserati parked across the parking lot. He reached inside the car and handed Roger an envelope. Roger gave it a quick count. One-hundred grand. "This your last freebie run for Rizzo?"

"Might be."

"Should be. You break free, you got my digits."

CHAPTER THIRTEEN

Phoenix
September 1996
· ·

Roger decided he now needed two things: an additional supplier and a driver. Things had grown fast after he'd run his final load for Tony Rizzo. After he'd met his obligation to Rizzo, Tony asked him if he wanted to keep going, you know, make some real cash now that he knew how things worked. But he wanted to cut loose from him. He was going to get back in the game, he was going to do it on his own terms, and he was not going to be tied to an idiot like Rizzo.

Juan White had set him up with a connection in Detroit, a guy who regularly wanted product a deuce at a time. He'd pulled some connections together from L.A, and after he re-connected with Chico Martinez, he was making regular trips back to Cali to pick up product. His reputation grew quickly, a guy who could get quality product, fast and efficient. Just like before. But now he was moving serious weight.

He pulled into the short driveway of the pink stucco shack at the end of the street. The last time he'd been in this neighborhood he was driving Roger Rabbit, tunes booming hip hop bumps that echoed off the chipped stucco and chewed asphalt of the urban Mexican barrio. Now he was sitting in the freshly broken leather of a Mercedes 500 SEL, bought in a cash deal at Scottsdale Benz.

The sun-splintered front door opened and the wiry figure of Arnulfo stepped out onto the porch. He held a gun in his hand, not sure who this was or why this vehicle was in his driveway. Roger popped the door open and got out, leaning over the car door. He slipped his sunglasses from his face and said, "'Nulfo, man, it's me!"

Arnulfo couldn't get over it, sitting there in the passenger seat playing with every electronic gadget within reach. All Roger had told him when he called was that he had an opportunity for him to make some serious coin and to pack a bag and be ready to head out of town with him for a few days. Then he shows up in this bad ride, steps out, all tailored and looking real dime in new threads. Now they were heading toward the airport, Roger telling him all about it, all about the trips he'd been making to Detroit, making connections up there, moving some serious weight—up to 800 pounds of weed a month.

Roger took Sky Harbor airport exit off the I-10. He valet-parked the Benz at terminal 3 and they were soon sitting in the Northwest World Perks lounge. 'Nulfo ordered himself a Heineken while Roger ordered an Absolut and orange juice. Roger continued explaining things to him.

"We're heading to L.A. I'm going to introduce you to my connection there. We're going to run a load together, up to Detroit. I'll show you how it's done. First few trips I'll be there, then you'll be running the loads yourself."

Roger was smooth, man. He was always cool, but now, man, the way he dressed now, the ride he was driving, the way the chicks looked at him around here. It was like overnight, the way he became a rock star. A real rock star.

Oooh yeah!

"I pay you five large per load to start." He was listening with real interest as Roger explained, impressed by his gold cuff links glimmering off the Arizona sunshine coming through the Perks windows as he tipped his crystal glass. *Yeah, real cool.* "You'll do two runs a month. I don't do nothing on spec. My supplier in L.A.; I buy the product right from him and move it. I don't move product and hope I don't get ripped off and not be able to pay my supplier. That's how people get hurt. I get a solid order from Detroit, get it set up with my guy in L.A., pay him in full. Understand, you get ripped off, you owe me. Watch me, do it the way I do it, and you'll be okay."

Sounding confident. Arnulfo liked it. If he was gonna do this, Roger was the guy to run with. They flew to LAX and Roger introduced him to a guy named Chico who ran an auto parts store just outside of Hollywood. The store had a four-lift garage attached to it and Roger walked back and grabbed a set of keys from a rack that belonged to a new maroon Mountaineer. He popped open the hatch and Roger showed him the bad speaker boxes back there.

"Great bumps! Man, custom fit? Serious coin," he said.

Then he watched as Roger reached over and pulled one of the speakers out of the box. There were no wires. The box was a fake. Inside he saw a burlap bag.

"We've got a hundred twenty-five pounds of grade A hemp loaded here and another over there." Roger pointed to the speaker's sister next to it. "We're moving two hundred and fifty pounds today. You ready to see how this works?"

What else could he say? The answer was yes. Roger had put them up in a five-star hotel on the beach for the night and at 5:00 sharp the next morning they were on their way to Detroit.

Roger was about to find out why they called her Big Mama Su.

Lazy Su's Fish & Chips sat on the southeast corner of 7th Street and Portland among a cluster of taco stands, thrift stores and shacks advertising "Payday Loans." The sign over the paint-chipped awning was sun-faded and bowed from the intense Phoenix sun. The filthy windows were tattooed in handwritten cardboard signs advertising today's specials, a neon "Open" sign that only glowed with the O and E in flickering red and a sign that said, "We Deliver."

When he walked in, he saw Su's brother AB sitting at the counter, hunched over a greasy basket of breaded fish parts and oil-saturated french fries. AB pronounced phonetically by two letters of his name, Aye-Bee. He originally met AB and the rest of his Chaldean clique in the Empire Club's VIP lounge, and he'd heard that AB was well-connected. As it turned out, AB's prime connection was his own sister, Suhad.

It was after 2:00 in the afternoon and he could feel the coagulated grease engulf his shoes as he approached AB. "Quite a place," he told

AB, deciding against taking a seat when he noticed the grease swirls in the shredded red vinyl of the swivel chair next to AB.

"She actually does quite a business here," AB said, his jowls wet and goatee matted to his chin in grease. AB dipped his last fish stick in tartar sauce and wolfed it down. "Suhad!" he shouted toward the back.

Behind the counter hung a set of swinging double doors, the kind you saw in the bars in the old west. Su's enormous frame filled the entire doorway, lintel to lintel, frame to frame. Her fleshy jowls stretched into a grin of sparse, gold-rimmed teeth. She let out a laugh that sounded as though it had been let loose from deep within some desert canyon as she pushed her way through the door.

AB said, "Big Mama, this is the guy I was telling you about. Roger."

The tree-trunk sized arm extended and he found a hand to shake somewhere in the outreached mound of blubber.

"He's cute. Can I keep him?" Another bellow sounded up from deep within that bosomy canyon.

He felt himself instinctively going for his gun, not yanking it out, but casually sliding his hand within reach, especially when he saw the chiseled black dude come in through the side entrance. A powder blue T-shirt bearing the Lazy Su's logo fit tight over his broad torso and a pick-comb stuck out from his thick afro.

Su said, "You look sharp, Roger. Too sharp for around here." She had rancid halitosis from the mounds of rotting food left sunken in the inflamed gums that held rotting teeth loosely in place.

"I dress my part," he said, his eyes meeting her beady stare. She smiled, seeming to like what she was seeing.

"Hey, Big Mama," the black dude shouted from the rear door. "Did that Yid come through yet? My money here?"

"Nothing yet, Mo', okay? I got people working on it."

"Hey, I need my money. You knew that Jew had a history of runnin' on his bills like this. Look, me and Gibby, we been talkin'. We know where his mama is. He keeps his little Yid kids there most nights, okay? Me and Gibby, we go by and pop a few caps through the front door. We take out the Yid's kids. We take out the mama, okay too. Man, I'm out nearly ten grand because of that Heeb! I don't care how I get it."

"Mo'" Su said. "I'm conducting business here."

Mo turned and left. From the window, Roger watched as he yanked the Lazy Su's delivery sign off from the top of his car, ripped his "Lazy Su's" shirt off and got behind the wheel bare chested and peeled off.

"He'll be back," Su said. "Hey, you need a driver? Mo' Wilson's a bit of a loose cannon. But he gets the job done. Real name is Maurice. Mo' for short."

"No, thanks. I'm set." He only trusted Arnulfo. He could control Arnulfo and could count on him. Mo' was the kind of moron that Rizzo would hire.

Big Mama showed him some samples of her product and he liked what he saw. They came to terms and he now had a new supplier, negotiating a deal with Big Mama that didn't require him to eat one greasy fish stick.

CHAPTER FOURTEEN

Tucson
February 1997

• •

Rizzo was in trouble.

Roger had gotten a frantic call from him begging him to come down and help. *Please!* Telling him Carlos was going to put a bullet between his eyes.

The way Tony explained it, his guy up in Detroit, Robbie the Jew, stiffed him on several loads. Roger asked what did he mean *several*? Get stiffed once by a guy and pop a bullet in his knee cap and maybe give him another chance once he learns to walk again. He does it again, silence him permanent with one between the eyes.

But Rizzo was an idiot. Now he was into Carlos for over two hundred grand.

"You got the money?" He asked Rizzo.

"Yeah, I got it, yeah. I got arrangements to pay Carlos off. He wants his money but he don't want me no more. After I pay him off, he's gonna pop me."

"So what do you want me to do about it?"

"Man, I need someone with irons here. Even if you're just in the background, you know, just there, letting him know he tries anything he's got problems. Look, the exchange will be quick. I get square with him, break things off clean and he goes away quietly."

"And if he starts something?"

"Well, that's your department. Man, I need you. Roger, he's gonna *kill* me!"

He was driving on I-10 toward Tucson, cruising smooth in his latest acquisition: a Mercedes 600 Coup, vanity plate reading "Hrach." The surrounding bulletproof glass pushed the final sticker price past the buck-fifty range. Bulletproofing his ride seemed like overkill, but since he'd nabbed Simen Semma as a customer up in Detroit, the stakes were running higher. The Chaldean cartel did not play games. He'd seen guys get popped, one .22-caliber behind the ear, for nothing more than complaining about the price of a load.

He was moving over five hundred pounds of marijuana a month now and the cash was rolling in. Real estate was his favorite method of keeping his drug enterprise laundered. Drug transactions were also easily lost in ventures with car dealerships, auto body shops and night club partnerships, which also came with VIP perks like the Empire Club. The night club babes always smelled the money man in the operation and Roger wore his silent ownership like a fine musk.

Despite the insurance business's cash-rich potential for laundering money, Roger kept Diamondback Insurance clean, ensuring his parents' safety from his criminal enterprises. If anything went wrong they could take it all from him—except Diamondback Insurance. Not that anything would actually *go* wrong. Things were going great and he felt as slick as Teflon. He was untouchable and nothing was going to stop him.

Nothing.

He pulled the Mercedes into the driveway and parked next to the black Saab belonging to Carlos. The way Rizzo planned it out, he had the $200k mailed to him, sent the way Roger liked to do things, always cautious, the money broken up and sent in increments to various addresses he owned. Rizzo figured that once Carlos arrived, he would tell him that he didn't have the money on him but it was coming by courier.

He reached under the front seat and grabbed his Colt .45, then grabbed the leather pouch containing Carlos's money and stepped out of the car. He pulled open the screen door and knocked, then pushed the door open and entered fast in case anyone was waiting inside ready to put a few slugs through the door.

He knew they didn't hear him knock or come in, not over Carlos's shouts and Rizzo's girly whimpers. He saw them in the kitchen, Rizzo sitting at the table, Carlos standing over him, gun barrel stuck to Rizzo's temple.

"I said gi'me the money, Tony! You got ten seconds!"

"P-please, Carlos, I told you, I ain't got it here. It's coming! I promise you, it's coming!"

Putting his thumb on the Colt's hammer, he said, "Put the gun down, Carlos," saying it calm, stepping into the kitchen, fixing the gun site directly between Carlos's eyes.

Carlos' mouth moved up and down but no words came out. He was a short, thin beaner with a beak nose and a haircut that reminded him of Moe from the Three Stooges. Carlos pulled the gun away from Rizzo's temple and slowly lowered it to his side.

Slowly pulling the Colt's hammer back, he said, "That's not what I asked you to do. I said put it down. Do it slow, otherwise I'm going to wallpaper that kitchen wall with what little brains you got rattling around in that mindless head of yours."

Ferocity burned behind Carlos's eyes as he slowly placed the gun on the kitchen table.

"Good." He tucked the Colt between the small of his back and his waistband. "Sorry I'm late, Tony."

Carlos said, "What are you doing here, onion? This is between me and him."

He unzipped the pouch and pulled out the cash. "I'm here to broker the settlement of Tony's debt."

"What do you mean *broker*?"

"You want your money or not, Carlos?" He dropped the cash on the kitchen table. "Take your cash and leave. That's all you gotta do."

Carlos stood for a minute, a stupid, puzzled look on his face, Roger knowing that he was not sure of what to make of this as he picked up the cash and counted it, not liking the first count and counting it again.

Carlos said, "One-hundred-eighty. Stupid onion, where'd you learn your math?"

He stepped forward, getting in Carlos' face, making sure to stand between him and the table, keeping him out of reach of his gun. "I only let my friends call me 'onion.' I tell you that once, not again."

"You're twenty K short!"

"Two hundred K minus my ten percent."

"*Ten* percent?"

He saw Rizzo go wide-eyed, saying, "Ten percent? Holy sh'…geeze Roger…wha'…'"

Carlos said, "For *what*, you stupid onion?"

He said, "I warned you. I only tell you once." Then he drove an uppercut hard into Carlos' groin, doubling him over. He grabbed a fistful of his Moe hairdo and slammed his head into the table multiple times, then slammed him hard to the linoleum floor. He grabbed the wad of cash from the table and shoved it into Carlos' mouth, using the barrel of the Colt to wedge it securely. Blood seeped down the corners of Carlos' mouth as he grabbed another fist full of his hair, yanking him to his feet, bouncing him from one wall to the other, his head cracking plaster as he ping-ponged him down the hallway and tossed him headfirst through the screen door.

He watched Carlos collapse on the front porch, hearing his pathetic whimpers as he tried to scramble to his feet. He shoved him forward with his foot, then grabbed him by the head again and dragged him to the Saab, slamming his head into the quarter panel.

"Nice doing business with you, Carlos," he said, tossing Carlos into the front seat, Carlos spitting the wad of bloody cash out of his mouth as he cranked the engine over and squealed out of the driveway.

Rizzo was still soaking in his own sweat at the broken kitchen table when he came back in.

"I think I need a new connection," Rizzo said. "Can you set me up?"

"I'll see what I can do."

"*Brokerage* fee?"

"I never work for free, Tony. Never."

CHAPTER FIFTEEN

April 30, 1997
Sevier County, Utah

• •

Arnulfo had just crossed the border from Arizona into Utah, heading northeast on I-15. He'd picked up a load in L.A., a small one this time, 120 lbs. Roger had bought a new ride for him. A nice one. A white Grand Cherokee. This shipment was going to a new connection in Denver and he was on his regular route, I-15 out of California, up through Utah to the I-70 split and into Denver.

He loved what Roger had become. He was a hotshot before, but, man, look at him now. Wow. Roger had customers all over the place, keeping him hopping nonstop and even trusting him with his prize customer up in Detroit, that rag head cartel big dog named Simen. He admired the way Roger could stay one step ahead of the law, keeping a low profile but always slick. Roger even got married recently, wanting to keep a clean image. The wedding was a big deal, his parents throwing a huge Armenian gig. But the image was short-lived, Roger getting antsy after just a few months, needing to set his loins free, getting the divorce proceedings going, closing the marriage down quick like any other business transaction. Get it done quick. Move on to the next big deal, living fast. Living large.

Yeah, that was Roger all right. Living big. Larger than life.

He was impressed with the way Roger was able to quickly make connections, making regular trips down to Mexico, checking out the dope farms, making sure the product was quality and the delivery routes clean. And Roger was generous, always paying him large and paying on time. Roger even kicked in a bonus for him last year when he recruited a new driver, his adopted father, the guy everyone called Pops.

He also noticed that the more successful Roger got, the less he used. It wasn't like the old days when Roger moved his product all red-eyed and jagged out on his own supply. He was real cool about it now, the entire operation a well-run machine. He dressed sharp, looked cool and reinvested his dough, not stuffing it up his nose or sucking it down his lungs. Yeah, Roger was unstoppable.

Arnulfo was relieved when that idiot Rizzo got out of the business last year, having crawled, tail between his legs, back into the pool business. He never liked delivering product to that guy, things always unstable around him, a bunch of crazy drivers always working for him. Rizzo had gone broke, the way he kept getting ripped off, always needing to borrow money from Roger to cover his losses, keeping his connections from blowing his head off. He also heard that Rizzo's cute little tart, Paulette, had finally left him and went back to California. Rizzo snapped, going loco, using more dope in a week than he could move in a month.

Arnulfo tried to imitate Roger but just couldn't shake the dope need. Money was rolling in and the more he had, the more he spent. He blew through his entire wad month after month, getting into the hard stuff—cocaine and meth. He knew he was out of control but he felt invincible. Roger *was* invincible and being around Roger made *him* feel invincible.

He exited I-15 and headed east on I-70 at the split, holding the needle right with the posted speed limit. The I-70 curved northeast just outside of the city of Sevier, and he was getting uncomfortable with the amount of state police cruisers that had passed him in the last hour. It was a bad omen, and as he approached the city of Joseph he decided to get off the freeway and take State Route 118.

It was not a wise decision from what Roger had taught him. Roger said to always stick to the interstates. You get pulled over on a back road, you look more suspicious driving a detoured route with out-of-state plates. They pull you over on the interstate, your cover story makes sense. You're a vacationer traveling across country or a business man driving his territory. On the back roads, your story doesn't always stack up and they always wanna check out your story a little further.

State Route 118 became Route 120 just past the Richfield Municipal Airport and was Main Street through the little town of Richfield. Not more than five miles out of town, he saw brake lights up ahead and a long line of traffic inching along in the northbound lane. After about ten minutes stuck in the crawl-like traffic, cars stacking up behind him, he saw the blue gumball lights of sheriff cars up ahead. He counted three of them up there and could see about four tan-uniformed deputies, wearing those Smokey the Bear hats, stopping each passing car, asking the question that if you answered right, you were waved through; if you answered wrong, there was a spot on the side of the road where you pulled off and they examined you further.

He was now ten cars from the roadblock. He looked in the rear view mirror and saw a few cars split off from the line and head back south, taking an alternate route rather than waiting in this mess. He knew that he could go the other way, backtrack his way into Richfield. But he'd lose a lot of time that way and, besides, he was only five cars away from getting through the check point. He didn't see any K-9s around and the deputy just seemed to be waving cars through. He straightened his tie, the one he wore because Roger always insisted he wore a shirt and tie running loads in order to draw less suspicion. He checked his hair in the rear view mirror, sat up confident, and got ready. All the windows in the vehicle were cracked open, making sure the Jeep was aired out. He could do this. He was invincible.

He rolled down his window and the wiry deputy who looked like Barney Fife nodded at him with his Smokey the Bear hat. "Afternoon, sir."

"Afternoon, officer." He practiced that, restraining his Hispanic accent, especially when greeting the heat. Roger made him work on it regularly.

"Where are you driving from?" the officer asked. Dang—he even sounded like Barney Fife.

"Arizona. Phoenix area."

"Where you headed?"

He knew he had to keep cool. Keep the story simple. "Denver."

"For?"

He felt himself getting nervous. The guy was obviously asking him more questions than he'd asked the last fifty cars he'd let pass. "Business. It's part of my route."

"What kind of business?"

He was prepared for the question. Roger had the SUV registered to the name of a dummy corporation in the construction supply business. "Tools mostly." He grabbed a glossy brochure of power tools from the passenger seat and flashed it at the deputy. He kept the brochure handy, hoping it would be enough of a distraction to keep a curious cop from asking further questions. "National sales rep. I cover the entire United States."

The skeletal deputy scratched his chin. He peeked in the rear view mirror and could see another deputy standing at the door of his cruiser, speaking into the radio mic, staring at the back of the Grand Cherokee, calling in the plates.

He heard the deputy say, "On the road a lot, I suppose?"

"Oh, it's brutal," trying to keep the conversation short. Simple.

"So, up I-15 to the I-70 split right into Denver?"

He hesitated longer than he should have. "Usually, yeah."

"You know, I'm getting the scent of something in your vehicle there that doesn't exactly smell like tool oil."

"What do you mean?"

"If I was to be a betting man, I'd say if I popped open the back of your vehicle we'd find a few bales of dope back there."

Now he started feeling cocky, so he said, "Okay, I'll bet you the $500 bucks I have in my wallet." And he showed the deputy a wad of one hundred dollar bills. The deputy got the hint, but didn't like it.

"You wanna pull off to the side over there for me, sir?"

Pulling off, he knew he'd made a serious mistake.

CHAPTER SIXTEEN

Roger did not need this. Not now. His phone rang shortly after midnight. Arnulfo, finally getting a chance to make his call, up in the Sevier County lock up, the bulls up there telling him to either give up his source, or face hard time alone. Play ball and things may just go his way.

"Roger, they're talking Class 2 felonies … four of them! Fifteen years a pop! They're telling me they're gonna bring the Feds in on this one … you know … cause they wanna make an example of me."

He knew that Arnulfo was on a recorded line and being careful with what he said. They were giving him the standard business but he had coached both of his drivers, Arnulfo and Pops, in what to expect and how to deal with things if they ever got nailed. First thing he told them to do was to stay calm. Second thing, call him right away.

Arnulfo had given him a call, but he did not sound calm.

"What'd they set your bail at?"

"It's nuts—thirty grand!"

Thirty grand? Ten K was standard.

"Jay'll get that brought down. You'll be out within forty-eight hours." His retained attorney, Jay Anderson, was among the best. "In the meantime, remember your rights. You don't gotta tell them anything till you get an attorney. You will remember that won't you, 'Nulfo?"

"Yeah, yeah, Roger, yeah, of course."

"Let's hope so."

It was a veiled threat, one that he knew was not necessary with a guy as loyal as Arnulfo, but he had to make it anyway.

But he still didn't need this at this time. He was too busy dealing with supply issues, crazy customers and keeping his network hot. And there was the divorce thing, trying to break away from the stupid mistake he'd

96

made, the mistake of getting married in order to keep his image clean and his parents happy. They wanted him to settle down but he didn't want to settle. He'd met Karine at an Armenian wedding reception, saw what he wanted and, as usual, got it. But marriage turned out to be a prison sentence to him. She hadn't been served her papers yet but the moment he'd told Jay to start drawing them up, he felt free—back in the fast lane again.

Things were moving fast and growing large, but not fast enough and not large enough to satisfy his lust for more. More money. More women. More power.

More.

It was kind of like that line from Scarface. He could hear Al Pacino as Tony Montana saying it, when Manny asked what he thought he had coming to him. Montana telling him he wanted the world—and everything in it.

The world was out there for him to get. He wanted what was coming to him. Not only did the future represent more money and power, but it also represented something equally enticing: the erasure of the past. The imagery of a young immigrant boy, barely able to speak English, wearing the same clothes every day, cereal-bowl haircut, afraid, no self-esteem, faded like the road in a rear view mirror with the acquisition of things and power. The faster he pushed it, the faster the lowlife image of who he once was vanished. It started its fade with his first hit of dope, passed to him by Ernesto, and continued to fade as he found his niche in the world of money, drugs and power. Now he knew who he was. He was "Hrach" Roger Munchian—a man of infinite money, wealth and power.

When he got the call from Arnulfo he had an endless agenda and he really didn't need to put a call into Jay at the top of his list. But it would be necessary to ensure that he yank Arnulfo out of jail quickly before he broke and started spilling his guts.

He had too much at stake now. Too much to lose. But he was Teflon slick. Nothing was going to stop him.

Nothing.

With a few punches of the dial he would take care of everything.

Sevier County Jail
Tuesday, July15, 1997

• •

The thick metal door rolled open and a rush of hot air carrying the stench of spoiled garbage and un-flushed sewage rushed from the jail pod. The pod was quiet, the inmates in their cells on lockdown. The detention officer gave him a little shove forward, and Arnulfo, wearing striped clothing courtesy of the Sevier County Sheriff's Office, stepped past the threshold into the pod.

The D.O. followed him up a flight of metal stairs. Halfway down the narrow catwalk lined by a metal rail and jail cells, a door rolled open. He looked at the big, black etchings on his door: C-18. Jail pod C. Cell 18. Sevier County Jail, Richfield, Utah. His new address for the next three months.

The cell door slammed shut behind him. He looked around at his new home. A wafer-thin mattress on a metal slab; stainless steel, seatless toilet and a metal sink; cold air blowing in from a vent above.

Three months. He could do this. The date was etched in his brain. Signing his papers, he'd looked at the release date: October 20, 1997. Yeah, today was the first day of the countdown to that date. Pops was taking over his loads while he was here. But the next day after he'd get sprung, October 21, he'd be back at it. He was sure of that.

But what he didn't know was by the time that date arrived, things were going to be different.

Very different.

August 29, 1997
Sky Harbor Airport

• •

She still had that dumbfounded, shocked look on her face when Roger pulled up to the curb and told her to get out of the car. He drove Karine here in the Porsche just to give an added dig to her soul. His soon-to-be ex-wife, Karine Munchian, still had the plane ticket that he bought her, a one-way trip, all expenses paid, to Burbank, California, clutched in her dainty, sweat-beaded hand.

"Jay filed the divorce papers this morning. You'll be getting your copy to sign in the mail. Be sure you get them notarized. If you don't sign them, I will have you served. Good-bye, Karine. Sorry it didn't work out."

"But what about the baby? Roger, your child!"

"Karine, you're nuts! You miscarried—there is no child."

"But my pregnancy was a sign that God wants to bring us children, Roger. You can't do this!"

"Don't bring God into it. God's got nothing to do with my life, Karine. I run my own show. God can sit by and watch if He wants. It's over. Goodbye, Karine."

She loved the lifestyle he had introduced her to. She loved the wealth. She loved the things. He knew that she had no idea where it all came from. She'd gotten pregnant and it was really looking like fast-times-Roger was getting domesticated. But after the miscarriage, he saw it as a close call. The wedding included something called vows. Something about "for better or for worse, in sickness and in health, till death do us part." But what was that all about? They were just words, spoken in front of some guy wearing a fancy collar and robe. In reality, marriage was a simple business transaction, right? Nothing but a contract, right? Business was business; contracts were contracts. Yes, a deal was a deal, but a deal could be broken with the right lawyer.

As he pulled away, he looked in the rear view mirror and saw her still standing there, a look of disbelief in her eyes as the baggage guy loaded her luggage on the cart.

Hitting State Road 51, northbound from the airport, he looked down and saw the needle clicking at 120 mph. It wasn't fast enough. He pushed the accelerator down further, pushing the Porsche to its limit, getting away from his past as fast as he could. He felt good, riding hard and fast again. Faster. Faster. But as the road signs whizzed by—faster and faster just wasn't fast enough.

No. Nothing was fast enough.

Now that the marriage was over, he'd push harder. He'd push faster. And God could sit by and watch.

CHAPTER SEVENTEEN

Thursday, September 25, 1997
Phoenix
12:58 a.m.

His hand covered hers and he could feel the heat of Alma's palms warm his inner thigh as he helped guide her hand to where he wanted it to be. Alma giggled, a throaty laugh, telling him she meant business. Roger punched the S600 Coupe's accelerator to the floor, the lane lines of eastbound I-10 going from dotted to solid white, the speedometer leaping behind its glass. Alma sunk back in her seat at the rapid acceleration but was not to be distracted from her task.

He looked in the rearview mirror at his two passengers in the back seat, watching the blood drain from Jaxie Soto's face. The front of Jaxie's shirt was soaked, the half-empty bottle of Heineken still poised under his gaping lips.

"Don't you dare lose it back there, man!" Roger shouted over the hip-hop thud pounding through the speakers. "Dude, I'm telling you, you puke in here, you're forking it over to get this car detailed!"

From the corner of the mirror, he saw a dainty, ruby red-tipped hand glide over and gently begin stroking Jaxie's cheek. Then he lost sight of him in the thick, hairspray-coated dark mane that tipped toward his neck. He heard Jaxie give out a little moan and could picture Marianna's tongue sensuously snaking the side of Jaxie's neck, the same way she'd been doing all night long on the dance floor. They seemed to be hitting it off well.

Through a world aglow in a soft Absolut-and-orange juice haze, his mind absorbed it all. The laser stream of street lights humming by overhead; the green swirl of exit signs dashing past; the throaty flow of Alma's juicy drink-fermented breath warming his neck; the glistening touch of tongue; the subtleness of her perfume, tainted in a nicotine stain from Empire Club VIP Lounge. She curled her legs up on the seat, the hemline of the skintight sequin dress gathering to her thighs. His heart raced. He wanted to get her home fast. Like everything else, he wanted it fast. There was no time to wait. Nothing could wait. He punched the accelerator again, and the speedometer leapt past 120.

Like all the women in his life, Alma wanted more out of the relationship. He liked her, perhaps a bit more than the others. But his life was unbridled now, the way he liked it—fast-paced and full of the carnal revelry of new conquests. The conquest of another deal. The conquest of another chick. The conquest of another million. He was going to get there, and get there fast. He wasn't about to slow down.

"*Slow down!*" he heard Jaxie scream and he peeled his eyes from Alma's legs and saw the semi's taillights racing toward him. He cranked the wheel left, the right bumper just inches from grazing the trailer. He looked in the rearview mirror and saw the truck's headlights fade fast. He saw Jaxie take another deep slug of Heineken and Marianna continued to giggle in sodden revelry, clueless as to what had just happened.

He didn't know Jaxie real well, only that he was the deep-dimpled crowd pleaser of the group of regulars that had been drawn to Roger's generosity that evening and it didn't take him long to peel himself from the open tab at the bar to make his move on the leggy Marianna.

To the Empire Club management, these were regulars; valued customers; guaranteed revenue for the evening. To him, this was his village, his people. They had their own special zip code in the Empire Club, a gold-studded exclusive section known as the VIP Lounge. There was always the ebb and flow of strangers, unknowns, vagabonds, but the core group of natives gave him a sense of belonging, a sense of meaning, a sense of purpose. He took care of them. In flashes of green and plastic-coated platinum, he kept the taps behind the bar primed, the pour-spouts flowing and the ice-bins full. Money ensured he spent very little time alone. Money ensured that he moved along unscathed by the indifference of the world. As long as he kept their veins flowing in liquid courage, their loins churning in guiltless potential, he had everything he needed. Hooking Jaxie up with Marianna tonight was just one more pious act of service that added meaning to his life.

He had wondered, for a brief moment at some point tonight, how 'Nulfo was doing in the Sevier County hole.

He punched the accelerator down harder and looked past the upended bottle of Heineken tucked in Jaxie's mouth, watching the road glide away, the mirror acting as some oblong mystical window into the past, the retreating dotted lines mere time clicks measuring how fast he could leave the past behind. It felt good. It felt right.

"The world, Chico—and everything in it."

God can sit by and watch.

Ahead, mile marker 148 flew by in a green swirl. Two more miles to go before his exit, and it was coming up fast. Adrenalin pushed his last drink rapidly through his veins and the road narrowed in a comfortably familiar vodka haze. Alma whispered something in his ear, a steamy promise of sorts as he pushed the accelerator further down. How much faster could he go?

The road was suddenly distorted in a mist of rain twisting from the black-shrouded desert sky. It was a light, pre-shower sprinkle, but at his speed the drops rushed at the windshield in horizontal slats and he subconsciously flipped the wiper switch.

The dash lights were bright, illuminating the speedometer dial that pointed to a fuzzy 130 mph as Exit 150 rushed toward him. Alma turned her head to reposition her lips on his neck, and through the forest of her silky tuft of hair, he saw the yellow sign at the sharp curve. It was an amber blob but he knew that it read 45 mph, a warning of the sharp curve ahead.

Any speed less than 100 mph and the past caught up to you. He slowed down just enough to compensate for the sudden wet conditions before hitting the curve with that euphoric vigor that accompanies defying the odds.

His hands and body would have registered that something had gone terribly wrong long before his booze-addled brain caught on. The shutter of the steering wheel; the counterclockwise fishtail of the rear end; the bouncing squeal of tires; the stench of burning rubber seeping through the wheel wells.

He noticed that the revelry in the car had gone silent. The shoulder harness sucked him deep into his seat, shutting off a cry of alarm. Despite his fight, the steering wheel was ripped from his grip as the car hit the curve, silencing the screeching of car tires. He heard metal shear and felt the floor buckle, shoving his knees hard into the steering column as the curb surgically gutted the car's underside and sent them airborne. His head snapped forward, harness garroting him, choking off cries from the white-hot pain that fought against the tide of vodka numbness from his shattered knees as the car landed in the gravel gore point with unstoppable ferocity.

The car slid sideways, leaving the gore point where I-10 ended and northbound I-17 began. His ears ached in the roar of squealing tires echoing off the concrete, the car skidding across three lanes, the raw stench of burning rubber igniting in his nose. A cauldron of shredded rubber and road debris poured from the wheel wells, the hood vanishing in a billow of slick, black smoke.

He looked up into the rear view mirror. Jaxie's face, paste-white, slack-jawed in horror, was turned toward the window, watching the cement barrier wall, bathed in the sodium glow of street lights, storm toward them. The fender buckled on impact, the crushed hood rising through the smoke-like mountain peaks in a volcanic furry, spewing glass, metal shards and debris high into the air. The window shattered, Jaxie's face turning skeletal, dotted in blood that was not his own.

He heard Alma scream. A cordite smell followed a shotgun-like blast, the passenger-side airbag shooting from the dash like a ravenous beast, swallowing her whole.

The car continued its tumble along the wall. A fireworks display exploded in the car, the shower of spark lighting the gray barrier wall, igniting the interior in a fire-blaze of incandescence. He watched the wreckage play along the wall in the shrinking shadow of the car demolishing itself along the barrier wall, the centrifugal force sucking him deeper into the leather seat, palms fusing to the steering wheel.

The car, spinning in a counterclockwise whirl, caused him to wish the twirl would defy time, taking him back in time. *How far back would you go? Moments ago, when the rain hit, a warning to slow down? Back to the Empire Club, never gotten into the car? Back to the first hit of dope—never taken that first drag?* Even time offered no hope. They were all going to die tonight, right now, it was happening—and he knew he'd just killed them all.

And God could sit by and watch.

The bulletproof windshield splintered, turning to powder in its next wicked impact with the wall. He watched the world spin by through the distorted, powdery view. It came in snapshots, like looking through a child's toy, a broken Viewfinder dropped long ago: the lines of the northbound lanes contorted in the shattered glass; then the cragged desert foliage marking the edge of the far shoulder; southbound lane whipping by, the car twirling out of control as though sitting upon a spinning top. Inside, the shredded interior illuminated in the explosion of spark, the surgical screech of tearing metal and the maraca-like sound of shattered glass churning, cutting, and tearing life away. The crunch of bone followed another impact with the wall, accompanied by a scream, whisked away into the rushing night air. A fragile life sucked from the car.

Through the frosted windshield, an orange strobe of spark revealed a bloody apparition floating by, twisting disjointedly in its path. A rag doll, he thought, a *papier-mache* figurine caught in a desert whirlwind.

It can't be real. It can't be her.

The fragile figurine, a China doll duplicate of Alma, turned over in mid-flight, peering through the windshield, the pulpy face staring at him in a frozen look of anguished shock. Her crimson tipped hand reached out to him …

…pull me back! Pull me back!

He fought the force adhering his hands to the wheel, trying to reach for her and then the explosion, and she vanished in a billow of white, his exploding airbag shutting her from view.

The sulfuric stench of the pyrotechnics that deployed canvas hard into his face filled the air. He felt the car ricochet off the wall and go wheels-up in a rolling tumble, the shoulder harness digging deep, tearing tendons, fracturing bone. He couldn't breathe, the airbag suffocating him, the harness choking him. A white-hot display exploded in his head, then dwindled away, shutting his world down like the shrinking white dot of an unplugged picture tube.

And his world went black.

PART II

God Calls

CHAPTER EIGHTEEN

Thursday, September 25, 1997
Phoenix
1:33 a.m.

· ·

Jenny saw the wreckage but it was Jason who saw the victims first.

"Awe, man! There's bodies! *Bodies!*" she heard Jason from the passenger seat.

It caused her to hit the brake, stopping her little Honda Accord right in the middle of the exit ramp. A car laid on the horn behind her, then in the rear view mirror she saw the four-ways suddenly come on and the doors pop open, two guys rushing to the guardrail to get a better look at the carnage.

"Oh, man, I gotta check this out," Jason said, and threw open the door and got out.

They were on their way back to Jason's place from a frat party at Arizona State. She was driving because she was in better driving shape, but not by much. Now they would be talking to cops. Cops would be here soon and they'd smell the booze on her breath and make her take a breathalyzer or something. *Oh, man!*

She rolled the window down and shouted, "Come on, Jason, let's just go!"

Jason looked back at her, teetering there next to the guardrail, eyes glazed, trying to hold himself up straight. "Hey, hon', maybe you should, like, call 9-1-1 or something."

Yeah, he's gonna get us busted for sure. "Jason, come *on!*"

"Where we gonna go, babe? The road's, like, totally blocked with bodies and stuff."

She heard a scream, coming from down there. Wow, it was a horrible scream. She got out of the car and joined the guys at the guardrail. There were two guys down there around the wreck. One was on a cell phone, walking around in a tight circle, waving his arm around frantically. The other she assumed must've been the driver because he dove back into the driver's side. She couldn't figure out what he was doing, on his knees digging around on the floor of the car for something. One of the guys at the guardrail said he was the one who'd screamed, before diving back in the car.

"Now what's he doing?" she asked.

"Writing something … leaving a note on the windshield! Hey, he's leaving! He's fleeing the scene!"

After the guy tucked the note under the windshield wiper, he started limping up the northbound lane. She could see him, white shirt, beige pants reflecting in the streetlights, staggering over to the shoulder. He hiked a leg over the barrier wall and disappeared down a ravine.

"He's getting away!" she heard one of the guys at the guardrail say, and then both of them started running down the ramp past the wreck, chasing after him.

"Come on," Jason said, and staggered down the ramp.

She could tell that Jason was entranced by the wreck, walking around it, saying things like, "Ah, man!" and "Oh, geez!"

Jenny looked at the dead girls, then over at the only surviving passenger, the guy who'd been walking around talking on the phone. She thought she heard a voice say the name Jaxie through the phone. He didn't seem to notice her and jumped when he heard her voice.

"This your car?"

The guy she assumed was Jaxie whirled around, eyes wide, face and white tux-style shirt all speckled in blood, blood not coming from any noticeable gashes on his face, obviously splatters from one of the girls lying outside the wreckage. He took his phone from his ear and held it at arm's length, dialing another number, out of breath and in a panic.

"No," he said between breaths. "No. It's … it's…" trying to come up with a storyline, she could tell. "My cousin's. It's my cousin … Scott's."

"How'd it happen?" she asked.

"Man, he was stupid. Stupid for what he did. Look at what he did." The guy was talking, not looking at her but off the road somewhere, down at the service drive below. Suddenly, Jaxie ran, hopped the barrier wall and slid down the gravel embankment. A white Pathfinder came to a screeching halt on the road below, and he jumped into the back and the truck took off, tires squealing.

In the distance she heard police sirens, coming this way. She cupped her hand in front of her mouth, breathed and sniffed, smelling stale alcohol and said to Jason, "You got any mints?"

1:48 a.m.

Officer Ken Rossie, driving K-9 Unit 021, stood on the accelerator and hit his lights when he spotted the subject racing across the street, heading for the railing of the Salt River bridge. He had been southbound on 16th Street, responding to the call of a subject matching the description a witness had given of the driver who'd fled the scene of a serious 962 at the 1-17/I-10 split. The subject was clear in the spotlights from the Firebird helicopter circling overhead and it was certain his intent was to leap over the rail. He knew the ravine floor below was a four-story drop and he immediately called in a suicide risk. Then he shouted into his mic, hopelessly, but out of proper protocol: *Police! Stay where you are!*

Over the radio he heard DPS Unit 320 respond and saw the unit's lights coming fast up 16th Street from the south. Rossie was halfway there but he knew that neither unit would make it in time to prevent the jump. He hit the brakes, fishtailing the cruiser, and reached down, flipping the switch to the K9 Door Popper. The rear door flung open, and Digger darted out of the car. He whipped open his door and sprinted after, shouting into his mic, alerting responding units, "K-9 released! Suspect going over rail!"

His world had not gone black for long. The anguish of guilt had jolted him back to reality like a splash of Arctic-cold water in the face. He'd pulled his battered body from the car, saw what he'd done, attempted to end it there with the bullet of his own gun only to shred his hands to ribbons rubbing them through the shattered glass covering floorboards in a frantic search for the weapon that was not there. In an eternal distance he saw the bridge. He'd jump—end this nightmare in a leap to his death. It was his only feasible option.

They'd closed in fast, police spotlights from above turning the night into day as he made his limping dash to the rail.

"K-9 released!"

His leg ignited in fresh pain from where the mutt ripped a gaping chunk of meat from his calf—but he'd broken free from the beast's fangs, the momentum sending him upended over the rail.

He heard the desperate cry of the hunters about to lose their quarry as he felt his legs fly into the air. Sharp rocks, dotted in sage and the spiked foliage of the desert and lit up in the spotlights of the police chopper, rushed toward him as he went over the rail.

It was all over.

God help me! God help me!

His plunge abruptly stopped as the throaty growl of the beast filled the air again. He felt the fangs sink back into his butchered calf—the beast seeking fresh meat—and he heard his anguished cries echo off the desert floor below. Tumbling to the sidewalk, he looked up and saw the gnarling teeth of the German shepherd, the beast whipping its head back and forth, grisly saliva flying from its vise-grip jowls, sparkling in the bright spotlights as it showered him and the bridge in a kibbley stench. Black shoes raced toward him from every direction. He heard the shouts, orders—warnings not to move as he desperately clamored back to his feet.

Arms engulfed him as he reached for the rail, hurling him to the ground, sandpaper grit of the sidewalk chewing the side of his face. A metallic clank, pop of shoulder socket, all-too-familiar feel of cold metal surrounding his wrists, tight, the painful twinge in his fingertips, denied the flow of blood.

The blinding light burned white-hot inside his head, questions being asked of him, questions he didn't understand, couldn't hear in the garbled confusion of the snarling police dog, the overhead roar of the helicopter, the muffled chatter of radios.

Arms pulled him to his feet. He still couldn't see, eyes pooled in tears and the white blindness of the police lights. He felt the metal roof of the police cruiser against his cheek, winced at the sharp pain from the kick to the ankles, spreading his legs. More questions. Garbled commands. Questions about the car. The wreck. The victims.

A head slam against the hood and he was told, "They're dead, sir! How does it feel? How does it feel to have taken two innocent lives?" Two more slams against the door, orders barked, *"Get in the car, you maggot!"*

The door slammed shut and he was looking through the mesh caging at another police cruiser approaching. He knew this was how he would see the world from now on. Distorted in bars and caging.

The cop intentionally drove slowly past the wreckage, forcing him to view the damage he'd done one last time. Through the mesh cage he saw the gold-framed vanity plate on the bumper of the wreckage, distorted in pool of tears: Hrach.

Who's Hrach? Who are you now, Hrach? Who are you now?
God help me!

Madison Street Jail
4:01 a.m.
• •

His nose burned in the cloying stench of stale urine and jailhouse grime. They'd booked him on two counts of Vehicular Homicide, his rage descending to primal fear when they told him how much he was going to enjoy the view from Death Row.

As they dragged him down the horseshoe-shaped intake hallway, he bent over, breaking free from the grip of the two detention officers and wretched. Bile pouring uncontrollably from his stomach, the visions of the scene came back as vivid as if happening all over. He saw it again, through the mesh caging, the golden-framed "Hrach" vanity mocking him from the wreckage; saw the wadded bundle of bloody clothing—the sequin dress—lying next to where paramedics worked on Alma's naked body—frantically working to restore her life; heard the cop say, "*They ought to inject your veins with pure acid, you maggot!*" spitting his words into the windshield as he punched the accelerator and raced straight to the Madison Street intake.

The D.Os cut off his retches by slamming him into the cinder block wall and yanking him upright with a fistful of hair.

"One more drop of puke hits my shoes, maggot and I'm making you lick them clean!"

Pain seized him, shutting off cries of anguish and rage as they yanked his joints to the point of dislocation, dragging him by the arms down the hallway. His anger returned, an unbridled rage intensifying his fight, pain tipping him toward unconsciousness as they strapped him into the "crazy" chair. Fighting against the restraints, threats and obscenities poured uncontrollably from his mouth, echoing off the intake walls, prompting whoops and hollers from the holding tanks, egging this *loco* fresh fish on, the guy still dressed all fly in his nightclub duds, fighting like a spoiled rotten brat not wanting to get into his striped jammies.

"Let me out of this thing!" his voiced echoed off the cell walls. He tried to rush forward, a feeble attempt to get at the two D.Os stepping back into the hall, wanting to wipe the smirks off of their faces; but the straps gave only an inch, cutting deep into his arms and legs, forever numbing the hope of freedom. "*I said let me out!*"

The pain from his shattered knee surged as electric anger forced a trembled pistoning of his legs. He felt the saliva bubble from his throat and watched the officers jump back to avoid the rabid strands of spittle flying as obscenities flowed from his mouth like a Tourette's patient on steroids.

The D.Os gave him one last knowing smile as they turned and left.

He fought against his restraints until he tilted on the edge of sanity, feeling the darkness of an inhuman abyss rise from the depths of Hell. He felt helpless as it engulfed him in an eternal anguish and he knew there was no escape. Nothing could rescue him, not even the gods he'd served so faithfully. The gods of sex, drugs, money…and power…were nowhere to be found. They had no place in this pit of hopelessness— because they'd led him here.

And abandoned him.

He was now eternally alone with the one person he now hated more than death itself: Roger "Hrach" Munchian, aka "Roger Rabbit."

"*God!*" he heard the name echoing off the walls. Blood ran thick in his head, pumped by a grieving heart, broken by anguish. "Are you there, God? *Are you there?*" His screams ripped his throat and he tasted blood.

He fell back in the chair, the restraints easing as fatigue overcame him.

God!" he cried again. His chest trembled infirmly, the pain of cracked ribs and bruised muscles searing a deep, convulsive gasp. His heavy sobs roared out uncontrollably, tears saturating his cheeks, burning the jagged gashes that disfigured his face. An unbearable guilt tormented him as he fought against the reality of what he'd done, the nightmare flashing uncontrollably in his mind like snapshots in a photo album of horror. A snapshot of himself staggering from the car; Alma lying on the blood-slick pavement, cold, lifeless, reaching out to him in death; a shot of himself responding to her reach, feeling her touch again, the coldness of her outstretched hand as he took it in his.

From the cold stench of his cell, he relived the anguish as he knelt beside her, feeling the softness of her hair as he brushed curly locks from her face, gently wiping the blood from her cheek, kissing her blood-freckled eye—kissing her goodbye. He knew he could never bring her back. Nothing in his riches, in his wealth—nothing in his control could undo this. Not even his high priced lawyer could negotiate Alma back to life.

Roger Munchian, aka Roger Rabbit, was nothing more than a murderer, a caged monster soon to be properly disposed of by a system of justice.

"*They ought to inject your veins with pure acid, you maggot!*"

The shaking came uncontrollably now, tearing muscle and bone, his skin burning, his lungs unable to draw enough air to support the sobs that echoed remorsefully throughout the entire jailhouse.

"God—if you're there God—*help me!* Oh, please help me!"

...help me ... help me ... help me ... Oh, God—

Help!

CHAPTER NINETEEN

Madison Street Jail
September 25, 1997
Early Dawn

• •

The amalgamated stench of urine, vomit and bile greeted him when he awoke. His stomach heaved, throat burning, followed by the stink of bile shooting from his mouth, soiling his shirt and pants in yellow disgorge.

Good morning, world.

The heavy clank of the cell door jarred his eyes open. Sometime during the night they'd moved him to the isolation cell across the hall from the "crazy" chair and chained him to a ring embedded in the cold, cement slab that became his bed. The donut-gutted form of the approaching D.O. was a blur. He was speaking to him, words coming from his mouth, the words garbled like a scrambled message from an ancient telegraph. "…lucked out … here's … new … intake … lucky SOB. … Let go man!"

The D.O. was trying to take something from him, something he was gripping in his hand. He struggled to keep it. Something in his hand. Something important.

Then he heard the D.O. say, "Just let go, man! Okay, fine, you want the old one, fine, maybe arrangements can be made."

His eyes came into focus. The D.O. had his meaty fingers wrapped around the bile-soaked intake papers that had been clasped in his hand all night, clenched in a rigor mortis grip. They were the papers that read HOMICIDE, the ones they'd handed him after intake, officially branding him a murderer.

He let go. Handing him a new set of papers, the D.O. said, "You sure lucked out on this one. Never seen nuttin' like this before in all my years working the zoo."

He sat up on the bench, head throbbing, on the verge of exploding, and looked at the new papers. The blurred words came into focus.

```
        Maricopa County Sheriff's Office
              Intake, Madison.


Inmate:    P443221, Munchian, Hrach "Roger".
Charges:   Count 1, Aggravated Assault with a Deadly
           Weapon.
           Count 2, Aggravated Assault with a Deadly
           Weapon.
```

The door slammed shut.

Assault?

Through the thick Plexiglas window he watched the D.O. walking away from his concrete cage, carrying the old intake papers.

What's going on?

His pleas from last night returned to him, as though the cement walls had absorbed them and were playing them back: *"God—help me!"*

He suddenly felt a comfort unlike he'd ever felt before as he heard God's answer, a voice telling him, *"I heard you. Trust me, Roger. Call out to me and I will show you great and wonderful things. You are not a murderer, Roger. You are fearfully and wonderfully made. All of my works are wonderful—and you are mine. Your journey has just begun— trust me."*

Saturday, September 29, 1997
St. Joseph's Hospital
Phoenix
. . . .

Antiseptic pungency stung his nose as he hobbled down the hall of the intensive care unit, leaning hard on his crutch. His knee had been shattered and ligaments shredded in the accident. His doctor had recommended immediate surgery but Roger had other things to do first.

It wasn't until after he'd been processed out of the jail that he was able to find out what had happened. As he was awaiting bail, he called his lawyer. Jay asked over and over what was he talking about? What homicide charges? The charges were two counts of aggravated assault. The victims were alive. Their conditions were grave—but they were alive.

Alive? How could they be alive?

"Jay, that's *impossible!* They were dead!" The cop's words still rang in his head, "*They're dead, sir. How does it feel to have taken two innocent lives?*"

"I don't have a full hospital report yet, Roger, but you're booked on aggravated assault. Which means they'd found signs of life in the victims. They could be completely brain dead from now until the day your boys shrivel with old age and it ain't changin' to homicide, babe. Don't get me wrong. These are still very serious charges."

He heard himself say, "They were dead, Jay."

"Let's get your bail settled and we can talk in the office."

"I mean, you should have seen them—you should have *seen* it, Jay! There's no way they're alive."

Bail was steep. Twenty large. But he'd gotten out by noon, as usual, and was sitting in Jay's office, Jay telling him how horrible he looked, all banged up like that, chuckling to himself, muttering words like we can beat this thing.

"I shouldn't even be alive, Jay. None of us should."

"The girls, both of them, are in critical condition down at Good Sam," Jay was sitting there behind his big oak desk, Roger's case file open in front of him. Roger shifted in his seat and winced at the pain shooting from his knee. "Man, you really should get that looked at. Looks like you got a cottage cheese-stuffed football shoved up your pant leg."

"What do you mean serious condition, Jay?"

"Comas. Both of them."

"They told me they were dead, Jay. How are they alive?"

"You keep saying that, Roger and I'm not sure what you're getting at."

God—help me!

"*I heard you. Trust me—I will show you great and wonderful things.*"

"In the tank. Down at Madison. I woke up, and they took my papers. Homicide. That's what they booked me for ..."

"You're sure about that?"

"Jay—they were *dead!*"

"*I heard you, Roger. Trust, trust, trust...*"

Jay shuffled through his file, shaking his head. "Look, Roger, this is a tight case. Aggravated assault is a Class Two felony. We're looking at ten years minimum per count. That's twenty long, Roger. If one of them does not make it, we add murder to that. And if both of them fade, that's two counts homicide, and we're talking Death Row."

The words Death Row didn't faze him. He wanted to be dead anyway. But he kept hearing a voice ... sensing it ... telling him, "*Trust me ... I have great plans for you ...*"

If you're real, God ... help me. Help me!

"*I'm here.*"

Who are you?

"*I'm God. I'm not just standing by watching. I'm with you. Always.*"

Jay continued shuffling through the file, talking about his defense. "I'm still waiting on the police report. We'll make an attempt for reasonable doubt that you were driving the vehicle. If anybody can beat this thing, I can."

He felt sick, the way Jay sat there, staring at his file, business as usual. He was tired. Confused. Ashamed. After leaving Jay's office, he had gone home and slept two days straight. Saturday morning he awoke, still dazed, thinking of Alma. He had to see her. He had to see it for himself.

Alma was in room 2231. He stood outside the door, staring through the small window, his heart breaking at the sight of her delicate, pulpy figure leaking tubes and wires. Fluids of all kinds ran in and out of her. Her delicate chest heaved in short, labored breaths, aided by the respirator that sliced paper-cut like scrapes in those ruby lips that once had been alive with laughter.

He tasted the salt of tears drenching his cheeks and flooding past his lips as he pushed through the door and hobbled to her bedside, seeing up close for the first time what he'd done. Plumb-colored divots of caved-in bone pocketed the un-swollen places of her face. A helpless gurgle bubbled in her throat with every labored breath while the blip on the little screen next to her bed recorded signs that Alma was in there somewhere, but just barely. Looking at this broken and pulverized child of God, he saw the intricacies with which God had knit her together.

"What have I done?" he whispered. "Oh, God … what have I done to your child?"

And yet there was an inexplicable peace beneath his anguish. God was fixing her. Only God could fix what he'd destroyed.

He stayed until they kicked him out and now he was sitting in his Porsche in the hospital garage, staring at his pager. He'd missed several calls demanding shipment statuses, pickups, and urgent needs for product. There were also several missed calls from Jay and one from Tony Rizzo.

He ignored the phone calls and drove to Rainbow Body and Repair where Jay had arranged for the Mercedes to be towed after getting it out of hock at the Maricopa County impound. He popped open the door of the Porsche and stepped from the car. Door still open, he leaned his arms over the window, the new-car waft seeping from the Porsche's interior, mingling with the burnt-oil-and-gas stench of the garage. The stench of dead and dying machinery.

Sitting under the tawny glow of the garage's only lit shop lamp, the crumpled mass that had been the Mercedes looked less deadly than it had at the murder scene. Back there it had been the center of attention, an air of importance in the way it was searched, probed, photographed, measured and scrutinized. It had purpose, meaning. Death trap. Evidence. Weapon. Now, in the oily surroundings of this automotive morgue with its windshield pulverized snow-white, wheel wells buckled in flattened rubber, crumpled hood clinging on a mere hinge, it was junk. The oily-death stench of the Mercedes mixed with the oaky new-car aroma pouring from the Porsche and he realized that both scents were the same. Emptiness. Nothingness.

Meaningless.

Why am I still here? Talk to me, God…help, oh please help! Show me the truth, God!

"Trust me, Roger. I have a plan for you. Just trust me. Now that I have your attention, trust me and watch what I am going to do…"

CHAPTER TWENTY

October 20, 1997
Sevier County Utah

• •

Roger watched Arnulfo step through the doors of the Sevier County Jail, his brown skin pale after three months of no sunlight. He got in the Porsche and let out a howl.

"Ah, fresh air at last!"

Roger released the clutch and laid tracks out of the parking lot, pushing the needle past ninety as he raced southbound on State Route 15. Arnulfo looked over at the speedometer.

"Man, Rog', ninety is grandma speed for this piece of machinery. Punch it, man. I wanna get out of this state as fast as possible."

He held the needle at a solid ninety, sensing Arnulfo staring at his swollen knee. After a minute of silence, he said, "I take it you heard?"

Arnulfo said, "Yeah, man. Pops, he told me about it on his last visit. Said you had some legal troubles."

"I ain't worried about the legal stuff, 'Nulf. I took the lives of two girls."

"Pop said they didn't expire or nothin'. Said you was lookin' at doin' ten large apiece for assault."

He was silent, staring out the windshield, watching the desert pass as he drove. He finally said, "No, I killed them. God saved them. God saved me."

Arnulfo was silent at first, waiting for the punch line, then not sure what to say. "What do you mean, Rog'?"

"They were dead at the scene, 'Nulfo. You should have seen them. They had me locked up, strapped in the crazy chair."

"But Pops said…"

"I don't care what Pops said, 'Nulfo! They were dead and I was the button man!"

"*Were* dead?"

"You don't know what it's like, man. If I could have died in their place I would have. 'Nulfo, for the first time in my life, I felt completely helpless. No matter how many millions I made. No matter how much power I had—I couldn't fix it. It was like falling into this big, black hole. An empty, cold, black hole where you got nothin' to live with except your own miserable self. Where the one person you now hate more than anything in the world—you're stuck with him. That's the guy I was stuck with in that cell. That's the guy I thought I was going to have to spend the rest of my life alone with."

"Man, Roger, you're freaking me out."

"I haven't shared it with no one yet, 'Nulfo. I haven't talked to no one about it yet except you. Down there in that hole, man, there was only one glimmer of light. Only one hope—God."

"Oh, man, you gone *religious* on me? Oh, that's great! That's just what we need."

"For the first time in my life, He was real, 'Nulf. Everything was going to be okay if I just asked Him. So I did. 'Nulfo, I was holding my booking papers in my hands that said homicide. They were covered in bloody puke, I tossed my guts so much. You know what it's like, 'Nulfo, to be so full of grief you puke till you don't got nothing left to toss up but your own blood?"

"Grief or tequila. It's called the dry heaves, dude. Take a couple Tylenol and get over it."

"They found life in the girls somewhere between the scene of the accident and the hospital. I called out to God for help, and He rescued me—by restoring their lives. I didn't get arrested that night, 'Nulfo. I got rescued. God rescued me."

"Roger, I just got a body full of goose bumps."

"Mariana came out of her coma a few weeks ago. For a while, it wasn't lookin' like Alma was going to make it. The prosecutor has been waiting around all breathless, wanting to be the first to slap the cuffs on me and tell me I'm under arrest for murder. But a week ago, she came out of it, too."

"Geeze, Rog'."

"It's got me thinking, you know, about all we've been doing. I just don't think I can do this anymore."

"Hey, now, be careful, Roger, okay? I mean, we got a good thing going here. Let's not go too far."

"Good thing, 'Nulfo? You forget already where you been the last three months? You've been eating maggot-infested tapioca, man, wearin' stripes and sleeping with your head six inches from where you leak and dump."

"Yeah, but Rog', that was only three months. County time ain't the best time, but it's over. I did it. Survived it. Ready to get back in the game."

He shook his head. "You ain't getting' it are you, 'Nulfo? Our luck is running thin. I was lookin' at Death Row. Two counts homicide and they fry you."

"Jay is good. He can get you out of this. No one does max with Jay."

"I ain't worried about that. I just sense God's got something bigger. Something better. Better than this. It's like, He got my attention. He used this to get my attention and He's calling me." He was silent for a minute, driving on, then swallowed hard and said, "He rescued me from myself."

"*Calling* you? Roger, He's God. He wants to call you, He can get your cell number even if it's unlisted."

He said, "Nulfo, I've been checking out a church and got talking to the pastor, a guy who wants me just to call him Pastor Frank."

"Wonderful," Arnulfo signed.

"He showed me a story in the Bible about a guy named Saul..."

"The *Bible*? Oh, man, Rog', don't tell me you became a Bible-thumper too?"

"Saul was killing Christians."

"Cool."

"Going through the desert on his way to Damascus, he got knocked off of his horse by a blinding light and he heard the voice of Jesus--"

"Oh, man. He went there. He said the 'J' word!"

"Shut up, 'Nulfo. God blinded Saul and knocked him down hard to get his attention. His name later became Paul. Pastor Frank said that God had a plan for Paul's life, and the only way to get his attention was to knock him to the ground. It was his Damascus moment. Funny. Saul's Damascus moment came at noon on an animal in the desert. Mine came at dawn strapped to a chair in the Maricopa County hole."

"Okay, seriously Rog'. Don't go soft, man. We got a lot of bad people around us. We built something good and there's guys that would kill to get a piece of it. They sense you've gone weak, they're gonna pounce. You can't just walk away from this. Not with all we've done. Not the way we've built this thing."

"*We* 'Nulfo? *We?*"

"Okay, man. Sorry. They're your connections. It's yours. But you understand, don't you? Man, Roger, the state decides to execute you, you can sit on Death Row twenty years. Any one of the punks we deal with decides you gotta go, you get popped in twenty minutes. And that's how it's gonna go down. They think you've gone weak, you become a threat. They pop you, pop me, and take it over. Man, they'll toy with you for a while, feel you out, then pop a cap behind your ear. We've seen it happen, man. I don't want to be no statistic, okay?"

He drove on, silent, thinking about it. Arnulfo was right. You just didn't get out of this business without making people nervous. Plus there was the envy. He could count more than a dozen homies and bangers who'd pop him in a second if they thought they'd have a chance at hooking into his suppliers, the moron Tony Rizzo topping the list. Rizzo had spent the last year trying to rebuild, going clumsy at it as usual. If he could find a shortcut, he would hesitate at nothing to get it.

But Roger knew God had something more. Something bigger.

A Bible passage he'd recently read came to him. Isaiah 46:11. "From the east I summon a bird of prey; from a far-off land, a man to fulfill my purpose. What I have said, I will bring about; what I have planned, that I will do."

God, is it me? Have you summoned me to fulfill your purpose? Why pick me, God? After all I've done? How can you possibly want me?

"*Trust me, Roger. Just trust me…*"

CHAPTER TWENTY-ONE

March 1998
Just Outside of St. Louis

• •

"I'm hungry," Arnulfo said, taking Roger out of his thoughts. "McDonald's next exit. Mind if I pull off?"

"Yeah, I think we got time."

"You hungry?"

"No. Not really."

"'No. Not really.' You know that's the most you've said in the last two hundred miles?"

They were running a 250-pound load up from the Mexican border to Simen in Detroit. He'd been thinking about his last court appearance. It had been five months since the indictment, the state prosecutor trying to send him down twenty-long for the accident— charging him with two counts of assault with a deadly weapon. He was wondering how God was going get him out of this one. He also wondered how God was going to get him away from an idiot like Rizzo, the guy getting dangerous, recklessly on the make for suppliers— putting the entire cartel in jeopardy. He knew it was only a matter of time before the moron sold to some narc and then they'd all be getting measured for the orange ADOC jump suits. So Roger connected Rizzo with Su, cutting him loose as a customer, but keeping control of his connections.

Arnulfo drove off the exit and pulled into the McDonald's drive-through. He ordered himself a Big Mac, extra large fries and a Coke. Pulling back onto eastbound I-80, Arnulfo dug into the McDonald's bag and took a huge bite of the Big Mac, Special Sauce oozing down his chin. "You know you ain't eaten since Amarillo," he said, shoving a wad of fries in his mouth. The grease absorbed the Special Sauce rolling down his chin.

"I told you, I ain't hungry."

Arnulfo drove along in silence for a while, finishing his burger, still working on his fries. He said, "Roger, man, you wanna know why you losin' so many customers?"

"Rizzo was no loss. He's a moron. And morons are dangerous."

"Okay. Right. Look, Roger, you need to dial the Jesus thing back a few clicks, okay? Listen, man, the Jesus talk was all over that hole up in Sevier County, guys talkin' that salvation smack all the time. Bibles were all over the place. We had so many Bibles up there, the cons tore them up and used the pages to roll joints, okay? They was tokin' God's word. Guys get thrown in the bucket turn religious real fast. They say they finally got Jesus, Jesus gonna help them turn it around, Jesus in the heart. We had one guy in our pod, man, he used to walk through the rec room on his time out, preachin' repentance like he had diarrhea of the mouth, his mouth runnin' right up till the day he got released. Thirty days later, he's back in the hole, not sayin' much this time."

"What's your point, 'Nulf?"

"This Jesus stuff, man, it's makin' people nervous. Just like I said it would. I know you been through somethin', Rog'. Like the guys up in Sevier County. It's okay you get a little religious. Look, Jesus is Jesus, but business is business. We gotta get back to where it's at—we gotta get back to business."

Roger looked up at the green sign that read, "Detroit, 500 miles." Arnulfo was right. In less than eight hours they'd be getting right to business—delivering a load of dope to nervous people wearing guns. *We gotta get back to business.* But deep down, he knew that the only business worth getting back to was Jesus—and the business of reaching His lost ones.

June 1998
Lazy Su's Fish and Chips

· ·

Tony Rizzo stared down at the plate of grease and breaded fish remnants that had come from Su's kitchen. It had been four months to the day since Roger had introduced him to this camel jockey blimp they called Big Mamma. But she turned out to be reliable, always getting him good product for his guy up in Detroit. Now he'd gotten another customer in North Carolina, and he was debating cutting her in. The guy was going to be putting in an order soon, a major load—Rizzo's biggest score ever. In the past, the one to trust with a load like this was Roger. Not anymore. Roger had turned Jesus freak and was jacking up everything he touched.

Su had been distracted ever since Rizzo walked in. She was dealing with a short Mexican dude who had come in ready for blood. Rizzo had never been formally introduced, but he knew that he was Jose Ortiz's little brother. Jose Ortiz, known as Big Ho', was Su's supplier down south of Tucson. They called the brother Little Ho', and Rizzo was never sure if that was supposed to be an insult or a play on names. He was a little guy, but his body was tight, his arms rope-like in powerful sinew. When he started getting physical, Su's delivery guy, a beefy black dude named Mo', sleeves of his Lazy Su's Fish and Chips T-shirt rolled up on his thick arms, stepped in and showed him out the hard way.

"Supply problems?" Rizzo asked.

"Got shorted on a load to South Dakota and Jose's threatening to pop me if it ever happens again. I gotta eat ten grand on this one." She pointed at his plate full of food. "You didn't eat much."

He looked down at his half empty plate and his stomach twisted another notch. "I ain't got an iron gut no more." He pushed the plate away. "My guess is Munchian jacked this up for you. Am I right?"

Su hesitated, Rizzo figuring she was wondering how much she should really trust the new guy. Finally she said, "Yeah, it was Roger."

"Su, you gotta start thinking about pulling clean from him. What do you need him for now, huh?"

"Tony, you're high risk, okay? Roger says you're dangerous, the way you push so hard to get new supply. Man, you talk to one wrong person, and you're done. *We're* done. I'm too fat and old to go to prison. They'd have to Crisco the walls before they could stuff me in any cell."

"And this is coming from Roger?"

"Yeah."

"The guy who just cost you ten grand?"

Su was silent for a minute, then said, "Let me think about it. I'm working on getting a load together now for Roger. Nothing can happen till after I get this done for him up to Detroit. He's kinda consumed with it since it's a heavy load—five hundred pounds up to Simen. This one's high stakes."

"Yeah? High stakes, huh?"

"Simen doesn't mess around. Chaldeans will slit your throat you come up short an ounce."

"When's the load scheduled to go?"

"Next month."

The smell of grease was making Rizzo's stomach want to heave and he'd been ready to go. But now he decided to stay a little longer. "Next month, huh? Tell me about it, tell me all about it," Rizzo said, thinking it was no coincidence Roger had a load scheduled right about the time he'd be needing the supply for his new guy in North Carolina.

July 1998
Provo, Utah

• •

He was told that Arnulfo would be a tough guy to tail. He could tell that Arnulfo had been well-trained in the way he started taking meandering paths once he'd pulled the Mountaineer out of Su's driveway. Watching the whole thing from across the street as Su's guys loaded the duffel bags into the back of the Mountaineer, he became anxious, not sure they were going to be able to pull this thing off. He had to chuckle, watching the guys try and stuff five hundred pounds of fresh harvest straight from Big Ho's fields into the tight space behind the false speakers—Roger's major load heading up to that rag head customer of his in Detroit.

He stuck to Arnulfo on his meandering path through Phoenix and stayed five car lengths behind once Arnulfo hit the interstate. He could picture Arnulfo's eyes darting back and forth from the windshield to the rear view mirror, knowing the guy would be watching close for a tail. He tightened it up to one car length as darkness fell, secure that the night would provide cover. He stayed tight to him, tailing him for nine hours until Arnulfo pulled off the exit and into the parking lot of a Motel 6. He drove to the opposite side of the parking lot as Arnulfo parked in the glow of the motel office lights. His heart sank when he watched Arnulfo crawl into the passenger seat, knowing that he was staying with the vehicle, not planning on leaving the load unattended.

When he was sure Arnulfo had dozed off he made his phone call and gave his location. He looked at the clock on the dash: 10:25 p.m. He shut the engine down, adjusted the seat back and waited.

He dozed off until a commotion outside startled him awake. His eyes came into focus and the clock on the dash read 12:43 a.m. In the wash of light spilling from the Motel 6 sign, he saw Arnulfo standing outside of the Mountaineer, the black dude and three of his buddies cornering him. He blinked his eyes in disbelief. The smart thing for Arnulfo to do would have been to just walk away, let this thing happen. But Arnulfo was looking spry, doing his boxer dance, giving the guys the bring-it-on sign with his dukes. He couldn't believe Arnulfo's speed, blocking a series of punches the black dude threw at him before laying him out with a counter punch. The two others converged fast and hard and for a full two minutes Arnulfo held his own until the black dude got back up, digging a bicycle chain from his back pocket. Arnulfo managed to swipe the first two swings away until the guy wrapped the chain around Arnulfo's head and it was over. He whirled Arnulfo around and slammed his head into the Mountaineer's hood. He gasped as he watched the others come in fast on Arnulfo, leading with knees to the body and blows to the head. He quickly realized that he was watching a simple ripoff turn into murder right in front of his eyes. Arnulfo collapsed to the ground, the kicks and blows continuing mercilessly.

Dang!

When the madness finally ended, he started the ignition and drove forward. In the spill of the headlights he could see that Arnulfo was not moving. The black dude, Mo' Wilson, approached the car as he pulled up.

"Ballsy little dude, I gotta give him that," Mo' said, rolling the bloody bicycle chain up and tucking it back in his pocket.

"He still breathing?" he asked, getting out from the car.

"A little. What should we do with him?"

"Stick him in the trunk and gift wrap him, special delivery to Munchian's front door," he said and walked over to the Mountaineer and got in. The keys were still in the ignition.

Mo' and his guys gathered Arnulfo up and tucked him into the trunk of the car. Sitting in driver's seat of the Mountaineer, Tony Rizzo watched in the rear view mirror as Mo' slammed the trunk shut and went to the back of the Mountaineer. Popping the rear hatch, Mo' said,

"Load's still here. You're all set."

Mo' slammed the hatch shut, climbed behind the wheel of Rizzo's car and took off. He didn't expect the ripoff was going to cost Arnulfo his life, but then again, he didn't really care. Rizzo cranked the engine to life and took off. He had a client in North Carolina who was going to be very happy.

CHAPTER TWENTY-TWO

August 1998

· ·

They literally had to re-break it. The way he'd neglected his shattered knee since the accident had caused it to heal wrong and the doctor told him that the only way he'd ever gain normal use of it was for them to go in, re-break it, and do the type of surgery on it that should have been done in the first place.

"Why didn't you come in and have that looked at right away?" the doctor had asked him. This was just three weeks after that morning his doorbell rang. Car tires screeched out of his driveway when he opened the door and saw Arnulfo's blood-soaked body on his front porch.

"Not sure why," was all Roger could tell the doctor.

"Well, my friend, you left your healing to yourself. A thing like this, it really needed the attention of a surgeon right away. I can fix it, but your healing is going to take longer and I'm not going to kid you, it's going to be more painful and require more therapy in order for you to fully heal."

"When can you schedule the surgery?"

"I suggest as soon as possible. Man, you really should have let a surgeon handle that."

He was now bedridden. Next to him on the nightstand, his pager buzzed unceasingly. He ignored it, knowing that it was another page from Simen. Rizzo had ripped him off and Simen was not happy that Roger failed to come through. He wasn't sure how Simen was going to handle this. Roger fronted the whole thing so the financial loss was all his, but the Chaldean drug cartel had a reputation of ruthlessness that it had to keep. They took ripoffs personally, regardless of who ate the loss.

I had to break you again, Roger.

He had experienced it again the moment he'd opened the door and saw Arnulfo splayed out on his porch, a pulpy mess. Instantly, he relived the moment he'd stepped from the oily wreckage of the car and realized the shroud of death he'd drawn, falling back into that same dark, hopeless abyss. He had nowhere to run. Nowhere to hide.

"I have great plans for you, Roger. Trust me. My Word shall not return to me empty. Trust me."

Arnulfo was still in the hospital, his brain searching for his identity through the fluid the bicycle chain had left sloshing around inside his head. Roger had visited him every day, reliving the moment he'd stood over Alma's hospital bed, staring down at the damage he'd done to one of God's own creations. His friend Arnulfo was in there somewhere, but the doctors couldn't guarantee he'd ever come back out.

For the first three days he didn't go home, sleeping on the hard, vinyl bench in the hospital lobby. When he did go home, he'd see his pager sitting on his desk. He'd missed over fifty pages from Simen. The deadline for the delivery had come and gone. Four days later his leg collapsed from under him as he walked down the hall toward Arnulfo's room, and he'd become a patient of the hospital himself, the sawbones doctor eager to get at his leg and start hacking and breaking.

The doctor was right. Recovery was more painful than anything he'd ever experienced. And it didn't have to be this way. Had he just let the surgeon fix it right the first time, recovery would not have been so slow, the pain not so agonizing, the scars not so deep.

God, you broke me. Then you re-broke me. He should have trusted the Master surgeon for his healing.

When will I get your full attention, Roger?

God brought back the memory of his first drug bust, the night that stupid cop told him he'd better call his parents at the airport and let them know that he was going to be ten to fifteen years late picking them up. It was his first time sitting in a Maricopa County tank, the stench still ripe in his memory. As he stared at the junkie, a shriveled mass curled up in the corner of the tank lying next to a puddle of his own urine, tracks all up and down his shriveled arm, he heard someone say to him, "You know, when God's got a lesson to teach you, he sends you a teacher."

He remembered looking over at the balding older guy, propped up against the cinderblock wall, feet stretched out across the bench, his designer jeans crinkled and his Tommy Hilfiger shirt matted in sweat to his round torso. His jolly face was whitewashed in graying stubble and he had a lost, defeated smile. However, the twinkle in his eyes gave light to a beaten soul.

Roger said, "I beg your pardon?"

"That's what my grandmother used to tell, you know, whenever I'd get in trouble. 'Jon,' she'd say, 'God has a lesson for you, and now he's sent you a teacher. Listen to your teacher, Jon.' Took me forty-five years to figure out what she was talking about. Grandma's been gone twenty years now."

"Nice. Thanks for sharing." The junkie rolled over and his head dipped into the puddle of urine, the guy's mouth twitching, leg trembling, aware only of the unseen demons tormenting him. Somewhere in the back of his mind Roger wondered if he was looking at his own potential future.

"Don't you get what I'm talkin' about?"

"I really don't care enough to try."

The guy, silent now, not aware that he'd just been dissed, finally said, "You've gone this route before. Walls aren't all that unfamiliar?"

"Look, I really ain't in a talking mood, okay?"

"Strange. Neither am I. But something told me that I needed to talk to you."

"Well, tell that something to shut up."

"What Grandma meant was the teacher was my consequences."

"No kidding? Only took you forty-five years to figure that out, huh? You must be some kind of genius."

"God let them happen to teach me a lesson."

"God's a spectator in my life. If that's the way He operates, He can just stay on the sidelines."

The guy got testy and Roger wanted to dim his lights but figured the guy was too old and pathetic to pop. "Took me forty-five years to figure it out, genius. Frank over there...," he pointed to the junkie, almost completely face-down now in his urine, "He ain't figured it out at all. It's too late for him now. He probably won't make it through the night. Drowning in his own stench may be the best thing for him. This time his bad trip has erased a mind he lost long ago. Yeah, took me forty-five years. How long's it gonna take you?"

"Alright, super genius, how's God teaching you now? You're back here in the County zoo. What's God doing with this?"

"God gives us warnings. Last time I was here, I got jammed for mouthing off to some cop when I got pulled over. Don't know why I did it. Just started lipping off, you know? But I was mad, you know, really irate because I was on my way to a meeting with this guy and it was going to be worth a lot of money to me. Cop pulls me over for a busted tail light and I go off on him, so he decides he smells booze on my breath, and does a roadside on me. Next thing I know, I'm sitting there like you, just kinda thinking, wondering if this wasn't God's way of stopping me, warning me to not to have that meeting. Watched two guys stick another guy's head in an open drain and snap his neck and I wondered if I was looking at my future.

"Yeah, it was like God gave me a time-out, made me sit in this hole for twelve hours to think long and hard about it, showing me how ugly things could get on my current path. Sitting in here made me miss the meeting and it got me thinking maybe I should just keep walking, moving on. But when I got out, I decided to look the guy up and set another meeting. For two years I thought it was a good move, 'cause the cash really started rolling in. Now it's all gone, and they're getting my reservation ready for my ten-year visit as an honored guest of the state. I wish I would have listened."

Then he closed his watery eyes and said, "I sure hope there ain't no open drains where I'm goin'," and didn't say another word the rest of the night.

By morning, Frank the junkie was dead.

His pager went off again and this time he looked at it, recognizing Simen's number. He ignored it and when his pager went off again seconds later he wanted to ignore it but decided to look. A rush of excitement flowed through him when he recognized the number as Chico Martinez.

A call from Chico meant serious business. He started reaching for the phone.

When God's got a lesson to teach you, he sends a teacher ...

Roger's fingers touched the receiver.

"God gives us warnings...I wish I would have listened ..."

He picked up the receiver, ready to dial. *Just one more dial and he could get out of this. Just one more dial.*

"I hope there ain't no open drains where I'm goin'."

When are you going to listen to me?

He hung the phone up. As he stared at the pager, it lit up again. Simen. Just one more deal, that's all he needed. The pager lit up one more time. Chico calling again. Wow, the guy was serious. Chico never paged you twice. This was big.

"Trust me, Roger. Trust me."

He grabbed the water glass on the nightstand and crushed the pager, the glass breaking in his hand. Staring at the blood dripping from his palm, he thought of the blood dripping from the hands of Christ, and he said, *Okay, God, you got me.*

Looking at the blood, shed by his decision to obey God, he felt completely at peace for the first time.

Tony Rizzo was sitting upstairs at Martini Ranch, a downtown Scottsdale hotspot, watching the action behind him in the smoky mirror behind the bar. Girls dancing on poles, the dance floor alive with bodies bumping to the thudding hard rock band. He was waiting on his new connection, being told this guy could provide large.

In the mirror he saw the guy pushing his way through the crowd, a burly forty-something with one eyebrow and a full black mane. Another damn Armenian, like Roger. The guy introduced himself as Papian, David Papian. He ordered bourbon straight up and they shouted a few pleasantries over the roar of the music and then went downstairs and out to the courtyard where it was quieter.

They stood at one of the high-top tables and he didn't make much of the fact that this Papian guy didn't seem interested in touching his drink. He just stood there and listened intently as Rizzo went on about how great things had been lately what with things getting bigger in

Detroit and his expansion in North Carolina and all. The only thing that was standing in the way of things getting really good was his unreliable supply base. He told him about the hot shot Hrach Munchian, the guy they called Roger, but he knew him all the way back when they called him Roger Rabbit. He told him the guy had washed out. In fact, he told Papian, he heard that Roger's last shipment got jacked, his largest shipment ever, and the guy was done. This Chaldean dude, Simen, is going to pop him to make a point.

"You know, I'm the guy who got Roger into the business in the first place. Yeah, me." Tony took a gulp from what was his fifth vodka tonic, feeling real mellow now, feeling confident, letting this guy know everything. He wanted to impress him. This guy could get him good product, and fast, he just knew it. "Yeah, that's gratitude for you, you know?"

Papian dug deeper with questions about Roger, asking if he was such a hot shot, why hadn't he heard of him before. "I know all the players, sport. Don't give me no straw man to make yourself look bigger. I don't deal with no one ain't in my league. I find out you ain't in my league, we got problems, okay? You get a real clear understanding of that up front, sport, you gonna be okay."

"Hey, I ain't jacking you around about Munchian, okay? The guy's just slick, real cool about his business. At least he used to be."

They ended with Rizzo telling him his needs up in Detroit and that he was expecting another order in about a week or so. Papian told him he only needed twenty-four hour notice and he'd get the load ready. Wow! They exchanged cell numbers and pagers, Rizzo giving him the numbers he reserved for business purposes only. Papian left as the server brought Rizzo another drink. Wow, things were looking great! As he reached down for his fresh drink, he noticed that Papian's glass of bourbon was still full. The guy never touched his drink.

Special Agent David Papian from the Detroit Field office of the Drug Enforcement Agency slid behind the wheel of his Suburban. He flipped his computer on and as it booted up he called in and gave the order for an electronic surveillance on the cell number Rizzo had given him. He'd finally made contact with his mark and the first meet had turned out better than he'd expected. The guy nearly spilled all his guts, and he had enough probable cause to order the taps on his cell phone and pager. The beauty of it was the idiot told him they were used exclusively for business, giving him probable cause to tap every outgoing and incoming number. Within twenty-four hours his analysts up in Detroit would have a complete list of calls and pages over the last month, expanding Papian's list of targets.

Papian's computer booted up and he signed into his case log. The pieces were slowly coming together. He sensed that Rizzo was a just a short bit in a major drug enterprise but his idiocy made him the key target in the investigation. He popped open the list of players that Papian's surveillance team had been able to gather so far.

Name:	Suspected Offense:
Anthony J. Rizzo	Conspiracy
	Illegally conducting an enterprise
	Possession of marijuana for sale
Robert B. Mankin (aka "Robby the Jew")	Illegally conducting an enterprise
	Possession of marijuana for sale
Simon A. Brash	Possession of marijuana for sale
Suhad Haddad (aka "Big Mama Su")	Possession of marijuana for sale
Gregory A. Gibbons (aka "Gibby)	Transport for sale, sale or transfer of marijuana
Maurice Wilson (aka "Mo")	Transport for sale, sale or transfer of marijuana

Papian stared at the list of players for a moment, visualizing the list growing rapidly as the investigation unfolded. The Rizzo wiretaps alone had the potential to snag at least a dozen more. He'd seen it happen. But for now, his meeting with Rizzo tonight had yielded at least one new name to add, and Papian sensed it was a significant one. A rush of adrenalin surged through him as he started typing.

Hrach R. Munchian (aka "Roger Rabbit") Conspiracy
                                        Illegally conducting an enterprise
                                        Possession of marijuana for sale

Shutting his laptop down, he chuckled, thinking to himself that he was about to catch a cartoon bunny—he was closing in, and was going to snag Roger Rabbit.

PART III

God Refines

CHAPTER TWENTY-THREE

September 5, 1998
Phoenix

. . . .

The meds eased the pain of his shattered knee but they could not silence the haunting nightmares of murder.

Strapped to the chair, heavy door slams, stench of vomit, bile and urine lace the dark cell. An endless struggle against restraints. Unearthly cries of anguish echo off cinderblock walls. He's so tired. He can't fight it any more.

"*Oh, God help!*" His cry bounced off the plaster walls as he shot straight up in bed, his sheets drenched, his body glistening in sweat. Roger looked over at the clock: 2:22 p.m. His Bible lay face down on his bare chest, stuck in a pool of sweat. He peeled it off, the entire chapter of Deuteronomy 8 soaked. He'd taken the pain meds as he started reading God's word, and, as usual, they knocked him out. He looked down at the ink staining his chest, God's word imprinted dead center. He chuckled, remembering what Deuteronomy 6 said about God's word and commands: …*tie them as symbols on your hands and bind them on your foreheads.*

Well, God, it's not exactly my forehead, but your Word is bound to me now.

Groggy, he reached for his crutches and slid out of bed. It had been over two months since the surgery but the pain was as fresh as the day they had to re-break his shattered knee to put it back together again. The surgery was extensive, the surgeon removing a ligament from his right calf to replace the shredded ligament in his left knee.

141

He made his way into the kitchen and checked the refrigerator, finding the pickings even sparser than he'd expected. He spotted a Domino's Pizza box and found two sausage-pepperoni slices left, bordering on petrification. His phone rang as he tossed the slices into the microwave. He checked the caller ID. Another collection call. He ignored it, pouring himself a glass of Coke, no fizz, and retrieved his slices from the microwave.

Sitting down at the kitchen table, he downed two painkillers with the flat Coke and seared the roof of his mouth with his first bite of sizzling pizza. The phone rang again. Knowing their pattern, always calling twice in a row, he ignored it, setting his pizza down to cool and grabbing the letter resting in the middle of the table. He'd received it yesterday, the letterhead reading, Lawton & Groves Law Firm.

Lawton had been recommended by Jay. Yeah, Jay was a brilliant criminal attorney who could have pled Charles Manson's charges to jaywalking. Eleven months ago, October 6, 1997, the grand jury handed down those indictments from the accident that threatened to send Roger away for more than 20 years. On May 19, 1998, after a seven-month battle in the courts, Jay won a plea of five years' probation.

"God has been with you all along," he remembered Pastor Frank saying. "He has been protecting you in order to work through you in fulfilling his purpose for your life. I'm sure if you thought back, you'd see where God spared and protected you."

Five years' probation rather than 20 years down. Chalk another one up for God.

But Jay didn't do bankruptcies. The letter from Lawton simply confirmed that his bankruptcy petition had been filed. The collection calls would stop soon.

The phone rang again. They never called three times in a row. He got up and looked at the caller ID and his stomach sank as he recognized the 248 area code. Detroit. Simen Semma.

God had broken him and he'd tried self-healing, seeking God but clinging to his worldly things and shattered remnants of a life God wanted him to leave. Like his shattered knee, he healed badly, wanting to cling to the riches of this world, keep everything his life of drugs and violence had gotten him. God had to re-break him. God used Rizzo, allowing Rizzo to jack a major load he'd pulled together for Semma.

Had he not heard God's voice that one morning, his Damascus moment at dawn in that rat-infested jail cell, he would have popped Rizzo within twenty-four hours of confirming that it was him behind the ripoff. He would have done it himself, making it personal, erasing Rizzo's existence with his .357 Mag, then gone ahead and popped Mo' and friends next, including Rizzo's bimbo Paulette, just make it all clean.

But God breaks. God calls.

He did not realize he was soon going to find out how God refines.

"Our journey is only just beginning. Trust me, Roger."

He could not keep up with the lifestyle of the criminal world. It was a fine line, the line between the criminal life and the straight life. He knew that God was blessing the insurance business. The insurance business was growing in ways that he could not explain. But he knew that he could easily pick up the phone, or answer a page, and score more in one phone call than he could in an entire year signing new insurance clients.

Worse, his connections were betting that his religious awakening was only a Bible-thumping temporary thing. His phone was constantly ringing, temptation always there. Looking at his bankruptcy papers, he knew that one call, that's all it would take, one call, and he'd be back at the Empire Club, back in the VIP lounge, back into positive cash flow, back in the game.

He would not be bankrupt.

He had been ducking Simen's calls for the last several weeks. He'd smashed his pager, so Simen could not send him his usual coded messages. But Simen anticipated that he knew the routine. He didn't know how it happened, but Roger found himself dressed and in his car, heading for the pay phone where he would return Simen's call

"So, you really doing this?" Simen's voice came through the line. He'd called Simen from his designated pay phone and Roger could hear the sounds of the busy streets of Detroit in the background. "See, I get a little nervous, guys like you, at the top of their game, thinking they're gonna get out. The Feds love guys like you and I gotta think, best thing for me is if I see them hanging from a bridge somewhere, dangling from their esophagus."

"I'm doing this, Simen. I'm out."

"I got a guy up in Washington state. Spokane. He's lookin' for a good connection. Steady. Be about three-four loads a month up there, nice weight, about two-fifty pounds a pop. I could give him to you. Be a nice way back in for you. West Coast. Easy runs. You get your guy Arnulfo back on the road, you're back in business."

"Just to clarify, we *are* square, right Simen? I ate it on that last load. Sorry it didn't work out. But it was my investment I lost. We're square, right? I really don't wanna spend the rest of my life looking over my shoulder, waiting for one of your homies to come up behind me and give me a twenty-two caliber headache."

"You sound tired."

"Pain pills."

"How's your boy Arnulfo?"

"Recovering. He'll pull through."

"From what I hear, the guys that did it are still above ground. As a going away present, I could get that taken care of for you."

"If I wanted it done, I would'a done it myself."

"I got a guy, likes to use a palm gun, you know, the kinda gun fits in the palm of your hand, stubby barrel poking between your middle digits. Walks up, shakes your hand with one hand, comes around with the other, pops a thirty-two-caliber round into your bean. Rizzo would never see it coming."

"Rizzo wouldn't see a freight train coming. Thanks anyway."

"So you're really getting out?"

"We square, Simen?"

"You know who you remind me of, buddy, buddy?"

"No, who?"

"Mac McKussic."

"Never heard of him. Listen, Simen, I am really tired--"

"The retired drug dealer from that Mel Gibson movie, *Tequila Sunrise.*"

"Never saw it."

"Oh, buddy, it was a classic. He's trying to get out of the drug business. His supplier, he don't want him to quit, so he starts lying to Mac when they used to trust each other. The cops, they wanna get his supplier and they can only get to him through Mac, so they're all corrupt. And his best friend, a cop, he's lyin' to everyone. Turns out, the only honest one is Mac, who simply wants to pay the money he owes his supplier and get out, ride off with his girl into the sunset, a tequila sunset.

"Like that guy Mac, there are no lies in you, Roger. Even as a crook, you was an honest crook. I guess that's why you're still alive, why you ain't dangling from some bridge. I can trust you. I just hope you don't give me no uneasy feeling in the future, especially, you know, if your past catches up with you. Cause it will, buddy, buddy. The past always catches up to you."

"My focus is on my relationship with God."

"Yeah, well, let's just hope for all our sake he's a big God."

"He is."

"Let's hope we don't have to find out just how big. Good luck to you, my friend."

Such veiled threats no longer worried him. He trusted through faith that he served a big God—a God for whose word would never return empty to Him and for whom nothing was impossible.

Simen still thought of him as a drug dealer—but an honest one. The Holy Spirit was teaching him different, bringing Romans 8:16-17 to his mind: "The Spirit himself testifies with our spirit that we are God's children. Now if we are children, then we are heirs—heirs of God and co-heirs with Christ, if indeed we share in his sufferings in order that we may share in his glory."

He was not a drug dealer. He was not a criminal. He was not a murderer. Because of the blood Christ shed for him—he was an heir to God's kingdom. But the Holy Spirit also revealed the fine print in signing on with Christ: "… if indeed we share in His sufferings in order that we may share in His glory." The Spirit told him if we are to share Christ's kingdom, we are also to share in His sufferings. *We are at war, Roger. We share in Christ's sufferings so that we can become stronger warriors to reach a lost world.* Christ affirmed what the Holy Spirit was telling him, revealing the true cost of being His disciple in Luke 14:26-27: "If anyone comes to me and does not hate his father and mother, his wife and children, his brothers and sisters—yes even his own life—he cannot be my disciple. And anyone who does not carry his cross and follow me cannot be my disciple."

He knew that God was preparing him for battle in a war that he did not understand, but a peace settled on him unlike he'd ever felt before when he decided that he would take up his cross—and accept his circumstances as God's training ground in preparing him to be a warrior for the kingdom of Christ. He found it fitting that his Damascus moment had come at dawn. The day ahead continued to brighten the light of Christ that grew within him.

But what he did not realize was that dusk was quickly closing in as the real battle ahead approached.

CHAPTER TWENTY-FOUR

Detroit

• •

A hint of the pleasant fall air momentarily penetrated the oily stench of the Detroit streets as Special Agent David Papian stepped from the Rick Finley Building. The dedication of the Finley as the DEA's Detroit field office was only three years ago and with the dedication came Papian's relocation from D.C. to Detroit. He wasn't sure if the move was meant to be a promotion or not, but given the divorce and ugly alimony battles he had been in the middle of at the time, even a move to a sewer like Detroit was a welcomed change.

He'd just received a call from Detroit Police Detective Buddy Fredericks telling him to meet him at Lafayette Coney. He had some information to share on the Simen Semma wiretap.

He walked to the V-shaped building where Lafayette Boulevard met Michigan Avenue. The building housed the two Detroit Coney Island icons, Lafayette and American Coney. Papian didn't get the hype surrounding the legend of the competing Coney stands. Apparently, on the eve of the Great Depression, some Greek immigrant opened American Coney as a nickel hotdog stand. He sent for his brother, taught him the business, and to thank him, his brother started his own gig next door. The competition between the two grew legendary and became part of the Detroit heritage. You were loyal to one or the other. Detective Buddy Fredericks was a loyal Lafayette Coney Islander and Papian was convinced that the loose cannon detective would blow anyone away who argued different.

Papian knew that Buddy Fredericks had good reason for hating drugs and drug dealers. Papian never got clear on how long ago the incident occurred but he heard that some bad seed had erased the mind of Fredericks' sixteen-year-old son when the boy experimented with the dope at a teenage party.

Papaian's first job was to pull together a joint task force with the Detroit Police Department's Narcotics Division and he knew that Fredericks had a style and the kind of gut-level vitriol that he needed on the team.

Blowing a scab away like Joey Giovanni wasn't exactly Papian's style but after the drug lord's body toppled backward out of a second story Greek Town restaurant, Fredericks survived the Internal Affairs investigation that followed. More importantly, Giovanni's poison wasn't erasing young minds anymore. Giovanni's network was well-connected to the Chaldean mob and known for targeting teens in the affluent neighborhoods in the area. One of those neighborhoods was where Fredericks' son played varsity football and word got back to Fredericks that they'd traced the mule who'd sold the stuff to the kid's clique to a Giovanni-owned farm. That night Fredericks, breath combustible with Jim Beam, strolled into Giovanni's favorite Greek Town restaurant and dropped him and both of his goons sitting with him. Word was that Giovanni barely got his hand inside his coat before the slugs from Fredericks' off-duty revolver sent the big Wop falling backwards, the restaurant erupting in applause as Giovanni's body toppled out the window. As the smoke from Fredericks' gun cleared, Fredericks strolled back out as though he'd just ordered a takeout.

While Fredericks was motivated to bring Semma down hard, Papian wanted to nail Munchian. He knew the guy was well-connected and believed that he could lead him to bigger fish. But he'd dropped off the radar screen shortly after Papian's team infiltrated the cartel through the Rizzo buy. Munchian's connection to Rizzo was still vague, yet it was the only solid link to getting to Simen.

Fredericks looked like an oversized playground bully sitting on a child's toy with his towering frame perched on the tiny stool. Wearing a tattered blue-jean jacket, he sat hunched over the counter, his powerful hands gripping a hot dog leaking chili, onions and mustard. Two more hot dogs sat waiting to be devoured on the plate in front of him. Papian slid onto the stool next to him. Despite the tang of chili and onions hanging in the air, Papian could smell the stench of this morning's hangover oozing from the big man.

"You have lunch?" Fredericks asked, not looking at Papian. He waved his hand in the air, catching the attention of the frail Greek guy in kitchen whites behind the counter. "Two everything!"

Papian waved him away, the Greek guy slinking back behind the counter, looking disappointed.

"Thanks anyway. Had a tuna sandwich couple hours ago."

Fredericks scoffed, a spray of chili shooting from between his teeth. "Tuna."

Papian ignored the gibe and asked, "So what do you have for me?"

Fredericks inhaled the rest of his dog and spoke while chewing. "Munchian finally took a call from Semma."

"Yeah? You got it on tape?"

Fredericks shook his head, picking up his second dog. "Simen's been dialing Munchian's digits nonstop. Munchian didn't take any of his calls till yesterday morning. They got a system worked out. Our surveillance team observed Munchian leaving his crib yesterday morning. He was tailed to the same pay phone matching previous calls to Simen. Based on the phone records your team was able to collect, his move correlated with the last time he and Simen connected, which was back in July. Both pay phones were sterile, so we got nothing on record, but we know they talked."

"Okay. So we know they're talking. We got something to go on."

Buddy inhaled his second dog in two bites, shaking his head again. "My suggestion. Drop the Munchian thing. It's a bad angle for you to work."

"What do you mean?"

"These two guys. Neither one of them will give the other up. Munchian got all whacked out on religion and decided salvation would come from splitting from the cartel. You kidding me? That's a death sentence—especially dealing with guys like Simen. The Chaldean cartel has a rep of making things very painful you cross them. Last one I saw, about four years ago, we got a call to check out a stiff down in the Warehouse District. What they did, they dragged him naked into a meat locker, jammed a meat hook up through the jewels and out the belly button and left him hanging there alive till his hands and feet started to turn black with frostbite. Then they cut him up, slowly, letting him watch himself bleed to death, which is a slow death, taking a long time when your body is the temperature of a Popsicle. I'm sure in the back of Munchian's mind there was a meat hook with his name on it, but he's been playin' it cool, working it like a simple business deal. Somehow, Simen respects that and now they're done."

"What makes you think neither of these guys can be rattled?"

Fredericks picked up his last Coney. "You need to focus on Rizzo. Rizzo will flap his jaws for a dime. Same with his squeeze, Paulette. But I suggest you move in fast and bust them both. Their days are numbered. You don't move, you're gonna lose them to a bullet behind the ear or a meat hook through their privates. Rizzo's clock started ticking the moment he got involved with China Mike."

China Mike, aka Mike Muldoon. Jamaican-born, charcoal-black with slanted eyes that no family tree could trace back to any Asian roots. A spade with a mick last name and chink eyes, growing up in Detroit. He had no choice but to get ruthless. Like Simen Semma and the Chaldean cartel, China Mike took his rep serious.

Papian didn't want China Mike. Didn't want Rizzo. He wanted Munchian.

"We've got more intel yet to gather on Rizzo before we move in on him. Keep digging on the Simen Semma angle."

"Bring Rizzo in. You got about ten counts to lead with. Show him he's looking at doing a dime apiece up the street. Once he realizes he's gonna be spending the rest of his life watching the tweetie birds through mesh, he'll turn on his own Aunt Tillie to save his hide from the predators inside who'd love a crack at him."

Papian tossed some cash on the counter and said, "Your heartburn is on me today."

As Papian got up, Fredericks said, "Rizzo's shelf life has about four to five months left. China Mike's angling to do a number on him soon. I wouldn't spend too much time on the Munchian-Semma hamster wheel.

You won't get much out of a lowlife like Rizzo but at least you can walk away from this thing with something."

Papian clenched his jowls shut, knowing Fredericks was right, but afraid of what he'd say in response. He didn't want to tick Fredericks off. As volatile as he was, he still needed him.

Papian put his hand on the door and Fredericks said, "No one hates them more than I do."

Papian stopped, pushing the door half open and said, "I know."

"Drugs poison minds. Erase lives. Young lives. Drug dealers, guys like Munchian, they should all go down for murder. Because that's what they do. They murder. Whether their victims end up physically dead or with their minds erased, they're murderers. They feed young kids the stuff that takes away their dreams. Takes away their future."

"You're sure about Munchian...going religious?"

"Yeah. Munchian should be glad he only has God to face in the next life. If he had to face me, I'd find a way to make Hell sound like paradise to him."

Papian had an especially difficult time dealing with the ones who went religious. Fredericks was right. These guys made millions, icing themselves out nice, putting stuff on the streets that was a disease spreading faster than cancer. And there was somehow a God that they believed could forgive them. Papian didn't believe in a God who would let someone like Munchian walk. Not after the minds he'd poisoned. After the lives he'd taken.

Fredericks said, "I know you don't like me. I know you don't like the way I do things. But I just want you to really understand the way it is and where I'm coming from. You got to the Munchian party too late. God got there first. Focus on Rizzo."

In reality, Papian envied Fredericks. For one brief moment, when he got that hip shot off at Giovanni and erased his existence, he had a chance to play the kind of God that made sense to him. The only kind of God that he could understand. The kind of God who would not let a guy like Munchian get away with all the horrid things he'd done.

"Stay on Munchian and Simen. I ain't ready to hang that one up yet."

I hope the God you found is a big God, Munchian. I hope, for your sake—that He is really big.

151

CHAPTER TWENTY-FIVE

October 1998
Grand Lake, Colorado

• •

Tony Rizzo kept his own private stash down in the hold of the ski boat he'd gotten from a connection who'd come up short on cash. Sitting in the spotter's seat, feet resting up on the cushioned engine hatch, he rolled himself a thick joint and blazed up, staring out at the lake. He'd bought this house, about 85 miles northwest of Boulder into the Rocky Mountain Park preserve, primarily because it was a perfect halfway point for the loads he was running from Phoenix up to China Mike's guys in Detroit. His driver, Gibby, was constantly on the road, the guy never sleeping, so Rizzo ended up hiring another driver, a friend of Gibby's, a guy named Jimmy Clay. Together they looked like a pair of paramilitary bookends. But today the place provided the kind of solace he needed as he realized what a bunch of dangerous idiots he was mixing it up with.

He pulled the toke deep into his lungs, dusk settling in, cool, crisp fall air feeling good as he stared out at the lake, not a ripple on the surface, glasslike, the flaming orange and yellow of autumn reflecting a mirror image of gold-shrouded timberland. After ripping off that load from Munchian, it had taken him a month before he'd stopped looking over his shoulder, expecting Munchian to come up behind him with one of his cannons and put him in permanent retirement. But after about a month, he figured Munchian's Jesus freak stuff was real and that he'd probably be getting popped soon himself. Getting out of the business this way was making too many big dogs nervous and he figured Munchian wasn't long for this world.

The load he'd jacked from Munchian made his guy in North Carolina happy and opened up doors real wide. His drivers were okay. Gibby and Clay. Between the two of them they had the IQ of an amoeba and they both looked like militia freaks the way they cropped their hair. But they were consistent and reliable. Rizzo had set things up real nice for them, purchasing each of them a Jeep Cherokee, fully loaded, with leather interior and Michigan plates since that was where most of their loads were going.

But he didn't like working with Mo'. The guy was nuts. One night Mo' had picked him up to go over to Su's to help bundle a load and on the way he pulled into some subdivision. Nice neighborhood, tract homes, stucco houses. Pulls into some driveway and says, "I'll be right back." Gets out of the car and out of nowhere, two more cars roar into the driveway full of black dudes. They get out and join Mo' on the front lawn, pulling out their guns and start blasting the front door and windows. For ninety seconds the entire house lit up in the blaze of their muzzle fire, then, as quickly as it started, it stopped, the black guys getting into their cars, Mo' slipping into the driver's seat, tossing his cannon into the back seat and driving on like he'd just delivered a pizza or something. The guy not saying a word about it again.

The real problems started when Mo' introduced him to a guy named China Mike. China's customers were high-maintenance and demanded quality stuff fast. Orders were coming in faster than either of his two amoeba-brains could keep up and they were slow-paying, leaving cash flow tight for new product. To keep up with product buys, Mo' went on the road and got sloppy. Rizzo just got the call that Mo's load to Kentucky got jacked. Two hundred pounds of grade A hemp, taken on spec from Big Ho'. Jose was going to demand his money and Rizzo didn't have it.

He took another hit on the joint, a deep hit, his mind relaxing, mellowness setting in. His problems with Munchian were now long behind him but he had a sick feeling knowing that his problems with Mo' and China Mike were only just beginning.

The church was a small, musty building in central Phoenix. Roger now attended regularly, learning praise songs and absorbing the word of God as it was preached through Pastor Frank. His knee was not quite yet at one hundred percent but he was no longer bedridden, getting around using a cane now. Like learning to walk again, his new walk with God was a daily struggle. He knew the life he did not want to live anymore. He knew that he wanted to learn more about this Heavenly Father that seemed to love him deep enough to come to his rescue in a rathole jail cell, strapped to a crazy chair like a discarded piece of human debris.

The night he was rescued—not arrested.

Service was over and the church was empty. He sat in the pew, second row, close enough to the front, but not quite the front row. He was thinking about Pastor Frank's message today. He talked about Psalm 139. About how deep God thinks of us. About His thoughts. If we could count them, they would outnumber the grains of sand on the earth. God doesn't choose to love us. God is love.

Suddenly, he felt the altar calling him. He slipped from the pew and found himself on his knees, elbows resting on the rail. He tried to pray but there were no words. He finally heard himself say, "God, what is it you want? God, where do I start?"

A gentle hand rested on his shoulder and he felt someone kneel next to him on his right side. He looked and it was Earl Swenson. Bald, middle-aged, plump in the middle, Earl was an elder in the church and wore the same gray pinstripe suit and fat, red knit tie every Sunday. Someone else knelt on the other side of him and he did not have to look to see who it was. He recognized the amalgamation of cheap perfume and moth balls of Earl's wife, Betty.

"It's a beautiful day outside, brother Roger. What keeps you here?"

"I'm not sure. Just thinking about the message today."

"Beautiful, wasn't it?" Betty said.

"I'm lost. I want so bad to follow God. But it's not going right. I'm not doing something right, and I can't figure out what it is."

"Roger, brother, give it time," Earl said. "You are still young in your faith."

"Yes, Roger. A newborn doesn't learn to walk over night."

Roger stared up at the cross, bathed in kaleidoscopic colors reflecting through the stained glass behind the altar. The cross suddenly became distorted as tears pooled in his eyes and the salty taste touched the corners of his mouth. "I just don't know where to start. I come to church. I read God's word every day. But sometimes, I just don't get what I'm reading. There's so much to learn. I just don't understand."

"You don't have to understand everything you read in God's word, Roger. Just thirst for God's word and let the power of His word feed your spirit. Don't get discouraged when you don't understand. Your spirit does. And it is being fed with every word of God's truth you read."

"What do you mean my spirit?"

Betty asked, "Roger, have you accepted Jesus Christ as your Lord and savior?"

"I, I guess so. I think so. I, I thought I did … that night I was strapped to the nut chair in the county jail."

Earl said, "Pastor Frank's message today, about God's thoughts—a God who thinks of every person, every individual regardless of what they have done, of how lost they are, of how far away they seem, a God whose daily thoughts outnumber the grains of sand on earth—is a God who would do *anything* to have a relationship with you. And He did. He sent His only son to die on a cross so that through His blood, your sins would be washed clean—and through His resurrection He could build a relationship with you."

And Roger realized what was missing. He had to begin a real and personal relationship with the only one who did not reject him.

"I'm ready," Roger said.

As Earl guided him through the prayer, he realized as he spoke the words, confessing with his mouth and believing in his heart that Jesus died for his sins, that his commitment must be real. Simen's words came back to him, "At least when you were a crook, you were an honest crook." Even as a crook, Roger's word was his bond. His commitment was always an unbreakable commitment. Now he realized that he was making a commitment to his Lord Jesus Christ—who shed blood and suffered broken bones to pay the price for all the awful and atrocious things Roger had done with his life. He realized that this was not only an unbreakable commitment to Jesus but a vow to whatever it would take to live for his Lord. Simen spared him his life because of his word. Now his Word was going to earn him eternal life.

As he followed Earl's lead in speaking his confession of sin, he felt the chains of over a decade of crime, arrest and incarceration fall free. When he was done, he heard laughter. Unbridled laughter that could only have been heaven-sent. The laughter filled the church as though coming from the packed pews of an overflowing congregation but he soon realized that it was only coming from the three of them. Their laughter was unstoppable. His gut ached; he felt tears rushing down his cheeks. Yet he did not want to stop. He wanted the joy and laughter to last forever.

When the laughter finally stopped they were no longer kneeling at the pews but stretched out on the floor in front of the altar. Earl was flat on his back, suit coat open, potbelly pointing to the church ceiling, chest heaving, trying to catch his breath, straining the buttons on his white dress shirt.

"I ... I never felt anything like that before," Earl said between breaths. "Now I know what it must have been like at the Pentecost."

"What ... what does this mean?" Roger said, an uncontrollable chuckle in his voice, like he used to get after burning a joint. But weed was always temporary. This, he knew, was never going to go away. This was forever, and he knew there was no amount of money, drugs or sex that would replace it.

Earl finally caught his breath and said, "It means welcome to the kingdom of Heaven, Roger. Welcome."

November
Detroit, Michigan
6:45 p.m.
• •

"He's actually lived longer than I expected," Buddy Fredericks said. "Mo's too stupid to figure it out yet, that Rizzo's there, in the house, probably hiding under his own bed, crapping his Daffy Duck jammies. But once he figures it out, Rizzo's popped and you're gonna lose your best lead." Fredericks grabbed the cup of bourbon that Papian had just refilled for him and held it up as though making a toast. "Hate to say I told ya so."

Dusk hung heavy outside Papian's office window, a light November snowfall swirling through the sodium glow of streetlights below. It was after hours, Buddy showing up, as usual wanting to discuss things over a drink at Cobo Joe's. Papian wasn't in the mood for the bar tonight, pulling the bottle of Jim Beam from his desk drawer and filling two coffee cups.

Sitting with his feet propped up on his desk, Papian read through the Rizzo wiretap transcript again, a conversation Mo' had when he'd called Rizzo's place from Detroit Metro, the time recorded as 6:17 a.m. Arizona time when Paulette finally picked up the phone. Mo' was catching the 9:00 a.m. Northwest flight to Phoenix Sky Harbor.

Begin Transcript

Paulette: Hello?

Mo':   Put that **expletive** on the line now!

Paulette: Mo', please stop calling here! I told you last night. I've been telling you the last couple days you been callin'— Tony ain't here!

Mo'   Yeah? You know where it is I am now? I'm on a plane in fifteen minutes and I'm gonna be right on your front step in a few hours. You tell Tony, he don't have that load, I'm gonna pop you, gonna pop him, and then I'm gonna catch a plane to California, find your mama, and pop her too. Yeah, that's right. Maybe you forgot. I know where you from, girl. And don't you try to leave. You like the present got delivered yesterday afternoon? Through the window?

Paulette: You mean the rock? But you're in Detroit.

Mo'   Man, you're dense. I just said I got people watchin'. Like the note attached to the rock? Clever, huh? My own idea. Bullet taped to it. Remember what the note said? 'This one went through the window. Next one goes through your head.' You think I couldn't 'a had them put that bullet through your head yesterday when you went up to Wal-Mart, you and your bratty kids, to buy groceries and those stupid cardboard turkeys you got hangin' in the front window now? Stay put, babe. Big Mo's comin' callin'!

End Transcript

Papian asked, "Why's Rizzo having such a tough time getting product?"

"Big Mama Su's been out of commission. She's gone to some quack in St. Louis to get a few sections out of her stomach stapled shut."

Apparently, China had snagged an order for a couple of high-demand big shot customers, real high-fliers with connections in Grosse Point Shores. From the transcripts, it appeared that Rizzo was having trouble getting a load together. China and Mo' were up in Detroit trying to keep the customer on ice, calling Rizzo on the hour every hour asking about the delivery.

"You think he'll be able to get the stuff together on time?"

"Think it'll matter?" Fredericks said, putting his feet up on the desk, crossing his ankles. "Mo' gets wise Rizzo's in the house, he's gonna kick the door down and you may as well close up shop and go back to D.C. Only other two you got are Munchian and Semma. Last report we got on Munchian he was rollin' around on some church floor. Hey, maybe you can get him for stealin' communion wine or something like that."

Papian continued staring at the transcripts. He wasn't sure yet if they had enough to move on Rizzo yet or not. He needed more time.

"We got people in place around the Rizzo place, anything happens."

Fredericks helped himself to another pour of Beam. "Yeah, well, let's just hope they can move quick. Really quick."

CHAPTER TWENTY-SIX

December 1998
Detroit
4:45 p.m.

• •

Gibby was proud of himself, the way he played it all up nice after Rizzo tried to fire Mo' and China as customers. Rizzo, playing the tough guy. He told Gibby that he set up a new connection—a friend of Simon's named Meyer—to replace China's guys. Rizzo, trying to put the pieces back together after he screwed that load up, nearly getting his house all shot up by Mo' and his guys. They'd kicked his door down and, after knocking his squeeze Paulette around, found him messing his pants in the back room. Rizzo managed to get out of having his knee caps blown off, agreeing to come up with a load within forty eight-hours, eating the cost himself for the whole thing.

Gibby knew that Rizzo wanted to keep him on after cutting Mo' loose. Rizzo pulled a load together for the new guy Meyer in Detroit and sent him to deliver it, but Gibby never knew that Rizzo had no intentions of paying him his ten K for the run. When he got back after dropping the load off, Rizzo was lame about it, saying Mo' stiffed him, telling him he'd flown Paulette up to collect but Mo's customers refused to pay. That's when Rizzo told him that he and Mo' were through. He owed him one more load and then that was it. He was cutting Mo' free.

At first Gibby had decided that he was going to go collect from Mo' himself, knowing the little dive in downtown Royal Oak where Mo' liked to hang out. He spotted Mo' at the bar and was impressed the way Mo' played it cool when he slid onto the barstool next to him, lifting his shirt and showing Mo' the gun butt sticking out of his waistband. Mo' simply told him to order himself a beer and he'd set him straight.

After listening to how it really went, Mo' asked him, "So, you wanna get double your payback plus a little bonus?"

"I'm listening."

So Mo' hatched up this thing, what was about to go down now. Mo' told him he knew that Rizzo had two serious loads coming up to Detroit. One load was going to be the final delivery Rizzo had promised him and China Mike, and the other one, two-hundred-and-fifty pounds of weed, going to the new guy Meyer. In order to ensure that both loads were in Detroit at the same time, Mo' explained that they had to cut Meyer in on this thing too. They also needed Jimmy Clay in on it, but Mo' could set it up so that Clay wouldn't know what hit him, Mo' telling him they'd split the whole thing three ways.

So Gibby played it out. The way Mo' told him to do it, once he got the load delivered to Meyer, give Rizzo a call and tell him he's quitting, striking out on his own and that he wants his pay for that last delivery to Mo', and tell him he wants it doubled, $20K. Put Paulette on the next plane up to bring it to him. The idea was to get him paid double for that load, rattle Rizzo a bit and to have Clay come in and help him with Paulette, getting Clay distracted and away from the load he was delivering. Mo' would take care of the rest.

"Twenty K! You crazy?" Rizzo said when he'd made the call. He was sitting there at Meyer's kitchen table, Meyer trying to hold back his laugh, snorting an orange spray out his nose of the bite of macaroni and cheese he'd just taken. "Just get back here and I'll pay you, all right?"

"You owe me ten K for that delivery I made last month. I figure, with interest, it's doubled. I checked the airlines. There's a Northwest flight leaving in about two hours. Plenty of time for you to kick her out of bed and make the plane. She'll be here by four, I'll meet her, Church's Chicken, Eight Mile and Dequindre."

"Gibby, I'll give you fifteen K when you get back. Just bring the cash back here, man! I need that. Man, we don't wanna jack Su's guy around, okay?"

"You got your choice. Meyer's sitting here. He's already offered to pay me fifteen K. He don't like the way you do business so much. Maybe

I should just take his offer, stay around here a while, run some loads direct for Meyer myself."

Meyer was really busting his gut now, unable to handle it.

"Gibby…"

"What's it gonna be, Tony? Anything left of you after Litte Ho' and his guys take care of you, you can come up here and talk with Meyer yourself about getting the rest of your money."

So there she was now, pulling into the Church's Chicken parking lot in a rented red Ford Taurus. Gibby looked at his watch, four-fifty-five, right on time. He got out of the Jeep and met her halfway. Paulette's big brown eyes always sucked him right in. She was carrying an oversized Gucci bag and she looked great, all wrapped snug in that puffy ski jacket, fur-lined hood pulled up, shaping her face in a soft pink frame. He loved her voice, like silk, and when she smiled, it was straight-toothed and bright. But she wasn't smiling today. The pulpy shiner swelling her left eye shut told him that Rizzo hadn't used the back of his hand this time. No, this time Rizzo had pistol-whipped her back in line.

"You slip on the soap in the shower this morning or what?" he asked.

"Where's the money, Gib? Tony ain't messin' around this time."

He chuckled. "*Tony* ain't messing around? I got three hun'red grand of Tony's money, sweets. Let's say we head back to the airport, pick a nice blue spot down in the Caribbean and sip Mai Tais with our toes in the sand while Tony gets devoured by the big dogs up here?"

"Where's the money, Gibby?" getting bold now, sounding serious.

"You know what happens to Tony, Little Ho' don't collect." He snapped his fingers twice. "Boom. Boom. Tony's done. We be back in about a week you want."

"Gibby, please. I'm cold and I wanna get this done and go home. Where's the money?"

"I should be asking you the same thing."

She opened the Gucci bag and he saw two wrapped bundles of one hundreds. He started to reach for them but she shut the purse and pulled it away. He smiled. "The money's nearby. C'mon, sweet stuff. Jeep's warm. Let's take a ride."

Jimmy Clay nearly lost sight of the Jeep when he looked down at the pouch of cash sitting on the passenger seat, a subconscious tick he had, making sure it was still there. He'd just dropped off the load to China Mike at 8 Mile and Woodward. Two hundred fifty K and he was jumpier bringing cash back than running a load of weed cross country. Cops pull you over with a load, you get jail time. Lose the cash, you get another smile carved under your chin or a prescription of .22-caliber lead injected into your bean.

They were heading north on I-75 coming out of the Detroit area and it had started to snow, flurries swirling around the rush-hour taillights ahead. When he looked back up he found the taillights of Gibby's Jeep cutting across three lanes, heading for the Royal Oak exit.

Driving down Main Street in downtown Royal Oak, he stayed five car lengths behind, the way Gibby told him. As Gibby approached the intersection of Main and 2nd Street, Jimmy pulled to a metered parking spot right in front of Mr. B's Pub. He tucked the pouch of cash in the glove box and locked it, got out and walked up the sidewalk, leaning against the Comet Burger, hands shoved in his jacket pocket, and watched.

The tires screeched and the Jeep bounced back and forth on its axles when Gibby hit the brakes hard right in the middle of the intersection. Exhaust stopped seeping from the tailpipe as Gibby shut the engine off and yanked the keys from the ignition. Jimmy could see the silhouettes of both Paulette and Gibby in the front seat, Paulette's arms flailing in protest, Gibby shouting back at her, pointing his finger. Cars lining up and horns blaring, the fight between them went on for a minute, and then he saw Gibby backhand Paulette across the mouth. As she fell back in the seat, he saw Gibby grab something from her and the door popped open. A curious crowd started to gather as Gibby ran from the Jeep, sprinting up 2nd Street, Gucci bag tucked under his arm.

He walked into action, playing his part, the way Gibby had told him to do it. Paulette ran to the curve, screaming for Gibby as he disappeared up an alley. Jimmy came running, coming to a sliding stop on the sidewalk ice.

"Paulette, what happened?" Acting confused, all concerned.

Paulette whipped around, tears running down her cheeks, black mascara frozen to her face in the swirling snowflakes. Gibby had left a nice welt on her right cheek.

"Jimmy! What … what…"

"I was having a brew at Mr. B's. Just made the drop and decided to drive back tomorrow. Sitting at the bar, I heard the commotion."

She said, "He's ripping Tony off! And he took the keys to the Jeep! Jimmy, I'm stranded—and he's got Tony's money. The *money!*"

Horns were blaring, traffic inching around the Jeep parked in the intersection.

"All right. All right. Let's think this thing through. First, we gotta get that Jeep outa the intersection, otherwise we're gonna be dealing with cops. Le'me see if I can hot wire it."

He popped the hood and, as he pretended to fiddle under there, he could here Paulette on her cell phone talking to Tony, all hysterical. Perfect. He felt along the car frame and, near the fan, found the little magnetic box Gibby had tucked under there. With Paulette still pacing back and forth arguing with Tony, he popped open the box and palmed the spare ignition key. Quietly latching the hood shut, he walked around and slid behind the wheel, fired up the Jeep and waved to Paulette as he pulled away. Looking in the rear view mirror, he watched Paulette drop her cell phone and rush to the intersection, arms flailing, screaming at the top of her lungs.

Weaving in and out of traffic, Jimmy got out of there as fast as he could. Gibby wanted the dope, the money and the Jeep. After all, the Jeep was registered in his name. Another gift from Tony Rizzo, the moron.

Mo' stepped from Mr. B's Pub and hunched down in his thick, longshoreman jacket, the wind picking up, snow falling heavier now. He'd gotten three beers down as he waited, feeling good now, real mellow but not out of control. He pulled the Slim Jim from inside his jacket and walked around to the driver's-side door of Clay's Jeep. No one noticed him jimmy the door open, all the attention on the screaming girl up the street, the Jeep racing away. He slipped behind the wheel and jammed the Slim Jim into the glove box, knowing it was locked, and yanked it open. He unzipped the pouch and his trained eye counted two hundred and fifty K without even touching the bundles. He slid under the dash and yanked the wires. Within a minute he had the Jeep started. He pulled away from the curb and slowed down as he drove through the intersection. Paulette's face flushed whiter than the snow swirling around her, jaw dropping as she recognized the Jeep. Mo' waved to her as he drove by, driving off with the rest of Rizzo's money.

And his other Jeep.

January 14, 1999
Detroit
8:35 a.m.

• •

The courier brought the two envelopes in and set them in front of him. Special Agent Papian was on his second cup of coffee and the blizzard swirling outside his office window shut off the morning sun. He'd watched the Weather Channel this morning before leaving his apartment and saw that it was going to be seventy-five degrees and sunny in Phoenix today. He envied the U.S Marshals in Phoenix who had just received full authority to make their move by the stroke of the judge's pen.

His gut told him that he was pulling the pin on this operation too soon, but he had no choice. Detective Fredericks was right. Rizzo got himself jammed up bad with China Mike and friends and now was in deep with the heavies out of Mexico. They could pop him anytime, up close behind the ear with a .22 or from a hundred yards out with a good scope and suppressor. Either way, his field agents would never see it coming. Things were falling apart fast, and it was time to bring Rizzo in. There was no protecting him from the Mexican armor about to be trained on him.

The envelopes contained copies of the arrest warrants just issued out of the United States District Court, Eastern District of Michigan. One for Tony J. Rizzo, the other for his tart, Paulette Powers.

His phone rang.

"Papian."

Special Agent Jane Hensley's voice came through the line, "Morning, David. Federal marshals are making their move on the Phoenix residence of Tony Rizzo."

Hensley was a special agent with the Arizona Attorney General's Drug Enforcement section, assigned to Papian's counterparts over at the U.S. Customs task force. She worked for the ruthless female Attorney General's office prosecutor Bobbie Rosenberg.

Rosenberg was every drug dealer's nightmare, famous for arranging steep bail on drug traffickers, keeping them locked up in the County hole while stringing their case along in legal red tape. It was a breaking technique and Rosenberg was famous for turning more punks into informants than any other prosecutor in Arizona. Getting snared by Bobbie Rosenberg became known as getting caught in the "JAP trap" — JAP for Jewish American Princess. After it was obvious that the Munchian wiretaps were going nowhere, Fredericks suggested that Papian drop the whole thing, let it go to State, snare the whole cartel in the JAP trap. Papian wasn't amused.

"You're up early."

"It's going to be a busy day."

He could tell that Hensley couldn't wait until the case got rolled over to the Arizona AG. She loved to watch Bobbie work.

"Paulette with him?"

"From what we've gathered, yeah. We should be able to get them both in one stop."

"Good. Thank you. Let me know when they're both in custody."

He sat back in his chair, both hands gripping his rapidly cooling cup of coffee as he stared out at the blizzard. Seventy-five degrees today in Arizona. In about five minutes, things would be heating up real fast at the Rizzo residence.

CHAPTER TWENTY-SEVEN

February, 1999
Federal Prison Camp
Nellis, Nevada

• •

Tony Rizzo had been wearing tan shirts and pants for the last month, cleaning crust-filth latrines that the fly boys at Nellis Air Force Base crapped in after finishing their aerobatic drills designed to keep the blue skies over the heat-cracked desert safe. The prison camp provided labor to support the base. Rizzo was here, looking at too many years wearing tan, working for free scrubbing skid marks off stainless steel toilet bowls.

The federal marshals were cool about it, showing up at his front door wearing their blue windbreakers, yellow star stenciled on the front, "Police" stenciled below, Glocks holstered. It all went down January 14, he would never forget the date. Four of them, official sedans parked in the driveway, knocked politely and told him they had a warrant for his arrest. They asked him if Paulette was at home and he was idiot enough to say, "Yeah, sure," and soon enough, they had them cuffed, in the car and on their way down to the Federal Building downtown.

He got dumped into a Maricopa County hold until they loaded him onto a rattling transport and bussed him up to Nevada where he met Special Agent Papian and it all became clear. He recognized the guy right away, the Armenian with one eyebrow stretching across his forehead like Munchian. The guy that had ordered bourbon and never touched his drink back at that swank Scottsdale martini bar. Now he knew why. The guy was on duty. Rizzo's face clenched, reddening, his arms shooting up from the table, wanting to cover his face in disbelief, but stopped short, trembling against the chains tethering him to the marred conference table.

"Easy there, sport," Papian said. "We got a long time ahead of us to get better acquainted."

Papian had shown him the charges, the case originating out of East District Court in Detroit. He was looking at 121 months unless he decided to cooperate. Turn narc, we might be able to get that reduced to 61 months. He took the deal and was soon before a federal judge in Detroit entering a guilty plea.

He was getting tired now, the cinderblock walls of this conference room closing in on him after three straight days of questioning, the hard plastic chair giving him a burning case of 'roids.

The door swung open and Papian walked in, all comfortable in his polo shirt and khakis, glad to be out of the cold slop in Detroit. A cute blonde stenographer came in after him, situating herself behind her equipment and poised her ruby-tipped fingers over the keyboard.

Papian looked livid, slamming the tape recorder down on the marred table while the stenographer situated herself at the other end.

"Your testimony about Munchian ain't lining up with your squeeze Paulette's story, Tony. You didn't exactly get a chance to get your stories in sync."

"Well, Paulette really wasn't involved--"

"Okay, Tony. Here's how it is. I am going to bust Roger. I am going to bust a lot of people based on what you tell me here. I hate to be embarrassed, Tony. I really hate it. So, if I decide I can't trust you, you'll be spending the next ten years cleaning toilets and sharing a cell with guys who fart two feet from where you lay your head at night. I have over eighteen potential co-conspirators in this thing, Tony. Any one of them can get me the information that I need to know. So, you need to decide now. Are you going to provide me with the information that I need or do I need to start planning my travel to other places besides sunny Nevada ... which, by the way, will only tick me off more."

He looked over at the stenographer, her ruby-red nails poised over her keyboard. Finally he said, "Okay. What do you really want to know about Roger Munchian?"

Papian reached over and hit record on the tape recorder. "Tell me everything. The truth this time."

August 1999
St. Louis

· ·

Her flight was scheduled for 6:50 the next morning. First stop, New York. Then non-stop to Charles DeGaulle in Paris and on to King Khalid International, Riyadh, Saudi Arabia. Suhad Haddad would be home in thirty-six hours.

The accommodations at the St. Louis Marriott were not bad. Clean rooms. Continental breakfast. Pool. Room service if she wanted it.

Both Rizzo and Paulette were flapping their gums to the Feds and the arrests were coming down. In March they busted Munchian and Mo'. They showed up at Mo's house with a search warrant and not only got him for the drugs and paraphernalia but they also found his stash of assault weapons, racking up the charges. She heard that they'd busted Roger in his office. U.S. Marshals walked right in, escorting him out in front of all his employees. Her brother AB had called her, telling her that it was just a matter of time before they came knocking and said they had to get out. Plans were in the works back home and all they had to do was get their travel all set. But while AB was trying to get his passport squared away, the Feds showed up and hauled him in. Su wasn't going to wait. She made arrangements to get a fake passport, booked her flight, got out of the apartment where she was staying and got herself to the airport, staying at the Marriott under an assumed name until her fake passport was delivered.

She was anxious, unable to sleep. She'd struggled to fall asleep most of the night, finally giving up and flipping the TV on, finding a replay of *Forrest Gump* on cable. Sitting up in bed, smoking a cigarette from her third pack of Newports for the day, she was just a few hours away from boarding a plane and getting out of here for good. Before she came to St. Louis for her surgery she'd sold Lazy Su's to her cousin. She hadn't moved any dope in several months and she had no debts to anyone. She was square with Big Ho' and the rest of her connections. The sale of Lazy

Su's left plenty of cash in her pocket and getting out while square with everyone meant she wouldn't be spending the rest of her life looking over her shoulder. She knew that her dealers had long arms. They could drop her any time any place, even in Saudi Arabia, she was certain of that. She was certain these people could get to anyone if they wanted to—which was why she didn't bet that Rizzo or Paulette had very bright futures ahead of them.

Lighting another cigarette and not paying much attention to Forrest or his box of chocolates, she thought about Roger, wondering what he was thinking of his God now. What a waste. Did the guy really think that he could escape his past? Get away from who he really was? If you're gonna go out, go out with a bang. Instead, the only bang at the end of Roger's run was the thumping he was doing on his Bible.

The knock at her door startled her. She shut the TV off and killed the light, sitting there in the dark, only the red ember from her cigarette giving the room any life. The knock came again, more forceful this time, and a voice said, "Hotel manager. I need to speak with you."

She stabbed the ashtray with her cigarette and slipped out of bed. Looking through the peep hole, she saw the plump little man, streaks of single black locks lining his bald head, wearing a red blazer and knit tie, standing in the hall two steps back from the door.

"I know it's a non-smoking room and I put the cigarette out. I'm sorry, I won't light up in here anymore," she called through the door.

"Open the door please, Ms. Haddad," he said. And she knew she was in trouble. She had booked the room under an assumed name. The gold badge on his blazer said, 'Paul Frazier, Manager.'

"I have an early flight. I need to get some sleep."

"Ms. Haddad, I am asking nicely. Please don't make me call security."

She unchained the door and opened it. Immediately, the door was filled with two men in blue, waving gold stars with 'U.S. Marshal' imprinted neatly in the middle.

"Ms. Haddad, we have a warrant for your arrest, issued by the United States District Court, Eastern District of Michigan. We need you to come with us, please."

September 1999
Phoenix

• •

Roger pulled up to the curb at Phoenix Sky Harbor airport and got out, helping his parents get their luggage out of the trunk. They'd be spending the next two months in Armenia, visiting family, and playing matchmaker for their son. Now that this case — something to do with the Federal Government, something they really didn't understand — was done and dismissed, they wanted Roger to meet someone and settle down. His last marriage had failed and they figured it was primarily because Roger had married an Americanized Armenian. What he needed was a sweet Armenian girl not influenced by the "me" culture of America.

They'd wanted to take this trip several months ago but he had stalled them, uncertain of the outcome of his legal problems. His parents were aware that he was in some sort of trouble, always talking to that lawyer back in Michigan on the phone, constantly traveling back and forth to Detroit, telling them that he had another "meeting" back there.

He couldn't believe six months had passed since it all went down. On a sunny Monday morning, March 15, he had been in his office at Diamondback Insurance, Bible resting on the corner of his desk, crown of thorns hanging from a nail on the wall behind him. He heard a commotion out front followed by his assistant's concerned voice first blurting out questions, finally saying, "Yes, he's back in his office."

There was a knock at the door. He said, "Come in," and his tiny office was suddenly filled with federal marshals, Arizona DPS, and U.S. Customs officers.

"I take it you're not here to inquire about a group policy?"

They escorted him out, tucked him into a government sedan and took him to the Federal Building in downtown Phoenix. They informed him of his charges, the indictments coming out of the U.S. Federal Eastern District Court Detroit. His arrest record also stated that the prosecutors in this case had in custody federal witnesses, one Anthony J. Rizzo and Paulette Powers, who were willing to testify to his involvement in conspiracy and drug trafficking. He was allowed to review the charges and he knew this was serious. Twelve Class-2 felony charges, almost as high as you could get. Two of the counts were for conspiracy and for conducting an illegal enterprise and the rest for possession of marijuana for sale or transfer. Class-2 meant twenty-to-life. He quickly added it up: 160 years.

He felt like he was back in the Madison Street hold again, looking at spending the rest of his life in prison.

"Trust me, Roger. Trust me."

He was surprised when they said he was being released on his own recognizance. He was required to surrender his passport and he'd be notified of his first hearing date in Detroit. He was back in his office by lunch, calling Jay.

Jay recommended a dago attorney up in Detroit, Frank Marcello, specializing in federal cases. He flew up to Detroit to meet Frank at his office on the top floor of one of the golden-glass twin tower buildings in Southfield. Frank was a barrel-chested, deep-voiced, bushy-eyed Italian iced out in gold bling. The guy put it to him straight. Yeah, this was serious. The gig was a joint task force of the DEA, U.S. Customs and the Narcotics Division of the Detroit Police Department. The Drug Enforcement Division of the Arizona AG also had their noses cocked in this direction as well, so watch your back once ol' Frank gets you cut loose from this.

"All right," Frank had said. "How much confidence you got that this Rizzo guy's got the goods on you? Him and his tart, what's her name?" He flipped open his file and looked at the report. "Paulette."

"Rizzo?" He suppressed a laugh. "Yeah. Right."

"Gotcha. He's a low-level. That's what I figured. Got nothing on ya but what his little pea-bean can concoct. Okay. Here's the way it is. They'd been on Rizzo for nearly a year up till ninety-eight when the moron arranged a buy from the DEA's lead investigator, David Papian.

"Okay, so, the way it's gonna go down, you're gonna meet with Papian. He's gonna play hardball. He's gonna try and get you to deal to turn government witness. Gonna tell you he's got a couple good witnesses, puttin' it to him straight, filling in the picture. He'll paint an ugly picture of what it's gonna be like to be spending the rest of your life in a federal hole. You don't gotta say a word and I'm advising that you don't say a word. The Feds ain't got a tight lid on you in this, Mr. Munchian. Keep tight-lipped, show up for all of your hearings and let me do my thing in the courts and get you untangled from this, *capiche*? Hey, when we walk out of that court for the last time, I'll take you down to Little Italy. We'll celebrate at Roma Café."

He pinched his fingers and thumb together and gave them a smacking kiss. "That place, even makes my mama jealous."

When he finally met Papian, God's true grace was revealed. Marcello was right, Papian painted an ugly picture, telling him they had eighteen conspirators in custody. He started throwing out names, watching for his reaction. Some he knew real close. Su Haddad. AB Haddad. Simen Semma. Others he'd only heard of, knowing they were tight with Rizzo. Greg Gibbons. Maurice Wilson. Simon Brash.

As he listened to Papian talk, he realized that everything the Feds had on the cartel happened after he had gotten out, after he'd made his decision to turn to God. The accident in 1997 was more than God's way of getting his attention. Had he kept rolling fast down that road, he would have still been in the cartel when Papian's team infiltrated. God saw it coming. God protected him, stopping him in a crumpled heap on that wet Arizona highway, using the wreckage to keep him from the threat of a lifetime of incarceration that was around the next turn up the road.

He stayed true to Marcello's counsel, never missing a court date, flying to Detroit once a month. At the end of August the Feds dropped the case against him. True to his promise, Marcello took him down to Roma's in Little Italy and they celebrated, Marcello having to drink the $200 bottle of Gaja Barbaresco himself while Roger stuck to his glass of water and lemon.

He pulled away from the curb at Sky Harbor watching his parents fade away in the rear view mirror, standing in the Delta curbside bag check line, waving to him. As he drove along the I-10, his pager went off. He'd gotten a new one, this one for legitimate business only, and he was shocked to see that it was a page from Simen Semma. How did he get this number? Something told him to return the page. He pulled off at the next exit and pulled into a Circle K.

"Okay, first off, you gotta know, Rizzo's a dead man. I don't care where he ends up. I got people all over. We either get him inside or we pop him when he gets back out of hock."

"That's your way, not mine, Simen. That what you called me about?"

"No. Wanted to thank you for holding true. You could'a caused a lot of trouble for me. We could'a caused a lot of trouble for each other."

"They dismiss your case too?"

"They dismissed everybody's. Rizzo was worth about as much as a turd floating in the courthouse toilet to the Feds. Last I heard, the Feds reneged on his deal. He's looking at a ten-year stretch, no time served."

"Too bad. I appreciate you, Simen, but I think this is it for us, okay? I don't see any reason for our paths to cross again."

"I wouldn't be so sure about that."

"What do you mean?"

"Just watch yourself, okay? Feds may have dismissed this but that don't mean the state of Arizona can't pick it up."

"State charges?"

"The ride ain't done yet, buddy, buddy. Good luck."

He walked back to his car, wondering if perhaps it was too soon for his parents to be traveling to Armenia to find him a bride.

CHAPTER TWENTY-EIGHT

Tuesday, April 4, 2000
Yerevan, Armenia

• •

It wasn't until after he stopped calling that she realized how much she'd started caring for him. The spring air had a chill, the cool breeze lifting the budding tree branches, the flowering meadow in front of her swaying gently. Behind her, the flowing waters of the Hrazdan River hissed over rocks and boulders. Off in the horizon, the ceramic blue skies framed the snowcapped peaks of Mount Ararat with a majestic elegance on God's infinite canvas.

Sirarpi decided to take her lunch hour in the park, away from crowds and noise, and spend time with God. She had her Bible resting on the worm-eaten picnic table in front of her, the pages blowing in the breeze, but her thoughts turned continually to Roger. Looking up at Mount Ararat especially reminded her of him, the way he talked about God and shared his faith with her on the phone. He was proud of his Armenian heritage and he was especially proud of the prominence of that mountain in the Bible where Noah's ark came to rest as the flood waters receded. He called almost every day since that first surprise phone call he'd made last October. Her family didn't have a phone at the time. Their neighbor was always kind enough to let her parents use their phone for emergencies and such. She'd just gotten home from work, working as a cashier selling office products in town, when her neighbor knocked at the door and told her that she had a call, hurry, it was long distance from the United States.

He introduced himself as Hrach, his fluency with the Armenian language strained. He'd grown up in America, a place Sirarpi heard about, especially through her uncle in California, but never visited, so his Armenian was not as fluent.

He told her she could call him Roger, the name he went by in America. As he talked she slowly put the pieces together. Earlier that month Roger's parents had come with her parents to her workplace to introduce themselves, telling her that they were distant cousins with her uncle in California and that they'd dropped by her house to visit her parents and wanted to meet her. They were jovial, talking about how long it had been since they had an opportunity to visit their country.

Their story was common enough. They'd had an opportunity to get out over twenty years ago through the luck of the draw in a lottery that granted their household visas. Opportunities to return were rare and only for the affluent even after the collapse of the Soviet empire. Though the iron grip of communism eased after Armenia gained its independence from the Soviet Union, the country remained war torn as tensions with neighboring Azerbaijan escalated into a bloody six-year war that paralyzed Armenia's infrastructure with rationed gas, constant blackouts and food shortages. Armenia was not on the top of many family vacation spots.

But as times got better in Armenia after the war, they said that their son, Hrach, wanted them to have a chance to go back and visit friends and family, so he had arranged for their travel. They spoke highly of their son, telling her how proud they were of him having risen from the dirt-poor streets of Armenia to the ghettos of Los Angeles to becoming a successful businessman in Phoenix. They took lots of pictures, making sure she was in every group shot. She did not understand what the draw was, taking so many pictures with her in the shop. But as her conversation went on with Roger, she figured it out. They had come to play matchmaker.

She was drawn to his faith, the way he talked about God. Armenians considered themselves Christians simply by their nationality. The country, nestled in a region of godless communism and theocratic radical Islamic republics, proclaimed itself a Christian country fifteen years before the Roman Empire converted to Christianity.

But most Armenians did not know God personally. They knew God as a name, worshipped on holidays and on special occasions by lighting candles. However, when Sirarpi was six, she came to know a different God. A God who loved her. A God who answered prayers. A God who heals hurts and wipes away tears.

It happened shortly after that terrible explosion that took Daddy away for a while. He'd gone to a place in the Ukraine, a town they called Chernobyl. She didn't understand what happened. But some kind of explosion killed a lot of people and Daddy and some friends went there to help fix things. Shortly after he came home he'd gotten very sick and whatever got him sick there made his hair fall out. He got skinny. He couldn't eat and she was scared. Her Daddy was going to die.

She prayed and found a God who comforted her and told her everything was going to be okay; told her that He was not going to take her Daddy from her.

And he got better.

She had to seek her relationship with God in secret. Having such a relationship with God was mocked by her family and relatives, so she had no choice but to go to underground worship services whenever she could sneak away. She knew that if she ever was going to marry, she was going to seek a man of God. A man who loved God the way she did.

Roger called every day, so frequently that her parents finally got a phone installed. She loved the conversations, finally being able to open up to someone about her faith. She told him how envious she was that he could so openly go and worship at a church that loved Jesus Christ intimately. She told him that she had to keep her Bible hidden and told him about the "gatherings" in her town, services where believers would get together and worship Jesus in secret.

They had become close friends. They would talk for hours and at odd times due to the ten-hour time difference. But now he wasn't calling. She hadn't heard from him since March 20 and she wondered what had gone wrong.

She looked down at her Bible and the pages had blown to Proverbs 3:5. She read God's message to her. "Trust in the Lord with all your heart and lean not on your own understanding."

"Okay, God," she heard herself saying. "I trust you. And I pray that Roger is okay."

Madison Street Jail

Roger's cellie, a guy named Ajax and a frequent guest at the Madison Street zoo, was obsessed with Salvador "Sammy The Bull" Gravano, the Mafia hit man who turned snitch and brought down John Gotti. Gravano should have been serving multiple life terms for the 19 murders he'd admitted to, but the deal he cut with the Feds got him off with five years for racketeering. He went into the witness protection program after serving his time but dropped out to hook up with some writer to do his book, making himself famous, saying he wasn't afraid of being in the crosshairs of any hit man. He also hooked up with a gang in Phoenix, a pack of white suburban nut jobs calling themselves The Devil Dogs, known for the way they barked like a pack of wild dogs at their victims.

Gravano used them to finance an Ecstasy drug ring that ended up cornering the Arizona market with the little $30 methamphetamine pills that looked like gumdrops stamped with a Nike swoosh. While Roger was working through his federal trial, the Phoenix police busted Gravano's drug ring. Now here Gravano was, a dog returning to its vomit, right upstairs in his own cage in the Madison Street zoo, a big, fat price on his bald head, working his way through the court system.

During his sentencing on the racketeering charges, the judge said that Gravano had "irrevocably broken from his past." Roger thought about his own struggle to turn from the only lifestyle he'd known, watching a guy like "Sammy the Bull" face the danger of turning snitch, then go back to a life of crime. Maybe he was drawn back to the fame. Or, worse, got pressured back. Maybe receiving a phone call, someone dotting a bull's-eye on his forehead, letting him know that he needed a favor. Do this for me, I un-dot your head.

Back in the stripes in the County hole, Roger wondered just how "irrevocable" the break with his own past would be. How long would it be before he got a call from someone in his past asking him for a favor, letting him know about the dot on his own forehead.

Or worse. What if they ended up threatening Sirarpi?

They kept Gravano locked up tight in protective custody, right upstairs, and everybody wanted a piece of him. Ajax believed he was going to be the one to slice him with the shank he'd made out of razor blades and a toothbrush handle. He was talking about him now, Roger trying not to listen, sitting up on his bunk, pretending to sleep, thinking of her.

It all went down two weeks before, March 20th. He'd promised Sirarpi that he would call her the next morning, calling her every day before leaving for work. She would be getting home from work as his day started and he looked forward to starting off every day hearing her voice. He loved her laugh. Her voice like a kiss from God the way it came through the telephone line, direct to his heart. They were supposed to be friends, keeping this casual, no expectations. But he was falling in love.

They came crashing into his office around noon, the Maricopa County Sheriff's Office S.W.A.T team not as polite as the federal marshals had been. Assault weapons trained on him, barking commands, slamming him to his office floor, handcuffs clanking shut—it was like the night he and Nunez popped caps at Frankie Richmond and his Dog Town homies all over again. They dragged him from the floor and hustled him past his stunned employees shoving him into the back of the police cruiser.

As he sat in the tank waiting to get processed upstairs he looked across the hall and recognized the cell where he'd been strapped to the crazy chair, where God had heard his cry. The chair was resting against the wall outside the cell as though mocking him, welcoming him back. He knew that outside the bars, wire and cinderblock walls, dusk was settling over Phoenix. Last time he'd faced that chair it was dawn, God answering him in a Damascus moment, the brightness of a new day—a new life—ahead of him. And now he felt a darkness coming, a stormy blackness that followed a heavy dusk, consequences he now faced for things he'd done in the past.

"Trust me, Roger. I am here. I am with you in the calm. I am with you in the storm. I am always with you."

By midnight he was dressed in stripes, stretched out on the top bunk in his maximum security cell, Ajax sitting on the metal stool next to the toilet asking him, "So what kinda bail did Judge Wapner set on you?"

"Half a mil."

Bail had been set at $440,000 to be exact, about three bills beyond his financial reach to make bond. He wasn't going anywhere for a long time. They didn't exactly have an international calling perk here at Sheriff Joe's Happy Hotel, so he could not contact her to let her know what happened. He knew it was over. Even if he beat this thing, she'd now know everything—know his real past—and never have anything to do with him again. He was a criminal. A druggie. A murderer. A poisoner of minds.

You are my righteousness, Roger. You are mine, bought with the price of the blood of my only begotten Son. Don't listen to the liar. Listen to me. Call to me, Roger and I will answer you and tell you great and unsearchable things you do not know.

"Half a mil!? *Whoa!* Man, they got Sammy the Bull upstairs—one-point-two-mil. You're in his territory, man! Wow. They are puttin' it to you, man. Here, you need some'a this."

Ajax reached his hand deep down in the stainless steel toilet and came out with a baggie full of brown liquid. He took a drink from the bag while it was still dripping with toilet water and offered Roger a slug. Roger could tell that his expression told Ajax all he thought he needed to know.

"It's hooch. Pruno. What, you think I'm drinkin' a bag of diarrhea? We make it out of what we can get around here. You know, fermented oranges, drop in a few sugar packets. Here, give it a shot. Takes the edge off."

"No, thank you. I never want to get in the way of a man and his pruno."

So here they were, cellies for the last two weeks, Roger curious the way Ajax was standing by the cell door, looking out at the iron-rimmed catwalk, mumbling strategies about getting Sammy the Bull.

There were no secrets inside. Roger had contacted Jay and told him that he needed his jacket—his legal papers —and after the pod leaders got a look at it, word spread fast that this fish was well-connected. But nothing in his jacket told them about the turn he'd made in his life. They simply tagged him as a big stripe and surely a guy like this could figure out a way to drop Sammy the Bull.

But he saw it different. Sammy the Bull, made famous by bringing down John Gotti, was none other than lost soul Salvatore Gravano, a man who needed Jesus.

The door lock suddenly clanked and he heard the cell door roll open. He turned around and saw the beefy frame of the D.O. fill the doorway swinging a pair of pink cuffs.

"Munchian. You got a legal visit."

Embarrassed by the pink cuffs as the D.O led him into the conference room, he was hopeful when Jay said, "Can you un-cuff my client, please?"

The D.O. shook his head, not saying a word as he cuffed him to the table and forced him into the plastic chair across from his attorney and left. The cement-walled conference room was as cold and empty as his cell.

Jay sat back in his chair and blew the steam off of a Styrofoam cup of coffee, took a sip, wincing at the burn as he set it down next to a spread of legal documents. The coffee smelled good and his head suddenly throbbed in caffeine withdrawal. His last cup of coffee was on the morning of March 20, fifteen days and counting. Jay said, "Pink cuffs this time. Maybe next time we should request fur lined."

"You can see that I'm not laughing." He rested his elbows on the rat-chewed table and it tipped on uneven legs, coffee splashing on his legal documents.

Jay started mopping them up with blank sheets of paper that he quickly tore from a legal pad, saying, "Okay, so the good news is I was able to get your case reassigned to another judge. Judge Wilson."

He asked, "Is he a Christian?"

"I didn't ask. I just know he ain't Judge Vernon, and as I've been telling you, Vernon is too tight with your prosecutor."

"What about the plea?"

Jay shook his head. "Bobbie Rosenberg doesn't plea with the money men in drug cartels, Roger. I've been trying to explain this to you. She's got all the testimonies from the Fed witnesses and your criminal history with Arizona, Roger. And you saw the way Rizzo and Paulette painted the picture, telling the Feds that he worked for you. The way Rizzo and Paulette set it up, she thinks that she's got two prize game fish in her net. You and Simen."

"But the Feds couldn't pull enough evidence together to do anything."

"Roger, you're in the state system now and you got a record here. This is the state's opportunity to close the book on you and maybe shut down a few heavies in the meantime. Yeah, the Constitution says innocent until proven guilty. That's all academics and civics class crap. As far as the system is concerned, you are guilty until proven guiltier. They're going to break the other yahoos from the cartel and they're gonna start testifying, forcing legal briefs, court motions, and hearings that are guaranteed to drag this thing out two, maybe three years."

"So much for the promise of a speedy trial."

"That's the idea, Roger. Bobbie, she makes sure she gets the high bail set on you, keeping you from bonding out so you've gotta fight this thing in this hole. She's taken away your freedom, already has you locked away, sitting in a hole somewhere until the system can run its course and find you a more permanent home where orange jump suits are always in fashion."

"Pink underwear and stripes are always in fashion here."

"And pink cuffs. It's all designed to break you. The others in the cartel, they're gonna break and testify against you. Bobbie wants you to break until you're ready to testify against the growers of the dope farms and the guys who fund them."

"Yeah, but with Judge Vernon out, can we get the bond knocked down? Jay, I don't want to spend the next three years in this zoo." He thought about Sirarpi, unable to bear the thought of never having the chance to speak to her again. If the state succeeded in convicting him on all twelve counts, he was looking at spending the rest of his life in prison.

"No, Roger. Sorry. Judge Wilson is ready to lower bail. But Bobbie is filing motions, delaying getting it done. Our chances are good now that we have Wilson. But, again, it's a matter of how much red tape we have to go through to get it done. Bobbie has a whole warehouse full of red tape that she can pull out at any time."

He sat back and slumped in his chair, feeling helpless. After a minute of silence, Jay said, "Don't torture yourself, Roger. We got a long haul ahead of us. I need you to have your head in the game. You will be ready for this, won't you, Roger?"

Isaiah 40:31 came to mind. "But those that hope in the Lord will renew their strength. They will soar on wings like eagles; they will run and not grow weary; they will walk and not be faint."

"I'm ready now.

A cold wind of fear and uncertainty continuously blew through the pod, intensifying at night. At night, the pod got unbearably quiet, the intense silence leaving a man with only his thoughts.

His mind was consumed with her. He could see her, thinking of his favorite picture of her, the one taken by the Hrazdan, surrounded in the purple bloom of spring flowers, the white peaks of Mount Ararat distant in the horizon. She was beautiful, her black hair long, flowing down her petite, curvy frame to her waist, accentuating every adorable slope and lift. Her deep dark eyes came alive in the picture, drinking him in and holding his heart captive. The thought of never hearing her voice again, of never meeting her, never brushing her hair away from that beautiful face, never kissing those lips, never wiping a tear from those soft cheeks or sharing a laugh tormented him. Unless Jay could work his magic with the bond reduction, he'd only see the light of day between court appearances. He'd go straight from county stripes to the ADOC peels.

"*Trust me, Roger. Trust me.*"

As his body shivered in the cold wind of fear, he tried to find God's word somewhere in his heart. Slowly, a verse worked its way free, comforting him with a sudden, inexplicable joy. "The Lord himself goes before you and will be with you; he will never leave you nor forsake you. Do not be afraid; do not be discouraged."

"*I will never leave you, Roger. I am here.*"

His body stopped shivering, peace and calm blanketing him. He felt a kiss from God, telling him good night, sweet dreams, and under his holy blanket, he fell into a peaceful sleep.

Tuesday, October 3, 2000
11:35 p.m.

. . . .

Travis "Cool Ray" Rayland turned the lowrider west on Madison Street, watching through the tassel-lined windshield as smoke from the recently extinguished reefer cleared, the dark outline of the Madison Street jail coming into view. The silhouette standing outside the intake door raised a hand up to shield its eyes as a single working headlight lit up the sidewalk. In the glow of the headlamp, Mason Brandon looked whiter than his usual cream white and did not look happy. And why should he? He hadn't seen the light of day in a year and a month, getting tossed in the County hole after they'd rolled Mason and five of his partners in on nine beefs for running weed up from Mexico, plus multiple dings for money laundering. This time down, Mason got tagged with a $1.7 million bail and he'd spent the last year coming up with the collateral to meet the three-hundred-and-fifty large on the bond.

The little dome light popped on as Mason yanked open the door and got in, his clothes smelling like the jail storage locker.

"Man, two hours I been waiting out there for you. What was the hold up?"

Cool Ray pulled away from the curb and continued heading west. "Boy, you need some sun. Never seen no white boy get so white."

Mason pushed in the lighter on the dash, reached over and dug inside Cool Ray's shirt pocket, the oil-soiled mechanic's shirt with the cut off sleeves and the name "Travis" stenciled on the pocket. He yanked out his crumpled packet of Marlboro reds.

"Man, ever hear of askin'?"

Mason didn't say anything, drawing a cork-butt from the pack with his jail-cracked lips, tossing the pack up on the shag-carpeted dash, staring out the windshield, waiting for the lighter to pop.

Cool Ray said, "So what's it feel like to be the million dollar man, my brothah?"

Mason dipped his cigarette tip onto the orange coils of the lighter. The glow of the cigarette turned his ghost-white face orange and with the boyhood scars, age-cracked face and jaundiced eyes, Mason looked like he'd put on an early Halloween mask. One year inside the razor-studded chain-link had aged him ten years.

"Million seven."

"Never thought I'd see the day my boy Mason draws a million seven bail."

"Bobbie Rosenberg!" Mason spat.

"Oh, man, you got caught in the JAP trap?"

"You ever get a good look at her, man? Butch. Only thing she's missing is a real brass pair and an Adam's apple."

Mason took a long drag on the cigarette and spit a lung full of smoke at the windshield, rattling the fluff ball tassels. "Gets a one-point-seven-mil bail on me and won't play ball. Then I hire a moron for an attorney. Guy'd leave me sitting three months, not a word on my case, me knowin' Rosenberg and my judge, Vernon, all in cahoots."

Cool Ray dug in his dread locks and pulled out a fat joint.

Accepting the lit joint from Cool Ray, Mason said, "You know. I was just wondering," he followed his hit on the joint with a long draw off the cigarette. "What happens to my case, you know, if Bobbie's wheels fall off her car on the way to work or she has a slip on the stairs or something and gets dead. What'll they do?"

"Aw, man, they just assign it to another shark in a suit."

"Yeah, but it'd get me out'a the JAP trap."

"Yeah, probably. But you move dope. You don't make accidents happen. Not your gig."

"Sure would solve things, though."

They rode in silence for a while, no particular destination in mind, Cool Ray thinking about what Mason said about offing the AG in his case. He said, "You know, making the wheels fall off a car or have someone slip on the stairs, they ain't such sophisticated ways of making someone go down. I mean, you ain't got no control of the outcome, you know?"

Mason let out a chuckle, the first hint of emotion the guy had let out since getting in the car. "Yeah? You suddenly the expert? Okay, Mr. Wizard, wha'do you suggest?"

"Well, we hire someone, you know, and make sure they can do it from a distance so they get away. Otherwise they get caught and roll over on you. Button man. See, you get someone good with a scope and a silencer, they squeeze off a shot. Pop. Pop. Problem solved."

"And you know a button man?"

"I got connections."

"To a button man? Cool Ray, you couldn't find a tailor to sew a button on your shorts. But, hey, say you get a button man. What's in it for you?"

"I get a percentage of what you pay the guy. You know, for brokering the deal." Cool Ray took a drag on the joint. "And I sell you the armor needed to get it done."

Mason flicked his cigarette out the window and sat back in his seat. "Crazy talk. Man, what I need is a drink."

Cool Ray rode along in silence for a while, pulling onto the I-17. Mason sat next to him, eyes closed, but Cool Ray knew he was thinking about it, about the hit on the AG. Up ahead, Cool Ray saw the lights of the place he was looking for, the place with the pink-fringed, leopard-skin-looking sign.

"We'll stop off at Jaguar's, get you a drink and a show."

Getting out of the car Mason said, "Cool Ray, the button man thing. You for real about that?"

"You let me know if you're for real, and I'll find out what I can. Attorney General prosecutor. That's big."

"Maybe you can work a two-for-one deal, we work something to take out my attorney. Doing society a favor. One less idiot walking around. Who's gonna miss him, right?"

"Still...an AG? You gonna need to go take out a loan on that one. A real big one."

CHAPTER TWENTY-NINE

Sunday, March 4, 2001
Sky Harbor International Airport

• •

He could see God's fingerprints everywhere in his case. Phoenix to New York; New York to Paris; Paris to Yerevan, Armenia. In thirty hours he'd be there. Thirty hours, a trip over the ocean, and he'd see her face to face. He'd be holding her. He'd be brushing her hair away from her cheek.

She would finally be in his arms.

He'd sat in the county stripes for twenty-one days before Jay finally managed to get the bail dropped to one hundred thousand. He bonded out on April 10, getting out early enough in the morning to call Sirarpi. The conversation didn't start off well. A chill came through the line. She did not ask for an explanation. Roger got right to it, telling her that he'd been away on business and had no opportunity to call. It was mostly true, he thought. His business had been drugs and the business had called him away. With no international dialing option inside the Maricopa County hole, he spoke the truth about not having an opportunity to call.

The state had nailed the entire cartel, Bobbie Rosenberg putting the same squeeze on everyone. One by one they went down. One by one they told their tales, and, as his attorney Jay had promised, painted an ugly picture of his involvement.

The court interview dates with Rizzo and Paulette were set to start on November 16, 2000, a Friday, in Vegas. He insisted on being there even with Jay telling him that it was next to impossible given the travel restriction attached to his bond. But Jay worked his magic and for the first time in over two years, he and Rizzo were in the same room together, Tony nearly wetting his pants when Roger walked in. It was also the first time he met Bobbie Rosenberg. She was bony and boyish with an Adam's apple and cropped black hair styled in Dutch boy bangs. Her veiny neck led to a body devoid of feminine bump or curve.

Rizzo choked, getting his lawyer to have Roger removed from the room as the interview started. He left, staring Rizzo down, seeing the guy visibly crumble, his former reputation clearly on top of the guy's mind. It had gone the same way for Paulette.

As Rizzo spewed his bilge and the court dates mounted, he and Sirarpi continued their daily conversations. He tried to arrange for her to come to Arizona, longing to meet her face-to-face, but getting a legitimate visa out of war-torn Armenia was impossible. In January, Jay nearly dropped out of his seat when he asked him to file with the court for him to make a trip to Armenia.

"Kiddo, I had to put my family jewels on an iron skillet to get them to approve to let you past Arizona borders to travel a few hundred miles up to Vegas. How am I gonna get Rosenberg to agree to let her prize fish travel to a third-world country that makes criminal extradition a fifty-year ordeal?"

"Tell them I'm getting married."

"You asked her to marry you?"

"Not yet. But they don't need to know that."

"You gonna ask her to marry you?"

"I'll know when I get there."

"Did you tell her you're looking at spending the rest of your life in prison?"

"I haven't exactly broached the subject yet."

Jay sighed. "I'll see what I can do."

A month later, Jay's voice was full of disbelief, bursting through his office phone line. He couldn't believe it. The motion for him to travel to Armenia had just been granted.

"You gotta be back in the country in thirty days. You don't make that next court date, your parents can say good-bye to the hundred-large they threw to bail you out of Joe's Happy Hotel."

Roger spent the next month making his travel arrangement and getting ready to finally meet her. Jay continued working his case, filing motions, keeping the courts busy with briefs and documents, working on wearing Bobbie Rosenberg down. It wasn't working. Two days before Roger was to fly out, Jay called and asked him to come down to the office.

When he walked in, Jay was sitting behind his desk, thick stacks of legal documents and depositions strategically placed around him.

"Big Mama Su copped a plea," Jay said, leaning back in his chair with a sigh.

"Ok, well, we were expecting that."

He pointed to the thickest stack of papers on his desk. "That's the transcript from the interview. The picture they're painting of you is getting uglier and uglier, Roger, and it's giving Bobbie the ammo she needs to dig in hard. Her testimony is significant, Roger. Rizzo can blab and can continue making up fairy tales. Out of all the state's witnesses, Big Mama worked closest with you. This thing goes to trial and she takes the stand, she's gonna be the hammer that nails your coffin shut."

"So you really think this will go to trial?"

"I can drag this thing out for another eight, maybe twelve months. But, unless a miracle happens and lightning strikes twice, my bet is by this time next year, we're gonna be making trial preparations."

"Lightning strikes twice?"

"We got the hack judge off your case. Now we need a miracle like Bobbie retiring. We gotta get Bobbie Rosenberg off the case, otherwise we get no plea. With no plea, we go to trial. You lose in trial and with a witness like Su who's a sure bet, you're looking at getting max. The state may grant a motion for a new judge. Replacing the prosecuting attorney—not gonna happen. Roger, we're looking at max on all twelve beefs."

Roger felt himself shrink in the chair. He said, "I still don't get it. We were ready, weren't we? I mean for Su to turn witness."

"Roger...and I'm speaking off the record now, okay?"

"Okay."

"Use your golden ticket."

"Golden ticket?"

"You ever read the book or see the movie *Willie Wonka and the Chocolate Factory*?"

"Yeah. Poor kid named, what, Charlie or something like that, goes to a factory where everything's made of chocolate. So what?"

"He won the trip to the chocolate factory, Roger. One day the poor kid Charlie finds a buck blowing in the wind, someone carelessly dropped. Goes into the candy store, buys a Wonka bar and gets the last golden ticket. One in a hundred million shot. Wins it."

"What's your point?"

"Your one-in a-hundred-million ticket, Roger, is your grant from the court to travel out of here and go back to where you came from. Armenia."

"What are you suggesting, Jay?"

"Off the record, right?"

"Absolutely."

"Don't come back. Whether you marry the girl or not, find a job shepherding goats or go on a lifelong pilgrimage to discover Noah's ark, anything to stay away from Bobbie Rosenberg and this whole thing. No way, Roger, no way are they going to come for you."

The thought didn't settle well with Roger. He said, "My parents will lose the money."

"Send for them."

"The whole family back in Armenia. A place we escaped from, finding a better life."

"No, Roger. You found an abundant life. Abundance takes two paths. Legal and illegal. You chose illegal."

"But not my parents. They didn't choose this."

"But you did. No man is an island, Roger. Your choices affect everyone around you, the guilty and the innocent. You decide to stay here and end up going down for the rest of your life, it impacts your parents. Sparks happen between you and the girl, it hits her. Stay in Armenia, you're a free man. Come home, well, you got a wardrobe choice. Orange jump suit and brown shoes, or brown shoes and orange jump suit. I'm just laying it out for you, letting you know your options. Yeah, the bond money will be gone, but certainly you can see that your freedom is worth a hundred thousand beans."

So now he was sitting in a plane, rolling along, jockey for takeoff and in just a few minutes they'd be wheels up and in about thirty hours, Phoenix, Arizona, his court case and Bobbie Rosenberg would be over seven thousand miles behind him. No man is an island. His decisions affect others. He could feel the attack from the enemy showing him what his past had done, the lives he'd destroyed, telling him he'd never be able to escape, no matter where he fled to, the enemy's promise was to keep tormenting him with his past.

His Bible sat on the open tray table in front of him, open to Psalms. He got to Psalm 107, his spirit stirred as he started reading verse ten.

"Some sat in darkness, in utter darkness, prisoners suffering in iron chains, because they rebelled against God's commands and despised the plans of the Most High. So he subjected them to bitter labor; they stumbled, and there was no one to help. Then they cried to the Lord in their trouble, and he saved them from their distress. He brought them out of darkness, and broke away their chains."

He thought of the prisoners suffering in chains, of the lost souls he'd met in his own incarceration. Ajax, worshiping at the stainless steel altar that kept his pruno cool. Arnulfo, knocking off his Blockbusters. Martin, his cellie from Tent City, recently drawing a ten-year stretch for trafficking marijuana. And so many more. He thought of the palpable fear that settled in the jail pods, especially at night, and the blanket of comfort he'd felt, knowing Christ was near, that he would never leave him. The peace of God's love was ever-present, even in the stench of a jail pod. Someone had to share with them, the prisoners suffering in chains. Someone had to share that only God could bring them out of darkness. The lost had to know, they had to know that Christ's love was in reach. That Jesus is real. They may have rebelled. But God's mercies are new every morning. They had to know that God is reaching to them. God's eternal love will never give up in bringing them back to Him.

The captain's voice came over the intercom, announcing they were clear for takeoff. They were soon in the air, banking eastward. As they flew over downtown Phoenix, Roger looked out the window, looking down at the little building that he knew was the courthouse. It looked so small from up here, fading away. He also recognized the tan brick of the Madison Street jail, just blocks away from the courthouse. Small. Insignificant. Fading as the plane ascended to cruising altitude.

He pushed his seat back and closed his eyes, wondering if that was the last he'd ever see of the courthouse, Bobbie Rosenberg and the Madison jail again.

"Trust me, Roger. Trust me."

Friday, March 9, 2001
Yerevan, Armenia

• •

The jewelry store was off Tumanyan Street, across from the Stanjslavsky Russian Drama theater in a cobblestone square where pink and blue lights set the square's fountain alive. A tiny bell over the door had announced their arrival and the short, paunchy jeweler guided them through his selection of rings.

His heart had leapt into his throat when Sirarpi greeted him as he stepped off the plane. He greeted her with a hug and a kiss on the cheek, gently brushing her hair away from her face the way he'd dreamt, feeling as though he'd known her all of his life. They talked nonstop through the night, not sleeping since the moment he'd arrived. Strolling the streets with her on his arm, he felt at home. He wasn't sure if it was just being with her or if part of his Armenian spirit found solace in reuniting with the place of his birth, with his true heritage. The medieval structures; ancient streets lined with ivy-covered vines, dormant in the winter freeze; grey-stone churches dome-topped, reflecting the volcanic dome of snowcapped Mount Ararat off in the distance. He could stay here. He could live here. He'd be free here. And he'd be with her.

He proposed and she accepted. They rented a hall at the luxurious Hotel Yerevan, the wedding date set for March 10, just two days to get ready. Today they picked out their rings.

The winter breeze was sharp as they stepped from the jewelry store, Sirarpi hunching into her fur coat, her long hair flowing, her brown eyes looking deep into his with a trust that warmed him inside, and then troubled him deeply. It was past the time. He knew he was lying to her in keeping his legal troubles secret. He had to tell her.

191

"You hungry?" he asked.

"Hrach, I don't think we've eaten since last night. We talked through breakfast, remember?"

A vendor was selling shish kebobs near the fountain and he bought two plates; they sat on the fountain ledge and ate. The skies were deep blue, the air crisp, the company perfect.

He said, "So, are you really ready for this?"

She smiled, taking a dainty bite of her sandwich, chewing softly and said, "Hrach, I've never been so happy and nervous at the same time in my life these last few days. I'm ready, Hrach. I love you."

"Well, listen. There's a couple of more things you need to know before we stand before God and vow to share our lives together."

He tried to hide it but he could tell that she could see that he was deeply troubled.

"Hrach, what is it?"

"First of all, I've been married before."

The blood drained from her face and the spark vanished from her eyes.

"She died?"

"Divorced."

"*Divorced!*"

The word caused several passersby to stop.

She said, "She...she left you, right? She's the one who did that to you?"

"No, Sirarpi. It was me."

She started to get up, wanting to leave. Roger grabbed her arm and gently sat her back down. "Sirarpi, it was before I came to know God. It was my previous life. I was living in the world and I wanted more of what the world had to offer. There just was no room for commitment."

Roger pointed to a church across the street. Gray. Cold. Tomb-empty, warmed only by the occasional lighting of a candle, not by the living spirit of Jesus Christ. "We got married in one of those kinds of churches, Sirarpi. Full of images, empty of Christ. That was our marriage."

"But God hates divorce. He says what he has brought together let no man pull it apart."

"I've struggled with that, Sirarpi, believe me. But take God by his complete word. 'What God has brought together.' *Brought* together. That marriage was not a marriage brought together by God. How could it have been? I was living a different life. I did not know him. It's different now. Sirarpi, I know that God is bringing this marriage together. I know it deep in my heart."

"Are there any…" she swallowed hard. "Any children? Do you have any kids?"

"No, Sirarpi. She miscarried and we didn't try after that. I wanted to chase after worldly things, so I asked her for a divorce."

She was silent, staring off, watching the crowd, thinking about it. "You said there were a couple of things. What else do you want to surprise me with?"

"I have some legal troubles back home."

"What do you mean legal troubles? Are you a fugitive?"

"I will be if I don't arrive back in the United States by the twenty-fifth. That month that I didn't call you, Sirarpi, I only told you a half-truth."

"A half-truth is a full lie, Hrach. How did you lie to me?"

"My business did cause for me to be away, where I could not call you. My criminal business. It had me away in jail."

"Jail!?"

Passersby stopped again.

"I am out on something called 'bail.' We had to come up with one-hundred thousand dollars cash to put on deposit with the court so I could get out."

"That's a lot of money."

"Money I didn't have so I had to borrow it from my parents. If I don't come back, they lose their money. And if I don't come back, yes, I will be a fugitive." He did not tell her that being a fugitive may be his only option for freedom. He had not yet made his decision on staying or returning. He wanted that decision to be made between himself and God. "Sirarpi, I left that life behind when I started pursuing Christ. It was my past. I'm done with it. Now all I want to do is move forward to my future. Right now, I can't imagine that future without you."

"Do they always let guys on bail leave the country?"

He thought of Jay's words: '…you got the Golden Ticket.'

"No, Sirarpi. It's next to impossible, especially with a case like mine. That's why I am convinced that God is bringing this together. Only God could have made this happen. Sirarpi, I've seen God doing incredible things in this. I am not promising that this is going to be easy, especially the next several months. But I know God has a plan, and I am trusting in Him. This is right, Sirarpi, you and I."

She was silent again. Roger cradled her face in his hands and looked into her eyes. "I love you, Sirarpi and I know God is going to see us through. Trust Him."

Slowly, the spark in her eyes reignited and her smile warmed him. "We haven't slept in over three days, Hrach, and we have a lot of work to do to get this wedding together."

He didn't think he could love her any deeper until that moment. As he kissed her deeply, the world ceased to exist. It was only them. Together as one. Together forever. Tomorrow, God would bring them together as one.

Saturday, March 24
Zvartnots International Airport
Yerevan, Armenia
10:10 a.m.

He wasn't sure if they arrived late because of Yerevan traffic or if it was because he simply did not want to get to the airport. He needed to be on that flight today in order to arrive back in the United States in time to prevent his default on the bail. His new wife, Sirarpi, would not be able to return with him on this trip. The paperwork for her to be able to leave the country was still being processed.

The wedding was beautiful, the reception an all-night affair. Roger and Siraripi fell asleep at the head table while their guests celebrated around them until dawn. Neither of them had slept in days and they both collapsed before ten at the head table.

When they arrived at the airport they were told that he'd missed his flight. Roger wanted it to be a sign. God telling him, stay. Build your life here. His next court hearing was scheduled for March 29. If he failed to show, Jay would know that he'd chosen to follow his advice. What else could he do now? Zvartnots International was no LAX. It could take up to a week for the next flight that could accommodate his U.S. visa credentials.

"Oh, you're in luck," the ticket attendant said as her fingers worked feverishly on the keyboard in front of her. "I have room on an Air France flight into Charles De Gaulle, departing here on the twenty-eighth. Then direct to Houston and a connecting flight with Continental Air at ten a.m. You'll be in Phoenix by noon on the twenty ninth."

He was scheduled to be in court at 2:00.

"Sir? Shall I book this for you? Sir?"

"He brought them out of darkness, and broke away their chains."

"Sir?"

"Hrach?" Sirarpi said, her hand taking his. "What's wrong? The flight. You have to go."

He didn't want to let her go. He had the Golden Ticket. He could stay. By staying, he could cling to her, keep her close. By going, he'd be letting her go, facing incarceration for the rest of his life. But he knew that she didn't belong to him. God brought them together as one but she still belonged to God.

In his heart a man plans his course, but the Lord determines his steps.

The theme of Willy Wonka and the Chocolate Factory was not about the riches of the Golden Ticket. Each winner of the ticket was promised riches by Wonka's enemy, a guy named Slugworth, if they were able to steal an Everlasting Gobstopper. All tried to steal from Mr. Wonka. All failed. Only Charlie returned the Gobstopper. And Charlie won. He won because he returned to the maker what was his.

He had to return her to God. He had to return to the Maker what was His.

And he had to return his own gifts back to God to use for his purpose in reaching the lost and the least.

"Sir?"

"Hrach?"

"Trust me, Roger. Trust me."

He said, "Yes. Book it please."

CHAPTER-THIRTY

Saturday, March 16, 2002
Scottsdale HealthCare Medical Center
Scottsdale, Arizona
7:55 p.m.

He looked down at his newborn son, Andrew, named not only after Roger's father, Andranik, but also in honor of the apostle. The hospital room was quiet. Sirarpi was sound asleep in her hospital gown, nestled under the sterile white sheets in a deserved rest. Andrew came into the world on March 14. They would be discharged tomorrow and Andrew would arrive in his new home.

Roger had finally gotten Andrew to sleep, sucking away on the pacifier, at peace. Cradling him in his arms, wanting sleep, he wasn't ready to put him in his crib, wanting to hold him a little longer. He never would have imagined experiencing the level of love that he felt for such fragile innocence in his arms. Holding his son, cradling him in his arms, was nothing less than the continued fingerprints of God's infinite love.

He'd stopped trying to figure God out, his case falling apart by the day. Last month Sirarpi had called him an onion, not knowing the derogatory association with the term here in the United States. He kept his case to himself, not sharing the nuances of the struggle, but as the news got worse and worse, he'd reveal a little bit at a time. Sirarpi said that learning about him was like peeling an onion. Every peeled-back layer brought more tears. She was not aware how bad this was but she continued to find out, one layer at a time.

Jay battled his case day to day, Bobbie not budging, Jay doing everything he could to negotiate a deal and keep it from going to trial. But the courtroom was where Bobbie knew her strength lay and she was either going to get Roger to turn witness or send him off to prison for the rest of his life.

Isaiah 55:8 told Roger to stop trying to figure God out. "For my thoughts are not your thoughts, neither are your ways my ways," declares the Lord. Let God be God. Don't try and figure Him out. We cannot possibly fathom His ways. But he read in Ephesians 3:18-19, "*Grasp how wide and long and high and deep is the love of Christ, and to know that this love that surpasses knowledge—that you may be filled to the measure of all the fullness of God.*"

He realized that God tells us that the only thing we need to figure out about Him is the depth of His love for us. As a father now, looking down at this young innocence in his arms, he felt the depth of a father's love. He could only imagine the eternal depth of the unconditional love the Heavenly Father has for His children.

Roger knew that he had to start making preparations for prison. She'd need to be financially secure, so he started the valuation process for Diamondback Insurance. He didn't want to sell the family business but the initial valuation came back at over $400,000.

He pictured the dinner table, an empty chair at the head, collecting dust, a family getting by without the head of the home. Holding Andrew tight, he closed his eyes and prayed silently.

God, you continually convict me with your word, reminding me of prisoners suffering in chains, your promise to bring them out of darkness. Lord, I pray for your intervention. I pray that somehow, some way, through your will and power, that this not go to trial, that my family remain whole, that I can remain with my family and be the husband and father you need for me to be. I submit to your will, though, God, understanding that you are all-knowing and all-powerful. If the mission field for me is to reach the lost behind bars for the rest of my life, then I accept. I know that there are no boundaries to the freedom that comes from your love. I know that even if I spend the rest of my life here on this Earth in prison, I will always remain free in your love. I accept, Lord, and will serve wherever you need for me to be. In your name, Jesus, I pray. Amen.

Andrew let out a little coo and then Roger heard his cell phone go off, on vibrate, sitting on the little table next to his chair. His heart sank when he saw that it was from Jay. Jay never called this late at night with good news.

He let the call go to voicemail not wanting to disturb Andrew's sleep by taking the call. When his voicemail light came on he gently put Andrew in his crib and stepped into to the hallway, dialing into his voicemail.

"Roger," Jay's voice came through the line, stoic, matter of fact. "You need to be in court this Thursday, March 21 at two o'clock. Roger, don't miss this one or you'll be back in jail on another half-mil' bail. This is going to be our only pretrial hearing. Call me back so I know you got this message. I'm sorry, Roger. I did my best."

Roger felt the tears soak his cheeks. He remembered his prayer but still had to fight the urge to cry out to God: *Why!?* Then from inside the hospital room he heard Andrew starting to cry. Colic, or he'd lost his pacifier. He didn't want for his wife to be disturbed. She needed her rest. He wiped away his tears and rushed back into the room to attend to his son's tears. His family needed him. His family needed Daddy.

Tuesday, March 19, 2002
11:52 p.m.

. . . .

The first time Edward "Eddie Boy" Ortez went down it was on a seven-year beef for aggravated assault. He and his road dog, Juice Cunningham, did a drive-by, turning the front door of some narc's house into Swiss cheese. Where it went wrong though, was there was a cop cruising the next block over and the gunfire and muzzle flashes got his attention. He had his lights on them before they got a hundred yards from the driveway. It was okay, though. While in the zoo, he'd gotten hazed into the Mexican Mafia—the eMe's—and became an effective torpedo, their top guy for cleaning up the hit list. The Big Homies still hired him regularly, only now he got paid cash rather than pecking order status for each drop. They usually used him to make hits on the outside but every now and then he'd get himself tossed back into the zoo to clean house inside. The eMe control over the prison system allowed them to move him around from joint to joint as though booking his stays using travel agents.

Eddie Boy wasn't going to get busted like that again. Not this time. Especially with the target being that high-flying AG prosecutor. He told Cool Ray that if he was going to pop a cap through this babe's window, he not only had to supply him with the heater but he also wanted a silencer, doing this thing up like a real professional button man. Cool Ray told him black market suppressors didn't come cheap what with the guy brokering this hit taking a piece of the action and trying to keep his profit margin. So what the guy did, he went down to the Home Depot and bought some PVC, cut to six inches, black paint, a button cap and copper pipe. He put the thing together and was able to screw it into the barrel of the Sig Saur that Eddie Boy had picked out for the hit. It took him four tries before his homemade suppressor was strong enough to take the 9mm load.

The way Eddie Boy understood it, Cool Ray's customer was some peckerwood named Mason Brandon out on bond from a drug running beef. The guy was all jammed up by a prosecutor putting it to him hard. He'd heard the name before and knew her reputation. The dykish AG prosecutor named Bobbie Rosenberg. The guy, Mason, figured that if he could have the AG taken out, plus his attorney for letting his case get all jacked up, his problems would be solved. So he got with Cool Ray and had him use his connections with the Big Homies to get it done. It was a tall order and going through the Mexican Mafia cost him seventy-five large. Most of the dough went to the big stripes. The guys doing the wet work, himself and his homie, Casper, got paid ten K for pulling the pin. Ten large. That was it for pushing the button on a top prosecutor at the state AG. Five K apiece.

The whole thing got set up right there inside the Madison Street clink. Eddie Boy got himself thrown inside on a minor beef and was busy cleaning house out on Main Street when he got word to come see Night Owl up in his cell. Night Owl, the eMe leader in the pod, told him he'd be getting a visit from a guy named Robby O, an investigator for some local defense attorney getting inside using fake attorney creds. Robby would be getting him sprung and would explain things in detail later.

A week later, he and Joey "Casper" Guajardo were sitting in Robby O's Caddie, driving through a high-end neighborhood on the upper west side of Phoenix, Robby pointing out the house where the AG prosecutor lived with her dim-bulb brother. Then he dropped them off at Cool Ray's apartment downtown where Cool Ray showed them their choice of guns, the ones with the serial numbers filed off.

And so tonight was the night. Casper waited in the pickup truck, keeping watch with the engine running. With Cool Ray's silencer screwed into the barrel of the Sig, Eddie Boy, dressed in black, moved across the lawn in the moon-thrown shadow of a tall oleander hedge, watching through the lit windows for movement inside Rosenberg's home. He moved around back and he heard fingers typing on a keyboard, coming from a dark room at the corner of the house, window slightly cracked to let in the cool March breeze.

He moved in as close as he could, the window not opened as far as he'd have liked. He didn't want to shatter the glass, make more noise, but he had no choice. The lights were off in the room, the window screen black, making it difficult to see much of the person sitting at the computer other than a silhouette in the glow of the computer. The shadow sat hunched over the keyboard, thin, no babe-like curves. It had to be her. The dykish AG prosecutor. He pointed the gun and squeezed the trigger, the PVC silencer reducing the 9mm load to a pop, no flash. The silhouette whirled in the chair, but didn't fall. Eddie Boy squeezed off three more quick rounds, expecting a full throttle explosion, figuring the PVC-rigged silencer would have been melted in the first round, but three gentle pops burped and the silhouette rolled out of the chair, disappearing from view.

Eddie Boy could feel the heat of the homemade silencer through his black glove as he urgently unscrewed it, letting it fall to the lawn and got out of there. As he crossed the street to where Casper was waiting in the pickup, watching him pull it into gear, he rolled into the truck bed. He'd crawl in the cab through the split window once they were a few blocks away from the house, not wanting to light up the cab with the dome. By tomorrow morning, the coroner would be zipping the body of Bobbie Rosenberg into a vinyl bag and Mason's troubles would be over.

CHAPTER THIRTY-ONE

Thursday, March 21
6:30 a.m.

• •

The house was still quiet. Roger had left for work early this morning, Andrew still sleeping. Sirapi was sitting at the kitchen table, no appetite for the cold scrambled eggs that sat on the plate in front of her. She looked over at Roger's seat, a half-eaten plate of eggs at his place setting, two nibbles off a piece of toast, and a near-full cup of cold coffee. He had no appetite either, preoccupied about his day, saying he had to go in early again, third time this week. He was losing too much weight and the worry lines deepened in his face as the preparations for trial proceeded.

Sirarpi couldn't imagine life without him, and yet, deep down, despite her denial she knew that she had to face the reality that he could be going away to prison for the rest of his life. For the rest of *their* lives. She thought of Psalm 112, verse 4. "Even in darkness light dawns for the upright." Those words described her husband. Even with darkness sinking in around him—around them—there was a brightness surrounding him. Hope was alive beneath those deep worry lines. He was everything to her. God couldn't take him away. He simply couldn't.

And yet, another psalm stirred in her heart. Psalm 91, God telling her in the first two verses, "He who dwells in the shelter of the Most High will rest in the shadow of the Almighty. I will say of the Lord, 'He is my refuge and my fortress, my God, in whom I trust.'" She tried to ignore it, not wanting to face the reality that God, a God jealous for her, wanted her to rely completely on him. And if He had to take Roger away from her to get her complete trust, He would. She did not want to face it but she knew it was real.

He was zombie-like, going through the motions of going to work, getting affairs in order preparing for trial. Roger left early in the morning, ignoring this morning's edition of *The Arizona Republic*, missing the front-page headline, below the fold, that read:

Attempt to kill prosecutor fails
Assassination try leaves brother wounded

A high-profile Valley drug prosecutor narrowly escaped assassination Thursday night when a bullet fired through a window of her home wounded her brother instead.

The shooting took place shortly before midnight at the north Phoenix home of Bobbie Rosenberg, lead drug prosecutor for the State Attorney General's Office, Phoenix police said Wednesday.

Driving south on I-17, his mind was elsewhere, the road and the world in front of him a fog. Two o'clock today he'd be back in court, different this time. This time, there would be no hope of a deal with Bobbie Rosenberg. There would be no more delays. They'd discuss process, jury selection, witness lists, trial dates and the summation of the charges. It all added up to one thing: prison time.

"He brought them out of darkness and the deepest gloom and broke away their chains."

In his fog, he only caught part of the news on the radio.

"...at this time, the condition of Arizona State Attorney General Prosecutor Bobbie Rosenberg's brother is being reported as critical. Phoenix Police spokesman Sergeant Michael Anderson said that police are still investigating the incident. Rosenberg's brother, Reginald Rosenberg, 40, was visiting Ms. Rosenberg at the time and reportedly was sitting at a computer in a back bedroom when at least one of four shots struck him.

"Investigators believe that a silencer may have been used to muffle the gunshots, which were fired through a screened back window. Anderson said that a crudely made silencer constructed of PVC piping was found at the scene leading investigators to suspect that the shooter was not a professional killer. No arrests have been made."

Roger wasn't sure what to make of the report or what it meant until Jay called him at the office later that morning.

"You hear about the incident?" Jay asked.

"About Bobbie Rosenberg, yeah, just what I heard on the radio."

"Your court date has been cancelled for today. Rosenberg's schedule has been cleared indefinitely."

"Jay, what happened?"

"AGs with brass ones like Bobbie make a lot of enemies, Roger."

"So how does this impact my case? What do you mean her schedule has been cleared?"

"Roger, an attempted hit on a ranking counsel with the state AG offices is serious biz. Investigators are going to be digging deep into every one of her case files in a royal anal exam. Who knows, this could be a blessing in disguise."

"Your guy nailed the brother, moron!" Mason's voice exploded through the line. Cool Ray was in a fog, sitting in his living room, chocolate crumbs of the Little Debbie dotting his bare chest, joint burning in the clip, Oprah on the TV. He was waiting for Jerry Springer, coming on in about ten minutes, so he wanted to get this call over with quick, never wanting to miss a second of Springer.

"How could he have helped it? The babe is dykish, you said so yourself. Our guy only shot at a shadow, yeah, looks like a dude, but she looks like a dude. How was he supposed to know she and her bro' throw the same shadow?"

"He left your little device at the scene. What was that all about?"

"Maybe he was in a hurry, wanting to get out of there, you know, in case anyone heard the glass break."

"He left evidence behind!"

He looked at the clock. Five minutes to Springer, Oprah wrapping things up.

"You gotta make this right, Ray."

Cool Ray inhaled a deep hit from the joint, holding it, saying, "Now how you propose I do that? Tell our guy to go to the hospital, apologize to baby brother, say, 'sorry, this was meant for her?' and pop big sis while she's standing there by his hospital bed?"

"I want my money back, Ray."

"Hey, this ain't Kmart. What kinda return policy you think I got?"

"It better be a good one."

"Let's sit on this for a while, okay? We gotta let this cool down." Three minutes to Springer. "We start wiring money all around, don't you think that's gonna draw attention?"

"I ain't going down alone for this, Ray. They trace this back to me, I'm bringing you down with me."

"Watch what you say, Mason. I can always make another silencer and your shadow my boy can't mistake."

"Are you threatening…"

"Springer's on. Gotta go."

Cool Ray hung up, turning the volume up, Springer announcing what the show was about today. Yeah, it was going to be a good one.

Saturday, November 2, 2002
10:30 a.m.
· ·

Roger was in the office on a Saturday morning trying to keep busy, trying to keep his mind off of the craziness of his case. He was still in a holding pattern, things still silent at the offices of Bobbie Rosenberg. He suspected things would get moving again as he sat at his desk, reading the story in *The Arizona Republic*.

2 INDICTED IN PLOT TO KILL STATE'S TOP DRUG PROSECUTOR

Two suspects have been indicted in the March assassination attempt against the state's top drug prosecutor.

The conspiracy's central figure, 39-year-old Mason Deacon Brandon, was arrested by Phoenix police on Tuesday in connection with the March 2002 assassination attempt on Arizona Assistant Attorney General Bobbie Rosenberg.

In 1999, Brandon was indicted by a federal grand jury in San Diego and by two Arizona grand juries for overseeing drug rings that smuggled tons of marijuana into the country. While on bail, Brandon allegedly contracted the killing of Rosenberg, who served as the lead prosecutor in Brandon's case. The assassination attempt resulted in the shooting of Rosenberg's brother while inside the Rosenberg residence. Rosenberg's brother was severely wounded in the assassination attempt but has since recovered.

Investigators found a homemade silencer outside Rosenberg's house. Trevor Alen Rayford, 30, of Phoenix, was indicted for manufacturing or providing the silencer. According to court records, Rayford, known by his street name "Cool

Ray," has at least three prior drug convictions and no previous weapons charges.

In addition to the charges by the state, a federal grand jury also indicted Brandon on murder-for-hire charges.

Jay called him in the afternoon. He said, "Rosenberg's schedule is moving again. She's staying on the case." Roger felt his stomach sink. "However, it looks like the AG, Janet Napolitano, is taking her off of her high-profile cases. She'll be listed as the lead prosecutor on this case but she's going after the low-hanging fruit. She'll be prosecuting Gibby and Clay, China Mike and Wilson, the ones the AG sees as the lower level of the cartel. Since the AG still considers you top management, your case is being moved to another prosecutor."

"A new prosecutor? Is this rare?"

"Like lightning striking twice in the same spot. But we ain't out of this yet, Roger. This could go either way. We could get a prosecutor willing to deal and keep this out of court, or this assassination attempt could force Napolitano's office to come down harder on drug dealers, sending a message that this type of intimidation won't play in the state of Arizona. Let's just look at this as a glimmer of hope that we didn't have before."

A glimmer of hope. The fingerprints of God.

CHAPTER THIRTY-TWO

Monday, March 17, 2003
2:20 p.m.

• •

The counsel that had joined the case was a longtime prosecutor named Louis Giovanni. He had a reputation of being old-school, tough on drug dealers, but Jay picked up rumors from the AG office that he didn't care much for Rosenberg. He'd started off playing hard ball but his caseload was swelling with the addition load from Rosenberg's office. Wanting to put to bed as many cases as he could, he let Jay know that he was open to negotiation on the Munchian case. Giovanni pushed hard to nail him on any one of the Class 2 felonies, but Jay held out. In the end, Jay got Giovanni to agree to amend Count 12, from "Transport for sale or transfer of marijuana" to "*Attempted* transport," reducing it from a Class 2 to a Class 3 offense and dismissed the rest of the charges.

Two days later the plea agreement was delivered to Jay's office and Roger came in and signed it. Seven years flat. He'd be spending nearly a decade in incarceration away from his family. But he trusted God. As much as it did not make sense to him, he would rather be in God's plan rather than out of God's plan.

I will never leave you, Roger. Never.

Roger sat in his office, going through the motions of filing paperwork and cleaning up loose ends. He'd just hung up the phone with the business broker, asking him to take Diamondback Insurance off the market. Even though he'd signed for seven flat, he wasn't sure the business would make it without him. He was about to let it go until the marketing rep of one of the companies he worked with walked into the agency. His name was Manny, a competent insurance rep looking for other opportunities. After interviewing him, Roger knew that he could only have been sent by God. He needed a good manager in order to keep the business. He hired him and Manny was able to start right away.

His phone rang. Jay's voice came through the line. "I just got word from the court."

"Yeah?"

"Your sentencing date. April eleventh. You need to be in the court by eight thirty." There was an undertone in his voice, telling him that he should have taken his advice and stayed in Armenia.

"He brought them out of darkness and the deepest gloom and broke away their chains."

"Thanks, Jay."

He hung up and before he had a chance to give it much thought, his phone rang again. Sirarpi's voice came through the line, a sobbing voice.

"Hrach…"

She stammered, her voice choked with emotion. It was emotion full of both grief and joy, of the darkness of fear and uncertainty, and of the light of newness.

"Sirarpi, what is it? What?"

"Oh, Hrach. I love you so much."

"What is it, Sirarpi? What's going on?"

"Hrach, oh, Hrach, I'm pregnant. You're going away—and we're going to have another baby."

Reality quickly set in that his new child would be getting out of the first grade by the time he could hold it for the first time as a free man.

"Trust me, Roger. Trust me."

PART IV

God Delivers

CHAPTER THIRTY-THREE

Friday, April 25, 2003
Alhambra State Prison Intake
Phoenix
1:35 p.m.

Sirarpi sat on the hard bench, the cinderblock walls cold and intimidating. She was just over one month pregnant, the stench of refuse and ripened filth not helping her nausea. Roger had disappeared from view when the cold metal doors closed, shutting them off for what she thought was forever despite his assurance that they would see each other soon. Metal clanked and Sirarpi jumped at the sound. A metal door rolled open and an officer stepped out, saying something she did not understand other than the name 'Munchian.'

"Me," she said, using the broken English she'd learned over the last few months. "I am Meesus Munchian."

The officer handed her a clear plastic bag containing the clothes Roger had been wearing when he self-surrendered this morning. She took the bag and the officer handed her a smaller package, again saying something that she did not understand. The officer stepped back behind the threshold, and the door rolled shut.

Sirarpi turned and started walking toward the door, opening the smaller package that the officer had given her. Resting at the bottom of the bag was the ring she'd placed on Roger's finger the day that they'd vowed for better or for worse, in a place over seven thousand miles from here. The ring became distorted in a pool of tears flooding her eyes. She felt herself running for the door, unable to make out its shape in the flood of salty anguish that filled her eyes. Somehow she'd rushed across the street and into the parking garage and was sitting behind the wheel of their car, trying to remember how to work the thing again. She'd just learned to drive, a two-week crash course that Roger had insisted she go through, telling her over and over that she had to learn how to do this. That she had to learn how to get around.

Street signs whizzed by at a dizzying pace. She was not used to such speed of things. Growing up she saw cars on the streets of Armenia. She watched them go by. But their pace was always slow. The pace there was always slow unlike here, where everything went fast. Everything a rush, except for the time she'd be without him. Except for the time it'd take for those metal doors to open again and they'd one day be reunited. It was only just a few hours ago she watched him walk down that narrow hall, the yellow tape on the floor telling her that she had gone as far as she could go. When he reached the end of the cinderblock hall, he turned, still in his street clothes, the wedding ring still on his finger, representing their oneness, and he waved good-bye. The metallic clank of the door echoed off the walls, the motors whirred and the big metal slammed shut.

He was gone.

For better or for worse. In sickness and in health.

She was alone. There was new life forming inside her, a life being knit together by God. She could go back to Armenia. She had family there, people who could help her raise her children. She could speak the language. She would not be alone. She would not be so frightened.

Till death do us part.

She made a vow. The vow was to God. As frightened as she was, as uncertain, she'd trust God. She'd simply trust God. She could tell God verbally how much she trusted him—but she would show him by sticking to her vows.

"Hrach," she said out loud. "Hrach, I love you."

Behind him another door slammed shut, the hissing of the seal echoing in the hall, the clank of the locks rolling into their chambers. He looked down at the intake papers in his trembling hands. He was no longer Roger Munchian, aka Hrach Munchian, aka Roger Rabbit. He was now Inmate 175948, Gender: Male. Height: 66 inches. Weight: 175. Ethnic Origin: Other.

It had taken over half the day for them to admit him. He had several character witnesses who'd testified on his behalf on his day of sentencing. Judge Wilson had also received several letters testifying to Roger's new walk in life—a life committed to walking with Lord—evidence of his newfound commitment to living a life as a contributing member of society and as a family man.

When the judge's decision time came he said, "Before I sentence you, Mr. Munchian, I want to ask you if you really understand, through the delivering of drugs and making this substance available on the streets, of the young minds you're guilty of poisoning."

"Yes, your Honor, I am."

"Because it's not really the distribution of drugs that you're guilty of here, Mr. Munchian. If the law allowed for me to find the victims, the minds you've destroyed, the futures you've ruined, the youth you've stolen, I would send you away for multiple lifetimes."

"Yes, your honor. I understand."

"However, this court listened to the testimony given here today." Judge Wilson referred to himself in the third person now, depersonalizing it. It's what judges did just before handing down serious sentences. He couldn't figure out where the judge was going with this. He'd signed for seven flat. But judges could always negate a plea. Roger braced himself for the worst. "This court has observed you and listened to testimony. There is strength and sincerity about you that cannot be denied. Mr. Munchian, it was the intention of this court to strike this plea and sentence you with the maximum punishment possible for this crime. However, in a rare moment of reconsideration, this court has decided to indeed strike your plea but *reduce* your seven-year sentence to two-and-a-half years to the Arizona Department of Corrections, with a pre-sentence incarceration credit of twenty-one days. Sentence to begin immediately on this date, April eleven, two-thousand-three."

After the judge's gavel struck the sound block, Roger was moved to an anteroom. Sitting, waiting for them to come shackle him and load him in the bus, he could not come to grips with what had just happened. The judge had struck his plea—and *reduced* his sentence.

The door opened and an officer came in, handed him a stack of paper-clipped papers and Roger was told he was free to leave. The papers were instructions for his self-surrender. His petition for a two-week reprieve to get his affairs in order had been granted. The papers instructed him to show up at the Alhambra State Prison on April 25 and surrender himself to state authorities.

It simply did not usually work this way. He should have gone straight from the court room into the orange jump suit. It simply did not happen to be sentenced—and to be given two weeks to get your affairs in order—given two extra weeks with your wife and family.

"Trust me, Roger. I am in every detail of your life."

The next two weeks went by fast. He had to make sure Sirarpi was able to get her driver's license, teach her the business and make sure their financial affairs were in order. Sirarpi would be taking over the business for the next two-and-a-half years, Manny there to help her.

He waved good-bye to her and the door slammed shut and she was gone. He stood there, looking down the long hallway, feeling completely alone, but knowing that he wasn't. A peace descended upon him. A peace beyond understanding.

I am here with you, Roger. You will not be alone.

He became aware of the smoke-colored dome hanging from the concrete ceiling above, telling him that he was being watched. He had to move on. The stretch of hallway that he covered on his way to processing would be the last fifteen yards he'd walk in his own shoes for a long time.

After trading his street clothes in for the orange jump suit, he was given a sheet of paper that listed his cell number. He processed through with about twenty inmates. They were told to line up in front of a metal door which clanked with a bang that echoed throughout the room and rolled open. They were led single file into the bowels of the prison, the cell doors shut tight on lockdown, the place as quiet as a library once the echo of the final metal door slammed shut. He found the cell with the numbers matching the digits on his paper. The door rolled open and the stench of days-old sweat and raw sewage hit him.

"Inside one-seven-five-niner forty-eight!"

Roger stepped passed the threshold and the door rolled shut, sealing him in the closet- tight room where two other inmates lay sleeping on their bunks, unaware that they'd just gotten a new roommate. One was a thin black dude, no thicker than the rails of his bunk, his snores whistling through a harelip, the raw stench of the streets seeping from his pores, content in the downy-comfort of the wafer-thin bed that was a king's luxury compared to the sewer grate where he likely laid his head last night. The other was a hunk of beef wrapped in the cell's only blanket, his gargantuan girth straining the bunk springs to their limit.

He had no idea what time it was, only that processing had taken an eternity and drained him. There were no windows to the outside, no sights of descending dusk or a midnight moon. All he knew was that it was late. He quietly crawled into the cell's only empty bunk without disturbing his cellies and quickly dozed off to sleep.

A sense that he was being watched, the eyes of an intense dark world boring into him, startled him awake. The gargantuan who'd been wrapped in the blanket last night snapping bed springs with every breath sat shirtless at the edge of his bunk. He was a bull-chested Chicano, his body a panoramic tattooed canvas representing every symbol of Satan's reign. Across his forehead stretched a gothic 666 and each side of his shaved head was covered in horns dripping in blood — a fork-tongued interpretation of Satan covered his bald crown. The center of his barrel chest bore a hexagram surrounded by pointed-winged representations of Satan's fallen angels, their fork-tailed bodies stretching across his thick shoulders, spilling over onto his back. Engraved thickly on each sinew-rippled forearm was an upside-down cross mocking the crucifixion of Christ with swastikas dotting each calloused knuckle. Looking into his black eyes was like looking into a cold abyss where deep within a soul struggled eternally against shackles of hate. The gargantuan smiled, revealing canines crudely filed into sharp fangs. His big nostrils flared as he took in deep sniff like an animal sniffing out its prey. Only this animal was not looking to devour meat. Its instincts sought only the saving grace of the Lamb of God. Then he spoke, his language one that Roger had never heard before, but one his spirit recognized as the guttural, underworld words coming with a hellish authority that penetrated his soul like an icicle through the heart.

Then he said in a language Roger understood, "You're a Christian."

Roger propped himself up on his elbow. "Yeah. I am."

"Paul wrote most of the New Testament in prison, didn't he?"

"His letters, yeah."

"Persecution. He wrote a lot about persecution, didn't he?"

"That's why he was in prison."

"House arrest. Romans. Wimp."

"So you know the Bible. You know of any way I can get one in here?"

He let out a laugh. "Here? Not a chance, Christian. What do you want a Bible for anyway? Bible's just a bunch of lies, written by Jews who wanna take over the world. They wanted to back then. They wanna do it now."

"You know, Paul wasn't just under house arrest. Some of his prison time was in dungeons. He was also beaten and left for dead."

"This your first time down?"

"Sort of."

His eyes bore into him, Roger feeling the cold, dark presence of the evil spirit within him. "You look like you only done county time. Yeah, this is your first time on the big boy yard. You think your God is going down with you?"

I will never leave you nor forsake you.

"He'll be with me wherever I go."

He chuckled. "If you was God, would you hang out in stink like this?"

"I believe that this is *especially* where God wants to hang out. This is where the lost are."

"First I was lost then I was found, sitting in a barbed wire sewage hole, amazing grace, huh? Okay, so let me tell you how it is here. Get used to this hole. Get used to the smell of piss, crap and the stink of body odor from every race God ever thunk of. The apes in here are the most rancid. You're sitting in this tiny hole twenty-four hours a day. Every other day we get two hours out. That's it. First hour you get to shower.

They cram about twenty of us in the shower room, jammed in line, scrot' to butt cheeks so get used to it, Christian, and hope you don't get lined up behind some guy who likes it.

"You're gonna be showering and sleeping stacked up in your cell with all types. Ain't no one been classified here yet, so there ain't no special yards where the killers go; where the chomos go; where the perverts go. Stripped naked or in the peels, we all look the same. But you can't mask the soul."

"Lost souls. Only Christ can rescue lost souls."

He smiled a fangy smile and said, "Things are different inside, Christian. Get used to it… if you survive long enough. People watch you, how you walk your walk. Say what you wanna say, but how you walk your walk, that's gonna determine if you get outa here either in one piece or cut up in ribbons." He lifted his pillow, revealing a shank, crudely made of a sharpened chain link cut from the yard fence, its grip fashioned out of yarn obtained through bed sheeting. Dropping the pillow back over it he said, "I hope your walk is solid, Christian."

He used the isolation time in the cell to talk with God, but he missed God's word. More than a week had passed and Roger heard nothing about his classification or where he was to be sent. He was eager to get to the yard. He craved Sirarpi's voice. He longed to read God's word.

After sleeping on the same stained and sweaty sheets for nearly two weeks he was given a fresh set of linens. When he yanked his dirty sheets off, a stack of papers that had been lodged between the wafer-thin mattress and cement slab fell to the floor. His heart sang when he picked them up. They were torn pages from a Bible. Four full pages—two from the book of Ezekiel and two from Psalms. The first passage from God's word that he'd read in over a week lifted his spirit from the abyss.

Ezekiel 34:16, "I will look for those that are lost, I bring those back that wander off, bandage those that are hurt and heal those that are sick."

He sat down on his bunk and started poring through God's word, his mind devouring each verse the way a starving castaway plucked off a deserted island would devour his first meal.

It was five-thirty in the morning the following week when his cell door rolled open. The correction officer's keys jingled on his hip as his huge frame filled the cell door.

"Roll up seventeen-five-nine-forty-eight!"

He was given his classification and informed of his new address: Arizona State Prison complex—Lewis, 5-E-6. Building 5. Run E, bed 5. Relief swept over him when he saw his classification: 3-3. Medium security, level three—just one tick shy of being tucked away in with murderers and lifers at level 4—maximum security.

"Trust me, Roger. Let not your heart be troubled. I am with you."

CHAPTER THIRTY-FOUR

Arizona State Prison Complex—Lewis
Stiner Yard
Buckeye, Ariz.
4:43 p.m.
• •

As they rattled through the prison gates, he watched the curl of the razor-ribbon barbed wire glide by through the narrow mesh slats that barely ventilated the sunbaked prison bus. Through the thick glass of the metal door sealing the inmates off from the air-conditioned cab he could see the blobbish frame of the uniformed driver working the wheel, his jelly roll back drenched with sweat despite the flow of cool air through the wide open air-conditioning vents. In the cab with him, a barrel-chested gun-bull sat in a jump seat bolted to the bulkhead, rifle resting in his lap, a burning cigarette dangling from his narrow lips. In the back, Roger sat bolted to a hot metal seat, chain-linked to his seatmate. There was no air-conditioning back here and the Arizona sun heated the hollow metal tube up to over 120 degrees. The hot, desert air blew in through the window slats like sulfuric dragon's breath.

When the brakes squeaked the bus to a stop, Roger and his seatmate jolted forward against their metal restraints. Diesel exhaust mingled with the stench of dried sweat as the driver left the bus idling. The gun-bull got up and jammed a key in the door and pushed it open. He dropped his cigarette to the floor and crushed it under his boot.

"Welcome to Lewis, ladies! Stiner Yard. Get a good look around before you walk in. For most of you, this is going to be the last view of the outside for a long time."

He squinted in the sun as he stepped from the processing house and started pushing his cart loaded with his mattress and orange clothes across the barbed wire-lined yard. The door to Building 5 was opened. As the wheels to Roger's cart bumped over the threshold he looked down and saw what was being used as the doorstop, keeping the iron door wedged open.

A Bible.

Roger stooped down and yanked it free, clutching it to his chest as the thick door slammed shut on its heavy hinges, shutting out the startled cry of the inmate who'd been behind him. Clutching God's word brought a sense of freedom that no chains or metal doors could seal shut.

I'm with you, Roger. Don't be afraid.

The door to Run E slid open as he pushed his cart across the floor of the semicircular room. He saw the silhouette of a single guard through the circular guardhouse in the middle of the room. Building 5 housed six runs, called 'jail pods' in County, labeled A through F. Thick glass turned each run into a fish aquarium of sorts, each tank stocked with orange piranha, their brawny scales stained in jailhouse art, gliding in deadly schools, searching for prey. The metallic clank and roll of the cell door for a fresh fish was like the ringing of a dinner bell.

The stench of raw testosterone hung thick in the air when he walked in, the run heavy with territorial strain. He left his cart outside, hearing the door roll shut as he walked down the aisle of bunks, mattress slung over his shoulder, boots and clothes tucked under his arm. He felt the probing tentacles of something that had crawled from a slit in the mattress and creep across his forehead, but he didn't dare flinch, feeling the eyes of hungry predators sizing up their game.

They were hungry.

And it was past feeding time.

He was unpacked and settled into his new home within minutes. Stretching out on his bunk, he wasn't expecting the ring of his doorbell with neighbors stopping by to welcome him to the neighborhood. He peeled open the tattered Bible and started reading until the fatigue of the trip overtook him and he dozed off.

He jumped when he heard his bunk springs creak and felt his bed rattle. A wiry Hispanic kid sat on the edge of his bed, yellow grin stretched across a pointy chin planted with a stringy goatee.

"Name's Gordo," he said, holding out a boney hand. His cold hand had a wet-noodle grip.

"Roger."

"I run with the Chicanos."

Without asking, Roger knew Gordo's role. They called them torpedoes. They were usually culled from the young herd, kids scared to death, the system moving them out of the sandbox in juvie and onto the big boy playground. They'd do anything to feel safe and that's exactly what the race leaders tasked them to do. Anything. Run drugs. Call out a snitch. Identify a strawberry for a homie whose loins were about to burst under pressure. Drive a shiv up through a man's kidney.

His task today was to feel the new guy out, see if he could add him to the Chicano numbers.

Roger asked, "What time is it?"

"Time here don't matter." He reached down and grabbed a sack between his feet. "Got some things here we thought you'd appreciate."

"We?"

"My homies. Chicanos, man. Thought you'd like to run with us, you know?" He reached in the bag and pulled out a four-pack of Ivory soap. "You see the skin-dissolver stuff they stock in the showers, you'll appreciate this. Got some shampoo. Pert. Good stuff. Stuff in the showers will rot your head. Some snacks from commissary. There's a few paperbacks in there, but I see you come in with something to read. That don't happen much. Also got a stamped envelope for you. Everyone wants to write someone right away. Takes time to get money on your books, you know. You can send something out next mail call you like." He tucked it all back in the bag and handed it to Roger.

"Thanks."

"What 'chew readin' man?"

"Bible."

He nodded, his gaze empty, his mind working on his checklist. He was obviously troubled asking the next question but he got on with it.

"So what's your story? You know, you tell me, I report it up accurately. You don't wanna share, you gonna end up talking with the big stripes anyway cause they gonna ask to see your jacket. Plus we can't guarantee you safety, we don't know about you."

Roger had been prepared for this. He pulled out his legal papers and handed them to Gordo.

Gordo went through them, his junior high education evident in the way he stared incomprehensively at the pages, trying to make out the things he understood.

"Marijuana, huh? Two years on this yard? Man, don't get caught whinin'. Average rap here is fifteen long."

"I'm just gonna do my time and get out. That's it."

"Okay, so, you run with us, we do our meals at the twenties. Breakfast is at seven, we go to breakfast at twenty past. Lunch is at noon, we go at twelve twenty. Get it? You're there hungry or not. Rec time, you head out to the jungle with us you wanna be or not. Think you can do that?"

"I don't exactly have any other plans in my social schedule."

Gordo smiled. "Chow is in twenty minutes. You wanted to know the time. In twenty minutes, it's chow time."

Over a month had passed and Roger fell into his routine. This morning, like every morning, he was up before anyone on the run, sitting on one of the metal stools at the rec room table, reading his Bible. For the first three weeks he used the tattered doorstop Bible until the package arrived from Sirarpi. She'd sent him a NIV New Life Application Study Bible, the commentaries and concordance instrumental in teaching him how to apply God's word to his life.

He read John 14:26, "But the Advocate, the Holy Spirit, whom the Father will send in my name, will teach you all things and will remind you of everything I have said to you." He took this scripture literally and prayed to his Father in Heaven to use the Bible to teach him the truth of

His word. Realizing that there are so many denominational perspectives and nonessential differences among Christians, Roger did not want to rely on human opinion for his teaching. He believed the Holy Spirit would translate God's truth to him and he asked with pure motives to know God and His ways like never before.

At rec, he was required to join the Chicanos when they congregated around their picnic table in the yard to show their numbers. Everything came down to numbers. To the state, he was a number: Inmate 175948. His neighborhood, a number: Building 5. His house, a number: Run E, Bed 6. But to God, he was not a number. Psalm 139 promised:

"How precious to me are your thoughts, O God! How vast is the sum of them! Were I to count them, they would outnumber the grains of sand."

His race thought of him when they needed the numbers. God thought of him nonstop, unconditionally. If he tried to count the amount of thoughts God had of him every day he may as well try and count the grains of sand on the Earth.

This morning, Roger was about to discover that his race also thought of him when they had other needs. Gordo suddenly appeared, taking a seat across from him.

"Jorge is expecting to meet with you in the *baño* in an hour."

Roger looked up, trying to figure out what he'd done to Jorge. A summons to the *baño* was an invitation to fight or get beat down. There were no cameras in the john. He'd seen how ugly things could get out of camera range. Beatings to the edge of death, near drownings in fresh-soiled toilet water.

"It's not for that. Jorge ain't got no beef with you. His area's gonna get tossed by the bulls and he's holding. He's gonna hand you some stuff. Stash it good. You probably won't get hit. They do hit you and find it, you don't know where it came from, got that?"

Roger was annoyed, this young kid talked down at him.

"I've moved my share of drugs in a previous life. No thanks."

Gordo's face registered shock, unable to comprehend the defiance.

"No one's asking you to do a favor. You're being told."

"Who told it?"

"Look, this one's coming all the way from Two-Pack." Two-Pack Garcia was the Chicano race leader for Building 5. The way the hierarchy worked, each run had a leader who reported to the yard leader. The yard leader reported to the building leader. The building leader was closest to the top, answering to the complex leader. Two-Pack was like a CEO reporting to the board of directors. "The whole yard's getting hit, man, not just our crib. You refuse, you're refusing a direct order from Two-Pack."

"You want me to hold Jose's bag, okay. I'll play. But I won't stash it. It'll get found. I'll take the heat for it and they'll toss me in cold storage for a while. I've never turned on anyone in my life. My word is and always has been my bond. But it's gonna come out the same. Jose's gonna lose his bag. He might wanna rethink who he wants as a mule." Roger turned his attention back to his Bible, making it clear that he was done with the conversation.

Gordo sat back, trying to figure it out. All he could say was, "You're *loco*, man."

"My handle used to be 'Insane.'"

Gordo sat for a minute, not knowing what to do. Finally he said, "Crazy preacher man." And whirled from the seat and left.

The *baño* was empty when he showed up for his meeting with Jorge. Obviously Jorge had picked another mule to stash his goodies. He wasn't sure what to make of it but he was certain that this was not the end of the issue.

After their show-of-strength meeting in the yard, Roger would hit the running track. Jogging allowed him to be alone with his thoughts while experiencing the freedom of movement within the caged confines of the yard. By the end of his first month he was up to three miles and trimmed down to the weight of his high school football days. Before hitting the track, he'd pick a Bible verse and meditate on it nonstop, every lap. The peace of the Holy Spirit enveloped him like never before. By his third month he was up to five miles a day.

He was usually alone on the track but today he sensed the presence of someone else. As he ran, he heard the pounding of feet crunching the gravel behind, gaining on him. He continued to run steady until he rounded the first leg, putting the sun behind him and casting the shadow of not one but two pursuers gaining on him. He thought of Jorge and the drugs and figured his time had come. Two months had passed since he'd refused to be Jose's mule. Jose didn't lose his stash, but Roger still expected his name to be added to the list.

He stepped up his pace, not looking back, but they closed in fast. Just as he was about to cut and run from the track, they drew alongside of him, one on either side, both winded and hacking, neither one conditioned for the brutality of jogging in work boots.

"You wanna slow it down for us a bit, bro'?"

Both were from his Chicano race and high up in the pecking order. Cheeks Sanchez and *Jefe* Torres were from Run A and hung close to Two-Pack. Roger slowed down just a little but didn't stop running.

"Two-Pack, he been watching you close, over a month now, right?" Cheeks huffed. "Okay, so now Two-Pack's ready to meet the new fish."

Roger continued jogging, not answering.

Jefe said, "He wants to meet the preacher."

Roger stopped. Both *Jefe* and Cheeks bent over, hands on their knees, coughing, gasping for air.

"Preacher?"

"Yeah, yeah," *Jefe* said. "That's what he calling you. Preacher Man. Two-Pack tag you with a name, it stick wit' you. You keep it. You ain't got no choice, nuh uh."

"I kind of like it."

"That's good," Cheeks said. "Because now it's yours. You got an invite to the head table tonight, Preach'. No RSVP required. See you there."

His handsome face was wind-burned, chiseled and ruddy, his brown tint grayed by a life sentence in the jailhouse air. Two-Pack Garcia could have been a Latino movie star had he not chosen a different path. But gangbanging led to drugs; drugs led to murder; murder led to a life sentence inside. Two-Pack got his name on the streets because of his rep of always packing two, only needing one, using one. One gun. One bullet. He'd put a rumored eleven guys down until he pulled the button on a cop's son, bringing the heat down on him hard. He'd spent most of the last twenty years up on the max yard. He was a lifer on a medium security yard now, two hours out, twenty-two locked down. That's the best he would ever hope for the rest of his life.

Thick, rope-like sinew pushed through the orange shirt sleeves rolled up on his biceps. His calloused knuckles dented the cork butt of the hand-rolled cigarette burning between his fingers.

"I ran a make on you and your jacket looks clean, Preach'," he said, taking a long drag off the coffin nail. "You ain't a snitch, least I don't see it or smell it. You was all cliqued up with some serious movers. You been out of commission for a while, from what I read. Tryin' to walk it straight. But straight don't cut it for guys like us, huh, Preach'? Past catches up with us, huh?"

"I made my mistakes. Now I'm paying for them."

Two-Pack flicked a long ash into the coffee cup he was using as an ashtray. He glared at Roger a long time through stone-hard eyes that could have been plucked out of a gargoyle. "What kinda debt you gotta settle on the outside?"

"What makes you think I'm still lookin' over my shoulder?"

"You got told. You dissed us, Preach'. I need to know why you done that. Takes real brass, pullin' something like that. Makes me think I'm dealin' with someone who ain't afraid of gettin' smashed in here. Someone with some backing gonna come in and bite ol' Two-Pack and his homies we try and issue some discipline."

"As a dog returns to its vomit, so a fool repeats his folly."

"Come again?"

"It's a Proverb."

"What's it mean?"

"It means I don't go near drugs. I stay away from them. If it means I get smashed, I get smashed. I only have the Lord to back me. That's it."

Two-Pack crushed his cigarette in the palm of his hand and dropped the butt into the coffee cup. His plastic tray of food was half-eaten and shoved aside on the table.

"I been in this joint nearly twenty years, Preach'," he said. "I see a lot of your type come in here. They find God on the way in, pray they'selves to sleep at night, jailhouse prayers. But it's one thing to talk it in here,

Preach'. It's another to walk it. I watch the jailhouse preachers melt right into the sludge that surrounds them. These gray bars, they kill a man's soul, chill it deep so it becomes as cold as these concrete walls. Yeah, they'll still talk the talk, but then you see them juicing their veins in the *baño*, scorin' hooch from under a toilet lid or hookin' it up with some strawberry in the laundry."

He cupped his hand around another cigarette and dipped the tip into a wooden match he'd struck with the scratch of his knurled thumbnail. "Hell, half the guys I put down in this joint were jailhouse preachers in hock for the gambling holes they dug themselves into supporting their habits."

"So why are you sharing this with me? Why single me out?"

"My eyes been on you, Preach'. Watching real close. There's not much room for error in here, Preach'. But I been pretty impressed by what I see so far. If ever the real deal come through here, it'd be you. That's why I decided to look away on the Jorge thing. But one step left or right from you, Preach', and I'm gonna have to reevaluate things, we understand each other?"

"I think so."

Two-Pack leaned forward, resting his elbows on the table, getting close and lowering his voice. "Okay, so here's the next favor I'm gonna do for you. There's likely gonna be a clash in here, chow time, tomorrow night. Tension's been brewing between the Woods and Brothers over some gambling debt. Ain't our beef, but this thing blows and this whole cafeteria's gonna be bangin'. You don't join in, Chicanos gotta put you down. If this happens, I know it's gonna go against your preacher walk. I'm tellin' you, hang back. Fall back behind it. Be ready to go, your brothers need you, but you hang back, you still supportin' us, you just got less risk getting pulled in the mix-up. You got that?"

"Yeah, I think I get the picture." Two-Pack leaned back and Roger read his face. "Something tells me you got something else on your mind."

"Yeah. You preacher types like to do your preachin' to anyone who wants to listen. We're all square as long as you stick to your race. And especially not the Muslims."

Roger was tempted to argue, to let him know that the word of God knew no skin color and was not restricted by racial boundaries. But he knew he had a narrow thread to weave here. He had to work within the politics of the system.

"I'll be mindful." Roger got to his feet and started to leave.

"Let's hope so. It's a rare thing, getting a meeting with Two-Pack you walk away from in one piece. Let's hope there ain't gotta be another meeting."

"I'm sure there won't be."

Tension was thick the following night at chow. The bulls must've sensed something was going down, or picked up the rumor that a score was about to be settled tonight between the Woods and the Blacks because they'd doubled their numbers tonight. Roger barely touched his food on his tray. Gordo suddenly appeared beside him, sliding a tray piled with slop on the table and plopping down in his seat.

"The big stripes are still negotiating. They got their torpedoes moving back and forth between the tables. They don't make nice in about fifteen minutes, the place is gonna blow. We got a wager going on you, you hear about that?"

"No."

"Whether or not you hang back or mix it up. We know Two-Pack gave you the okay to hang back. But, you know, in here, things start flyin', everyone's tempted to smash a Brother or two, you know?"

"Where'd you put your money?"

"That you'd bang."

"You didn't choose wisely."

"I think that I may have. I got information you ain't got. Two-Pack knew all about it, too."

"What's that?"

Gordo pointed over to table of Brothers and his heart sank when he recognized the short guy on the end, the one with the Chinese slant to his eyes.

China Mike.

Gordo said, "He just came in. Two-Pack knew he was on his way in a few days ago before he hit the yard. What'dya think now, huh? Place breaks out, all hell breaking loose, give you a chance, huh? Chance to put down the guy witnessed against you. Guy who helped put you here. Yeah, you still got that killer instinct, Preach'. Yeah, I think I made the right bet.

CHAPTER THIRTY-FIVE

Sunday, November 30, 2003
Arizona State Prison Complex—Lewis
Morey Yard
5:25 p.m.
• •

Ricky "The Rooster" Wassenaar, max security inmate number 16155, brushed the brown locks of hair off of the clear plastic apron pulled over his bare, tattooed upper torso. The buzz of the hair shears stopped and he felt the calloused fingers of Bones White brushing the hair clippings from his neck.

"Lookin' fine, my man, Rooster. The Rooster's lookin' fine in the pen!"

He pulled the apron over his head and got up from the hard, plastic chair and walked into the john. He looked at himself in the mirror, his pockmarked face still heavy with stubble that hid most of his ancient acne dings, but the long, wild hair was now shaved as tight as a necktied executive. He didn't like the look but it was necessary. And he had to establish the new look now. Initially he knew that the sudden, inexplicable makeover of "The Rooster" Wassenaar would raise a few eyebrows and he wanted to make sure all suspicion was gone by the time he pulled this thing off.

Wassenaar was seven years in on a twenty-eight year stretch for jacking a Tucson strip club. The deal went bad halfway through, someone tripping a silent alarm, police converging on the place within ten minutes. And The Rooster screeched out of there in his jacked up GTO, squeezing the trigger at the cops in pursuit. Last thing he remembered before waking up in cuffs, face sandblasted by asphalt, was aiming the nose of his car straight at a motorcycle cop coming at him. Refusing to accept the court-appointed attorney, he represented himself in Pinal County Superior Court and didn't do so well. The judge gave him max-plus.

As he cleaned a line of shaving cream from under his chin with the swipe of a razor, he saw the green, winding snake tattoos of two beefy arms reach over and turn the water on in the sink next to him. Cupping his palms full of water, his cellie, Stephen "Pony" Coy, lowered his head toward the sink and splashed cold water on his face and rubbed it over his shaved head.

"Package came early, Rooster," Pony said, the rush of water ensuring his message remained between Wassenaar and himself. "Stall three."

Wassenaar tried to control his anger but slammed his fist on the faucet, shutting the water off and tossing his razor into the sink. He walked over to stall three and sat on the stainless steel toilet and reached behind the toilet paper dispenser and found the weapons planted there: two shanks, one fashioned out of a sawed-off metal chair leg, the other from a snipped piece of chain link, both with thick handles made of shredded bed sheets. The third weapon was a razor blade that had been melted into a snipped toothbrush handle.

The weapons were what he'd been looking for but they'd arrived way too early. He'd dreamt of escaping since the moment he hit the yard. Landing the job as a cook four years ago gave him the opportunity he'd been waiting for. He learned the procedures, the movements of the COs, inmate workers and civilian personnel. He knew the weaknesses and the optimal time to strike. But if the weapons got discovered during some unannounced bunk tossing, the whole thing would need to be put off for at least another six months.

He slid a bladed toothbrush handle into a slit he'd cut in the elastic of his waistband and tucked the shanks into the folded cuffs of his pants. Pony was still washing at the sink when he came back.

"Bird's gotta fly," he told Pony, picking up his razor and resuming shaving.

"When?"

"Sooner than we was plannin'."

Saturday, December 20, 2003
Buckeye, Arizona

• •

The chain link fencing, curled in the razor-ribbon barbed wire, and the grey-block watch towers rising above the compound turned the majestic Arizona mountain ranges off in the horizon into an ugly thing. From the back seat, Andrew's excited voice rang out as he recognized where they were heading.

"Daddy's house! Daddy's house!"

Childlike faith. Yes, Lewis State Prison was Daddy's house. The sealed gates, the colorless buildings, the menacing fences, the orange garb that stripped identities away, revelry for a boy of two. It meant time with Daddy. Once a week with Daddy, Daddy wearing his orange pajamas. Always in orange pajamas. Daddy's house was so much fun.

Rachel, now just over one month old, cooed from her car seat, almost in an equally excited anticipation that she'd be in Daddy's arms again very soon. Sitting in the backseat with them, Roger's mother played along, making a happy voice toward Rachel's car seat, "Yes, Daddy! We're going to see Daddy soon!"

Sirarpi wished such childlike faith was contagious. But as they drove over the hill on westbound I-10, the ugly complex that rose over the horizon was only a reminder of time stolen from her. They'd taken her husband from her. They'd stripped him of his identity, given him a number and locked him away. How could they ever repay her for what she'd lost? How would they repay her for the nights around the dinner table when he was not there? The nights without him sleeping next to her? His companionship? The security of a God-fearing husband at her side? Time stolen. Time that could never be returned.

She'd never felt so alone. Even in church, the place where she had hoped to find comfort and support, she was an outcast. Yes, on Sundays she'd get the sympathetic smile, the clammy handshake and the obligatory "How are you holding up?" But after, they'd turn away, sticking their noses back into their hymns, forgetting about her and Roger until next Sunday.

Perhaps they just didn't know how to deal with the wife of a felon. Perhaps the blot of incarceration lent too much convenience in locking away the villainous, shaming them to a barbed wire colony, jettisoning them from amongst us like yesterday's lepers. Either way, once the organ sounded and the hallelujahs began to ring, Sirarpi sat in the pew surrounded by the "Body of Christ"—feeling abandoned and alone.

Visitation was every Saturday. She looked forward to the visits not only because it was time to spend with her husband, but it was also a time to drink the joy and peace that had settled upon her husband with an inexplicable reverence. He had a contagious glow about him, a deep peace that came with an intimacy he'd discovered in using his time to draw close to God.

"Draw near to God, and He will draw near to you"…James 4:8

Every week when visitation time was through she'd look back at Roger, waving goodbye just before the iron doors slammed shut. Although their goodbyes were tear-filled, Roger always returned to his cell with a peaceful look of anticipation. Like he had an appointment to keep, a love to meet. And he did. He was going back inside to spend countless precious hours alone—with God.

Sirarpi finally realized that although she wasn't physically behind bars, *she* was the one in chains—allowing her impossible circumstances to bind her tighter than the walls of Lewis prison. Her struggle was in trying to understand why? How could this happen? Then Roger told her to meditate on Isaiah 55:8.

"For my thoughts are not your thoughts, neither are your ways my ways," declares the Lord.

"What does it mean, Hrach?" she asked.

"It means, let God be God."

God had removed everything that she'd relied upon in order for her to learn to trust and completely rely on him. Isaiah 55:8 put it bluntly, God simply saying, *"Don't ask me why. Don't ask me what. Just trust me."* She decided to start asking God "what" and not "why," eagerly anticipating his answer, trusting his promise in Jeremiah 33:3, "Call on me and I will answer you and tell you great and unsearchable things you do not know."

She decided to let go and let God be God—and her faith grew amazingly stronger.

The expected chow hall riot between the Woods and the Blacks never went down. But Roger knew that Two-Pack continued watching, awaiting his reaction to China Mike's arrival on the yard. In Two-Pack's world, a guy helps put you away, you put him down. He lost his chance with the freebie, a chow hall mix-up that would have allowed him to drill the narc down in the chaos. But Roger quickly found that it wasn't going to be a revenge line that he'd cross. It was going to be the race line. Rather than reaching out with a fist in revenge, he reached out with God's word in love.

His first encounter with China Mike came two days later. It was during rec, China Mike strangely alone, isolated, sitting at the only picnic table with an obstructed view of the tower, making Roger wonder if it had not been arranged. Two-Pack pulling some strings, getting the guy alone, watching to see what the Preacher Man would do. Roger walked the tightrope, aware of the hidden eyes on him as he approached China Mike from behind. He kept it simple, pushing the race line, crossing just enough for Mike to get the message.

"Hi, Mike."

China looked up, his slanted eyes widening in recognition, first looking in horror at Roger, then darting left and right, suddenly realizing for the first time that he was dangerously alone. His mouth moved up and down, words unable to leave his lips, a man convinced that he'd just made his final mistake.

"God loves you, brother." And Roger reached out with a brotherly handshake, patted China Mike on the back and moved on.

Message delivered. Seed planted.

God loves you.

Sometimes, that's all it took. But he had still dissed his race and was out of line. Yet he was not about to sweat the consequences. Christ promised in 2 Timothy 1:7 that "God did not give us a spirit of timidity, but a spirit of power, of love, and of self-discipline." The Holy Spirit was not merely counseling him and teaching him the truth of God's word but living inside of him. He was going to let the same power that had resurrected Christ from the dead move him—refusing to sit idle as a Christian in name only. He'd spent the first 25 years of his life idle. Coming from a "Christian" country had earned him the Christian title by heritage—not by the sacrificial blood of Christ. Over the last six months, surrounded by twenty-four-hour temptation, darkness and depravity had intensified his Christian walk. He was surrounded not only by depraved and wicked hearts who were ready to pounce at his first misstep, but, more importantly, by contrite and broken hearts seeking hope and light in a wickedly dark place.

His Damascus moment had come at dawn, the light of Jesus Christ lighting a dark jail cell. Dusk had begun to settle as God allowed his past life to catch up with him. Darkness came in the encroaching shadows of the chain link-shrouded prison yard. But it was in the midst of the darkness—amidst the hurting, the lost, the helplessness—that he recognized the power and majesty of the light of Jesus Christ shining through him. In this place of constant lockdown, wicked prison politics and twenty-four-hour surveillance—by the gun-bulls and the race leaders—he knew that he could not afford to hide that glorious light. There were too many lost souls, too many eternities to save.

He had just dozed off after morning chow when the door chambers rolled, echoing off the walls, and the door slid open. The gun-bull's beefy frame filled the door and he started calling out the fortunate names who had visitors.

"Munchian, bed six!"

He popped up from his bunk, grabbed his Bible, and fell in line, eager to see his family. Today he had big news for Sirarpi.

The metal door to the visitation room slid open and Sirarpi and Roger's mom were sitting at their usual table. Andrew looked up from ramming his Hot Wheels race car across the scarred Formica table, eyes lighting up, and running to him. He leapt into Roger's arms. "Daddy! Daddy!"

Sirarpi's eyes glowed as he approached, holding Andrew with one arm, Andrew clinging to his neck. Rachel was asleep, bundled in pink swaddling blankets, tucked in her car seat. His mother smiled warmly as he approached.

Visitation was Saturdays. Once a week he had six full hours to spend with his family. Roger spent the first couple of hours playing Hot Wheels with Andrew. Today was special. Today Andrew let him be the Shelby. Andrew decided to be the black car and at one point he made a sound of screeching car tires and an explosion with his lip as he spun the car into a metal chair leg. The black car bounced off the chair leg and tumbled across the floor and Roger felt the tightening of the seatbelt around his chest, the white hot explosion in his mind, the suffocation of airbag, the haunting cries of life whisked away into the night.

"Hrach? Hrach?" He felt Sirarpi's delicate fingers on his shoulder. "Mama, he's burning up."

Roger saw the drip of sweat fall from his forehead and splash in front of the tiny car between his thumb and index finger, whitening in his grip.

"I forgive you, Roger. Let it go."

A calm swept over him, a peace beyond anything he could possibly understand. He looked up and saw that Andrew continued roaring the black car along the floor, unaware of the moment Daddy just had.

"I'm okay, honey," he said, and got to his feet. He looked over at his mother's concerned face and gave her a reassuring smile. Andrew had picked a police car from his Hot Wheels collection and was busy conducting a high-speed chase across the blue cinderblock wall.

"Let's visit a little," he said, leaving the Shelby parked in front of the puddle of sweat and leading Sirarpi over to a table where they could have some privacy.

They talked uninterrupted for over an hour, their conversation quickly going from housekeeping issues to God and their growing faith. They opened their Bibles and walked through scripture together, Roger leading, Sirarpi listening intently. His admiration for her grew deeper and deeper every day, watching the way her faith strengthened.

He flipped to Matthew 25:40 and read it out loud. "The King will reply, 'I tell you the truth, whatever you did for the least of these brothers of mine, you did for me.'" As he was about to comment, he looked up and saw that the look on her face suddenly turned distant.

"Aren't we the least of these, Hrach?" She said.

He was silent for a minute, looking into her eyes, the pool of tears magnifying a deep down hurt that only the unfailing love of Christ could reach. "You're still not going to church?" he asked.

She slowly shook her head, looking down at the table. "No, Roger. I just can't. I can't sit in that pew anymore. I feel like I just don't belong there."

"You need to worship, though, Sirarpi. It's part of getting to know Christ better. Worship."

"What about your worship here, Hrach? Where's your worship in here? Where's your church?"

He looked around the room, seeing the faces of the dejected dressed in orange, their joyless expressions cracked with strained smiles, momentary revelry in the restrained taste of freedom that comes from the limited touch that visiting day allows with the outside world. If he'd looked in the face of one, he'd looked into them all. Worry lines creased their leaden pallor; eyes were deep with the eternal thoughts that come with long, empty, bridled days surrounded by gray walls and menacing chain link.

The smiles could be forced and with the limitless time that sitting in stir allows for practice, those fake smiles could be made to look as genuine as the practiced art of a Hollywood leading man.

But the eyes, the windows to the soul, revealed the truth. Eyes, sunk deep in the pathetic, clammy mugs of the hopeless, came in all shades of color. Blue. Brown. Green. Hazel. Black. Each hue a canvas bespectacled in tiny black flecks, each peppery dot a story of remorse, of sorrow, of unhealed hurt welling up from a pertinent soul seeking an ear to listen, a compassionate voice to reassure, an outside touch to let them know that they are still human.

Through the window of desperately searching eyes, he could see the tiny flame deep down in each of them. A tiny ember of hope waiting to be fanned into flame. Drugs. Alcohol. Sex. All were fuel readily available behind bars, but their burn was only temporary. Only the fuel from the sacrificial blood of Jesus Christ could ignite an eternal flame that could never be extinguished even in the darkest crevices of this hollow place of bridled hopelessness.

They needed to be reached.

They needed to know the eternal hope of Jesus Christ.

He looked across the room and recognized the prune-like, liver-spotted head of Earl Watson, shuffling along without the aid of his bottle of oxygen today. A step behind him, his frail, silver-haired wife Bea followed. The thick, black Bible that Earl carried in his eggshell grip looked like it was about to snap his brittle arm right off. They belonged to a small church nearby that did not support their mission field. They held small services here, two Sundays a month, and came with a borrowed CD player and scratched, warped CDs for worship music.

"What about your worship here, Hrach? Where's your worship in here?"

Where? Where was the church? The faithful like Earl and Bea were it. Elderly folks, geriatric missionaries, pouring their failing hearts into the lost behind bars. But where was the bigger church? The whole church? Some guys had pen pals with outside faith organizations. Others took advantage of correspondence classes, busy work, offerings found pinned to the chow-hall corkboard, like lost puppy signs taped to a grocery store bulletin board. But where was the human touch? The willingness to reach out to the cast-aside, to be the hands and feet of Jesus Christ and reach out and rescue society's refuse?

In a place of such ripe harvest, a place brimming with the least of these starving for hope's eternal light, where were they? Where were the faithful willing to draw close and bring the light of Jesus Christ to the modern-day lepers? To the human chaff discarded and forgotten like yesterday's garbage?

Where?

"I'll write another letter to Pastor Frank."

Sirarpi shook her head. "No, Hrach. No more letters."

"Sirarpi, how many mortgage payments was Pastor Frank able to meet because of our giving? How many times did he call me directly, needing money to keep the church doors open?"

"All that doesn't matter anymore, Hrach, because you are here. You are in this place. They just don't know what to do with us, Hrach. They just don't know what to do."

He sat back in his chair, feeling the twist of gnarled muscle and strained bone that came with nearly a year of sitting only on backless metal stools and sleeping on metal springs poking through wafer-thin cotton stuffing.

"Things are going to get better, Sirarpi, I promise. I have some good news."

He could see her spirits visibly perk up. "What, Hrach?"

"I just got reclassified. I'm being moved to a minimum security yard. Probably Bachman Yard."

Her face lit up. "Oh, praise God! Hrach. How? I thought you said you would be here on Stiner for the rest of your stay? You said the way the classification system worked, by the time you could be moved to a minimum security yard you would be getting out?"

This was true. After his six-month reclassification hearing, he didn't expect to be reclassified at all. Reclassifications were unheard of after the first meeting. At best, he'd expected to be moved from a 3-3 to a 3-2 after his first year inside. By midyear next year, with good behavior and assuming he didn't get brought down by prison politics, he'd be at a 3-1, still sitting on Stiner. Before his next hearing after that, he'd be getting out. However, two weeks after his reclassification meeting, on December 17, he received formal notice that he was now a 2-2. He'd be getting his orders soon to roll up for his move to one of Lewis's minimum security yards.

"You got powerful friends on the outside, don't cha, Preacher?" Two-Pack had said to him in another rare meeting with the yard king. Roger had expected the meeting. The news spread fast that the Preacher man had skipped an unprecedented five classifications.

"I have only one powerful friend, Two-Pack. I'd be happy to introduce Him to you. There isn't any politics with Him. He doesn't look at skin color. He doesn't care what race you run with or where you fit in the pecking order."

"Yeah, I know, I know, Preach'. Jesus Christ."

"The only powerful friend you'll ever need."

"Good luck to you, Preach'. Don't expect no goin' away party."

Roger said to his wife, "It's all God, Sirarpi. All God. Listen…on Bachman, I get two visits a week. Saturday and Sunday."

"Praise God!" Her eyes filled with tears. "When do you get rounded up, Hrach?"

He laughed. "Rolled up, Sirarpi, sweetie. Rolled up. I expect in a month or so. At least by mid-January."

When visiting hours were coming to an end, Roger walked his family as far as he was allowed to travel within the visitation room. Rachel cooed when he kissed her applesauce-stained face good-bye and Andrew gave him a high-five with his tiny hand. He kissed his mother and took Sirarpi aside as his mother ushered the kids through the maze of metal detectors and uniformed guards.

"Sirarpi, even Jesus used his time of suffering to get closer to his Father."

"Hrach?"

"He showed us the way, Sirarpi. Jesus came here and was beaten and rejected. There's no depth of pain or loss that we feel that Jesus didn't experience. But the anguish He experienced here brought Him even closer to God, even to the point of sweating blood at the thought of becoming separated from his Father, of losing the intimacy His time here on Earth brought between Him and His Father. Sirarpi, you don't have to be in chains. This time of trial for you may be the only time you will ever have again to experience an intimacy with God deeper than you could ever imagine. Anybody can experience God, Sirarpi. He's all around us. We were made to be in tune with His existence. Only those who allow his love to free them from their own chains experience a *connection* with Him. Join me on this journey, Sirarpi. Join me."

A pool of tears magnified a flicker of understanding that sparked deep inside her eyes, a tiny flame that cast light on a freed soul suddenly released from the bondage of worry.

He felt a new level of love that he'd never felt before, a depth of love for her that he knew he never would have reached outside these walls of chain-link and razor wire.

"I love you, Hrach. I love you so much."

"I love you."

Sunday, January 18, 2004
9:30 a.m.

· ·

She was excited. She just knew that this would be the week. This week, Roger would get the word to roll up and he'd be on his way to the minimum security yard. She feared for him every day, knowing the dangerous line he walked on Stiner yard. Being from a battle-torn country like Armenia, she knew the savagery of war. She'd seen uniformed soldiers of both her countrymen and the enemy. She'd seen bombs, bullets, blood and death. The very fabric of Armenia was war and blood. But America was supposed to be the land of the free, a land of opportunity. She didn't know blood flowed here as well. Blood drawn in the turf wars and random savagery of soldiers uniformed in gang paint.

Until coming to America, she'd never heard of names like the Mexican Mafia, Aryan Nation, Bloods or Crips. They ran the streets where Roger grew up like the soldiers ran the streets of Armenia. And she was learning that they ran the prisons as well and that her husband was locked down in a cage twenty-four hours a day with them. Yeah, she knew that he'd grown up with them. He'd attained street wisdom and smarts that gave him an innate sense of survival. But what if those senses had dulled over the years? Minimum security was far from freedom but she felt at peace that her husband would be safer there and that God continued stretching His protection over Roger.

She flipped on the TV and screamed when the first story of the local news came live on the screen. She heard glass shatter in the kitchen, Roger's mother dropping a coffee cup, startled at her screams.

"No! No! Oh, Hrach—*no!*"

She didn't fully understand the words that the anchor was saying, but she knew something had gone wrong up at Lewis prison. Very wrong.

CHAPTER THIRTY-SIX

Sunday, January 18
3:10 a.m.

● ●

The smell of bubbling pancake batter on the griddle was always a welcome change to the BO and urine stench of the prison cell. The kitchen graveyard shift was sparsely guarded and generally with old-timer bulls months from retirement or fresh fish straight out of training. They must've figured no one would try to pull something off this early in the morning. Ricky Wassenaar was about to prove their theory wrong.

Wassenaar was the ranking crew member on the griddle. He scooped pancake batter out of a giant metal vat using a heavy, industrial-sized stirring paddle and used it to pour Frisbee-sized pancake batter puddles in straight lines onto the griddle. He looked up and saw Pony's hulking frame working an industrial-sized mixer, his snake-tattooed biceps bulging as he poured a sack of premixed batter into the giant stainless steel mixing bowl. Pony looked over and Wassenaar gave him a nod. Wassenaar watched him set the empty bag down and casually pull the shank out from where he'd tucked it in his sock.

Feeling the rush of adrenaline, Wassenaar set the vat down but kept the heavy paddle in his hand. With his other hand he worked the shank out of the slit in his waistband and crossed the kitchen, approaching the elderly guard, a hard-nose gun-bull named Martin Kennick smoking a cigarette over near the pantry, staring out at the early morning darkness through a barred window. Wassenaar knew the guy never sensed his approach. Strong-arming him from behind, he wrapped one arm around Kennick's neck, held the shank hard against the man's jugular and whacked him on the side of the left knee with the paddle. Kennick buckled, nearly hanging himself in his grip.

"Okay, here's the deal," he whispered in Kennick's ear. "I'm stuck in this joint till I'm older than you so I ain't got nothin' to lose, so the choice is yours how you want this to go down."

Kennick complied as he led him to a nearby office and ordered him to strip out of his uniform, down to his skivvies. It was snug but Kennick's uniform fit him good enough. He handcuffed Kennick to the office's tool room door and stepped out, dressed in a tan prison guard uniform, gun belt and everything. When he stepped back in the kitchen, he saw that Pony had already taken control by herding the civilian workers and locking them in the pantry.

Wassenaar brushed the wrinkles out of the uniform, checked his sidearm and walked out of the kitchen, crossing the yard toward the gun tower.

The jingling of the keys on his tool belt gave him a sense of power and authority as he climbed the metal stairs. The keys were the final authority between freedom and incarceration. Keys held the power to lock or unlock cell doors and loose metal chains. He patted the gun strapped to his hip. Control over freedom. Control over life. Control over death.

He was in charge.

He could make out the young, chiseled features of the officer on the other side of the tower window as he got to the top of the stairs. He was a fresh-fish gun-bull named Dan Auchman, age 21, just over three months on the job. Wassenaar pounded on the window, startling Auchman. He held up Kennick's radio and shrugged his shoulders, feigning a problem with a broken radio. He made a pushing motion with his thumb, signaling Auchman to buzz him in. Auchman turned his head and said something to someone else in the tower, then got up from his station and signaled to follow him over to the tower door.

Holding the metal paddle at his side, he stepped back. When the door buzzed, he sprang forward and threw the full weight of his six-foot frame behind the kick, drilling his foot into the center of the metal door. Auchman's startled cry followed the crack of bone echoing off the control room walls. Wassenaar threw his shoulder into the door before it had a chance to slam back shut and barreled into the room, poising the metal paddle over his shoulder like a homerun hitter gripping a Louisville Slugger. Seeing Auchman staggering back from the door, blood pouring from his forehead and down his face, he swung the paddle with the same energy and twist of wrist that grand slams are made of, landing the flat of the paddle with a sickening smack across the fresh-fish's cheek. Saliva, blood and powdered teeth showered the brick wall behind him, and Auchman collapsed to the floor. A feminine scream echoed in the tower and he saw the bullish female CO charging him. With a backhanded swing of the paddle, he dropped her. As she started to crawl away, snaking across the floor, he stomped her flat-faced into the linoleum with a boot to the small of her back and knelt down, pressing the shank hard against her eye.

"Girl, you and I gonna party," he said. "But business first. Unlock the weapons locker and show me how to work the controls in here."

5:35 a.m.

. . . .

Captain Betty Salmon, Morey Unit security chief, arrived at the situation room that her officers had set up after alarms had sounded that an escape attempt was underway and that Lewis prison was facing a serious hostage situation. Buckeye police officers and Maricopa County sheriff deputies had already arrived. She was informed that assault teams were on their way and that FBI hostage negotiators had been called. A young lieutenant, Roberto Garcia, handed her a cup of coffee and the prison files on the two inmates up in the gun tower.

"And you said one of the hostages is a female?" she asked after reading about inmate Stephen Coy's history of sexual assault in his file.

"Yes, ma'am. Officer Friedman."

"Louise?"

"Yes ma'am." Garcia continued his debrief. "We've confirmed one officer has been injured. Inmate Coy apparently was running through the chow hall on his way to the tower when he was spotted by officers Roy Kelly and Liz DuBois making their standard rounds. In an altercation with Officer Kelly, Johnson slashed him across the face with a shank and proceeded to rush into the yard, making his way to the tower. After Officer DuBois sounded the alarm, a half-dozen officers converged on inmate Coy as he ran toward the tower. Officers managed to stop him with pepper spray. As he was detained, inmate Wassenaar stepped out from the tower and fired an AR-15 assault rifle at the officers. As he fired, inmate Coy was able to make it to the tower."

"So the weapons closet has been breached."

"Yes ma'am."

"Wonderful. Was there any other exchange of fire?"

"Not that has been reported."

The control room's phone rang. The light on the phone told Captain Salmon that the call was coming from the tower.

"Captain Salmon."

"Sorry to have woken you, ma'am."

"Who am I talking to?"

"This is Wassenaar."

"How are my officers, Mr. Wassenaar?"

"Officer Kelly's gonna need a doctor. He decided to attack a heavy metal kitchen utensil with his head. Weird."

Captain Salmon held her tongue, knowing she had to leave things up to the negotiators.

"Please release Officer Kelly so we can get him the proper medical attention."

Wassenaar laughed. "Let's make a trade. Officer Kelly is a fresh fish. Gi'me a lieutenant."

"I can't do that, Mr. Wassenaar."

"Well, then give me a sergeant." Wassenaar let out a laugh. "Ain't you gonna ask for my demands?"

"That's not my job at the moment. My job is to make sure my officers are okay."

"Well, we're getting hungry up here. I'd like a pizza delivered right to the door." Wassenaar paused, then said, "In fact, make that two pizzas and a helicopter."

Laughing, Wassenaar hung up.

CHAPTER THIRTY-SEVEN

Roger figured today would be the day. He was expecting to get the order to roll up and he'd be hitting the minimum security yard by noon. Instead, he awoke to find that no one was going anywhere. The entire prison was on security lockdown. Twenty-four-seven locked down in a hole with twenty incarcerated men whose only glimpse of freedom was that small daily window out on the caged yard.

Gone.

Tension would soon be running thick, tempers short.

Lockdown on the yard was the final yank of freedom short of being put in the hole. Freedom was marked by clicks on the clock. Two hours out, twenty-two locked inside. Two hours of freedom, one hundred and twenty-four ticks. All you had was time in the joint and Roger realized that unless you found the real freedom found in God's word, you'd go crazy fighting for less than a handful of clicks on a dial.

Lockdown meant no commissary, no store. Which meant no sugary treats; no salty snacks. And no cigarettes. Nicotine was just as much barter for goods as it was nectar for life. Chow hall was also cancelled. Meals of stale sandwiches were served in brown paper sacks.

The only thing that lockdown didn't stop was information flow. The bulls could lock the joint down airtight but the brick walls remained as porous as sponges. Within two hours the word was out. Two cons over on Morey Yard, a lifer named Stephen "Pony" Coy and a big-stripe named Ricky "The Rooster" Wassenaar jacked the gun tower and took hostages. One hostage was a mickie hack just three weeks on duty, blazed with Wassenaar's shank and taken out of commission. The other badge up there was a toots and Pony and The Rooster had her in the pen all to themselves, assault rifles at the ready to keep the goon squads at bay.

The first day passed with an eager anticipation that this would be over soon. The two cons up there would either make it from the tower and escape through the Administration building and turn up as coyote fodder in the desert, or this would end with the both of them on the tower floor, each with a sniper bullet in the head. But to Roger's disappointment, the anticipation was not of compassion for the hostages or the two fellow inmates out there, but a selfish desire to end the lockdown and get those few clicks of freedom back.

Information about the standoff flowed in daily. During brown-bag dinner chow on day three, Gordo shared the latest.

"Okay, so, word up on Pony," he said, pulling his sandwich from the bag. "He played Wassenaar on this whole thing."

"What do you mean?" Jimmy Smith said. Smith was a peckerwood who was allowed to sit with the Chicanos today. The race restrictions were relaxed during lockdown.

"Ok. So, a while back ago, an eighteen-year-old fish comes in fresh after spending the last four years as a guest wearin' the yellow shoulder stripes for Uncle Joe."

Roger knew he was referring to a juvie who'd spent the last four years in the Maricopa County jail on an adult beef. The hard-core juvies didn't go to State wearing the tan sweaters and brown slacks. They served hard juvie time as a guest of Sheriff Joe, wearing prison stripes and pink underwear. The juvie shirts were marked by yellow shoulders.

"There's a trusty wolf hound at reception, targets him. The trusty's earned his good time by brokering mules for all races except the Chiefs."

What broke Roger's heart more than anything was the pack-wolf mentality in targeting the young kids coming into the adult system out of juvie. No matter how hard core their rep on the outside was or how much time in the Maricopa hole had hardened them, they all hit the yard as young boys, entering a world of adult predators, baby birds barely protected by their pin feathers, fresh and terrified. If there was only a way he could get to them before they got here. Before they recycled one too many times through the juvenile system and ended up here.

God, show me the way. Show me how.

Once you hit the block in your pinfeathers, your options were limited. You get targeted the moment you hit the block by either some well-connected trusty or a long-timer looking to make points with some big-stripe matching your race. You're gonna mule and you're gonna mule hard, targeting who they tell you to target, hitting who they tell you to hit, pushing what they tell you to push; otherwise you join the yard queens or get a false beef tagged to your jacket that eventually either gets you a shank jammed in your side or a series of unwelcomed visits in the *baño*. Either way, no matter how you ranked in the juvie, you're a sewer rat in here and the pecking order gets worse the more you fight it.

Unless you find God, the road gets ugly. Without a walk with Christ, you will eventually get used to your role as a torpedo for the crew chiefs. It becomes your lifestyle. Mueling. Stabbing. Killing. Cleaning up the hit list. You're not allowed to think for yourself. The guys with juice schooled you and erased your identity, made you what they wanted, what they needed. You're a real hard-core torpedo, seasoned and valuable to the big-stripes and your benefactors.

Then one day they ask you to take out a young fish who broke one too many of the hard rules. As he showers unsuspecting, your blaze hits its mark and as the shank drains his life from his body he looks up at you, and his boyish face, eyes asking you *why*, reminds you of someone you once knew. Someone you knew too long ago.

You were eight years down on a ten-year beef, two more to go down the road and the journey was going to be over. But your last drop went bad and got caught up in prison politics. Like a good soldier you took the fall and your dime turned into a life-term. Now you feel you've earned enough stripes to walk away and do the rest of your time easy. You notify your benefactors and they smile nice and say, "Sure, enjoy your life." Two weeks later you're beat into a coma while taking a leak. Waking up in the infirmary, spending the next month eating liquefied food through a tube the croaker attached to your throat, you realize staying in got you a life sentence. Getting out would be a death sentence. And for the first time, you look back on it all and realize the true hopeless abyss your life has become.

The individual scenes are as unique and plentiful as individual inmate numbers but the script is the same and there are no surprise endings. At the end of the line there's a prison graveyard or family plot flooded in mournful tears and the unanswerable question, *Why? Where did it all go wrong?*

It all goes wrong without Christ, Roger thought. There had to be a way to get to reach these young kids with the truth of God's love before it was too late.

"The fish don't bite," Gordo continued relaying his intel. "In fact, he disses the trusty all wrong. So the guy makes arrangements for the kid to get sent up the road with some bad beef on his jacket. Magically, the kid finds hisself on Main Street, not fish row where he was supposed to go, and he's on the yard alone, no one to run with. No one wants him. The kid's jammed up and the word out is he's narked on some Big Homie— Mexican mob—and the eMes put the green light put on him. The wolf pack started moving on him one morning in the *baño* and that's when Coy stepped in. The bulls ended up calling it a day for the kid. He gets put in PC and Coy gets put on the eMe hit list. Coy's been trying to get either checked into protective hisself or get taken off the yard. But the bulls have been playin' hard nose with him. They know what happened. Coy saved 'em from having a dead fish on their yard and they thank him by jammin' up his case. That's the way the system works, man."

"So how'd he play Wassenaar?" Smith asked.

"Wassenaar's been a rabbit since he hit the yard. You know. Someone's always talkin' about givin' hisself a permanent furlough. Word up is Coy knew this thing would go bad but as long he can keep a sniper's bullet out of his bean, playing this thing out with Wassenaar would get him off the yard. Maybe even transferred to another prison."

Smith said, "Once you're on the eMe list, they can find you anywhere."

"It's the best chance he's got."

The days dragged on slowly and tempers rose in the run—especially for those needing their nicotine fix. There was no laundry duty so the peels ripened daily with the stench of body odor and jailhouse sludge. The walls remained porous and rumors and information flowed freely. The bulls finally allowed the inmates to fire up their TVs and the run got to watch the hostage standoff filtered through the eyes of the news cameras like the rest of the world.

As he watched the news on TV, Roger felt the convergence of two worlds—two lost worlds—a barbed wire world inside gray walls and another, free of chains and razor wire, but equally shackled in selfish pursuit and worry.

The well-groomed reporters stood outside the prison and lent their expertise as to what was going on inside the barbed wire walls. They babbled on about the barbaric history of Wassenaar and Coy and, as they dehumanized the entire prison population with their rhetoric, Roger felt a sudden, unexpected flood of compassion not only for the hostages up in the gun tower—but also for the two inmates. Around him there was no concern for the innocent lives at stake up there or for what was in store for the two men. They only cared about getting out of lockdown. Their store. Their smokes. An hour of freedom on the yard.

Outside, they sat in their living rooms and watched with indifferent voyeurism. The networks got their ratings. The audience got their freakish fix. But did the prisoners get their prayers? Their barbaric act deserved the outrage he felt as he watched the news coverage, but why the sudden compassion? Then the Holy Spirit reminded him of Matthew 9:36-38:

When he saw the crowds, he had compassion for them, because they were harassed and helpless, like sheep without a shepherd. Then he said to his disciples, "The harvest is plentiful but the workers are few. Ask the Lord of the harvest, therefore, to send out workers into his harvest field."

How many Christians were sitting around their living rooms now watching these events unfold, oblivious to the rich harvest behind the gray, barbed wire walls? How many were moved to prayer? How many were moved to join the few workers—the so many few—and reach the lost and helpless behind these bars?

Considering his own church's response toward his wife and family—not many.

It was no longer just a matter of reaching the lost behind bars. Outside these bars and chains he felt there was a whole harvest of God's children walking empty lives as Christians in name only. Their hearts needed to be turned. Their purpose needed to be defined. They had to be found. They had to be brought back into the loving arms of God—where he and only he would clarify their purpose in the limitless harvest of winning souls back to Christ.

The hostage standoff lasted two weeks. On Super Bowl Sunday, Wassenaar and Coy descended the gun tower stairs with their hostages and turned themselves in to the FBI negotiators. They were granted what inmate Coy had been seeking all along. Not only did Coy get himself removed from the yard but he was eventually transferred to a state prison back east, closer to his family.

Two weeks later, Roger got the order to roll up. It was after midnight when the captain clanged his baton on the foot rail of his bunk and told him it was time to go. As he bundled his things and walked through the maximum security doors for the last time, the razor wire chain link of the complex was bathed in the soft sodium glow of the yard lights. A quiet desert chill settled in through his peels as he stepped through the same door where he'd found the Bible jammed as a doorstop just under a year ago.

Off in the distance, he could see the Morey yard gun tower looming over miles of chain link, lights aglow, fully operational again. The crunching of his boots on the gravel disturbed the quiet night as he walked across the complex toward Bachman yard. As the metal doors of Stiner yard slammed shut, he sensed purpose in his time on the maximum security yard. The quiet spirit of Jesus Christ moved in him, letting him know that the nine months of his undivided attention to the teaching of God's holy Counselor had prepared him for the next level of his mission within the harvest-rich confines of the prison yards.

CHAPTER THIRTY-EIGHT

Thursday, December 9, 2004
11:42 a.m.

• •

The denim itched horribly, the state-issued blue jeans hung baggy on his narrow waist, the denim shirt two sizes too big and swallowing him whole. But it felt good to finally be wearing something other than the peels. Sitting on the splintered bench in the processing room, Roger looked up at the clock ticking slowly on the cinderblock wall. In twelve minutes the metal door in front of him would hiss, the gates would roll open, and he'd be walking through them into freedom.

God used the strict confines of the maximum security yard on Stiner to hold him close and allow the Holy Spirit to teach him and give him his vision. He released him to the medium security yard of Bachman where he had just enough freedom to start making God's vision for his life a reality. Prison politics were still around him, but medium security meant that your stretch had three to four years left. You were too concerned with doing the rest of your time easy to get caught up in the power struggle of the prison politics and the race leaders were a bit more lenient with who you dealt with.

Bachman yard allowed him to start his ministry. He had the freedom to hold regular Bible studies, minister across races, and use his commissary to help clothe and feed the less fortunate inmates. The confines of Stiner yard allowed him to mature in the word of God. Bachman was God's commission for him to start doing the word of God. God's promise in Proverbs 3:5, "Trust in the Lord with all your heart and lean not on your own understanding," sustained him on Stiner yard. And James 2:26 "As the body without the spirit is dead, so faith without deeds is dead," inspired him on Bachman yard to put God's truth into action.

With Bachman yard also came the privilege of one extra visiting day per week. Saturday was family day in visitation. Sirarpi came by herself on Sundays, allowing them to spend the entire day together. It was during this time that Roger realized God's true blessing on their marriage. They grew closer despite the bars and chains. Their time digging deep into God's word together every Sunday not only brought them intimately closer to Christ, but closer together, their bond strengthened in ways Roger would never have imagined. He realized the truth of God's promise in Jeremiah 33:3: "Call to me and I will answer you and tell you great and unsearchable things you do not know."

The great and unsearchable things God was showing him in his marriage and the incredible depth of his relationship with Sirarpi was eternally unsearchable. Razor wire, thick doors and chains could not destroy or break what God had brought together. It was just the opposite. Their trust in God's love and mercy was rewarded with an incredible love and closeness—and an unbreakable bond of a cord of three strands.

As the clock ticked slowly toward noon, Roger sat with his Bible in his lap, reading Deuteronomy, chapter 8. On Bachman yard, he'd taught in his Bible studies that Deuteronomy 8 should be required reading for every inmate getting sprung. Deuteronomy 8 was God's instructions to Joshua and the Israelites before delivering them from their 40 years of wandering in the desert into the Promised Land.

> "Remember how the Lord your God led you all the way in the wilderness these forty years, to humble and test you in order to know what was in your heart, whether or not you would keep his commands. He humbled you, causing you to hunger and then feeding you with manna, which neither you nor your ancestors had known, to teach you that man does not live on bread alone but on every word that comes out of the mouth of the Lord."

For forty years, God held his people close in the wilderness. During that time God was faithful. He provided. He revealed His character, promises and unyielding love and mercy. More than that, He was preparing them. The Promised Land was to be a holy place of worship, yet it was full of idol worship and horrific sin.

God had used the time in the desert to test and humble His people to rise up great warriors like Joshua in order to engage in the battle ahead to cleanse and prepare the land for his glory. As Roger looked up at the locked prison door, soon to open to his freedom, he felt the peace of the Holy Spirit, letting him know that his training was complete. He was going to walk out those doors like Joshua crossing the Jordan, trained up and ready for the battles ahead. Outside that door was a lost world. A harvest field full of lost souls who desperately needed Christ. God had gotten his attention using a barrier wall, wreckage and death. He used a corrupted legal system, incarceration, and loneliness to humble and prepare him. Now, the God of eternal love and restoration was sending him into battle.

The clock hit twelve and the doors rolled open. He got to his feet and started walking toward his freedom, his blues chaffing his thighs, his peels in a crumpled lump on the prison floor. As he stepped through the prison gates, his heart sang when he saw Sirarpi walking toward him from the parking lot, free, her arms opened wide. Romans 8:28 leapt in his heart:

"And we know that in all things God works for the good of those who love him, who have been called according to his purpose."

"Here am I, Lord," he said. "The workers are few and I've seen the plentiful harvest. My training is complete. Here am I, Lord. I'm ready—ready for battle."

EPILOGUE

(A Personal Message from Roger)

How does a man describe the moment when he steps from incarceration into freedom, hearing the prison gates slam closed behind him, the metal chambers rolling shut, sealing his life of chains and razor wire shut forever? How does a man describe his first few steps walking in a free man's shoes, stepping into his wife's long-awaiting arms, kissing her deeply, this time free from the confines of cinderblock and chains, brushing the tears of joy away from her delicate cheeks?

I had always thought that the term 'bittersweet' was a worn-out cliché until I stepped through those gates at Lewis Prison for the last time. There really are no words to describe the joy I felt holding Sirarpi again as a free man and the euphoria of returning home to my family after over twenty months away. What I *wasn't* expecting was excruciating heartbreak. I was leaving something behind in that prison. Something that I would never get back again. Something that I would never experience again.

Time.

Nothing but time to spend with God. And it struck me hard, the moment the winds of a free man's world swirled around me, the first scent of desert bloom, the first whiff of Sirarpi's sweet perfume—that I would never again have the opportunity to spend such intimate time with my Lord Jesus Christ.

When you get inside, they school you real quick the way it is in the joint. The first thing they tell you is that time does not matter here. Get used to it, son—you got nothing to do and a lot of time to do nothing with.

They were wrong.

The reality is, time is *all* you've got in the joint, and I learned to get selfish with it real quick. All I had was time. Precious time—time to be alone with God.

My time of incarceration was not a punishment for my past life, but a time to become more intimate with Jesus Christ—building an intensely personal relationship with Him that I never dreamed possible. I knew that Jesus never would leave nor forsake me but as I stepped through those gates and into my wife's arms, I still felt a sense of separation from Him that left a pit in my stomach that still aches to this day.

The ache made me think of Jesus' own time here. Jesus left the right hand of his father to come down from the majesty and trappings of heavenly kingship to this mess that God's people had made of His Earth. It must have been like a prison sentence to Him. In fact He was imprisoned—locked in a cell in the shape of a cross with two cellies, one to his right and the other to his left. The first believer to enter Heaven was in reality Jesus' own cellie.

God broke Him, to the point where His bones were pulled from their joints (*Psalm 22:14*). He was despised and rejected for His calling, beaten down by the people He loved—a man of sorrows, familiar with pain (*Isaiah 53:3*). He boldly accepted a calling as an innocent man who was to be pierced and crushed for sins He did not commit (*Isaiah 53:5*). Jesus' calling was such a fatal blow to the enemy that Satan went to work immediately trying to knock him off of His game, first by getting him to doubt who He was ("*If* you are the Son of God," *Matthew 4:3*); then by getting Jesus to doubt and test His heavenly Father ("Throw yourself down, for it is written, 'He will command his angels concerning you,'" *Matthew 4:5*); and finally, by tempting Jesus with worldly possessions ("All of this I will give to you if you will bow down and worship me," *Matthew 5:9*). Jesus persevered over Satan's attacks and boldly accepted God's call. God then refined Him through trial and pain, from saddling Him with twelve bold-headed, misfit disciples, to ultimately having Him pierced, beaten, bound and nailed to the cross. God's refining prepared Him to finish His mission, and God delivered Him. He is now reunited with His heavenly Father, sitting at the right hand of the almighty God. His majesty restored. King of kings, His name above all names.

God breaks. God calls. God refines.

God delivers.

That is God's process for deliverance. God's method of rescue. There is no avoiding it. If this is how He called His one and only begotten Son to His mission, what makes anyone think that it will be any different for us?

God broke me by using precision machinery and a concrete barrier wall. I responded to His call and Satan immediately went on the attack. I doubted. I tested God rather than acting in faith. I was tempted back into the things of this world. But I pushed through, accepted God's call, thinking this meant things would get better—only to enter God's refining process. Bankruptcy. A harsh and often corrupt legal system. Incarceration. Separation from my family. God prepared me for His deliverance. He used my trials for His ultimate rescue and complete restoration.

God used my incarceration to plant the vision of reawakening the church of *Acts*. He handed me a vision to reach the least of these brothers behind bars in a unique way and to challenge the Church to love and forgive all sinners as the Acts Church did two-thousand years ago.

After my release, I immediately applied for badge access to return to the state prisons as a volunteer. I knew that the state law prohibited ex-felons from volunteering in the prison system, but I thought of the liver-spotted Earl and his feeble wife Bea, God bless their souls, coming into the prison, reaching the lost on the fumes of their aging bones. If God really needed me back there, He would provide a way. All things are possible with God. And by His grace, I soon received my acceptance letter in the mail with my badge. The next day, I was back on Stiner yard, bringing the word of Christ to my brothers without the constraints of chains, bars, or prison politics.

But God refines. And then He refines a little more. And a little more.

Not long after I launched my ministry on the very yard where I had spent 20 months of incarceration, the state suddenly recognized its error and pulled my badge. I was heartbroken not only for the brothers that I was suddenly prohibited from reaching behind bars—but also for the juveniles that I so desperately wanted to reach.

Pulling my state credentials meant that I was prohibited from entering the state juvenile complexes as well. Imagine that. I entered my life of crime as a teen. I took my first toke of weed as a sixteen-year-old varsity football player—and was facing death row just nine years later. The juvies needed to know my story. They need to learn from my mistakes. But I quickly learned that the walls of bureaucracy were thicker than the razor-wired walls of the prison yard.

But God refines.

God redirected me. The County jail system allows ex-felons to volunteer after two years clean on the outside. I was finally able to get badged with the Maricopa County Sheriff's Office and started one-on-one mentoring with jail inmates. It started off slowly at first but after my testimony made the cover story in *Prison Living Magazine*, the ministry literally exploded.

I started training volunteers and eventually my home church, Christ Church of the Valley (CCV), used my mission as the foundation of its prison ministry. CCV adopted my vision of reaching all sinners including sex offenders (who are the lepers of today's society) without judgment of past sins. In late 2012 our organization became a separate entity known as Rescued Not Arrested (RNA) through a CCV-sponsored organization called Mission Create.

Through this venture, God opened doors for us to reach churches nationwide, and soon, by God's great grace, worldwide.

We established a sound mission of bringing awareness of the real needs of the incarcerated and to educate churches in effectively ministering to all God's children without categorizing their sins. Our ministry team soon grew to over 100 volunteers and no paid staff. We quickly surpassed reaching over 3,000 inmates and loved ones each month and holding regular baptisms in the county jails. Through CCV's bookstore, RNA was soon the only prison ministry providing NIV Life Application Study Bibles upon request to any of our incarcerated brothers and sisters. Our Bible ministry distributed over a 1,000 Bibles in the first year.

The biggest challenge in launching my prison ministry was reaching the juveniles. For six years my heart broke daily because of my inability to enter the juvenile system. There were two juvenile homes situated between my home and CCV—Adobe Mountain and Black Canyon Juvenile Corrections. My spirit stirred every day as I drove by them on my way down to mentor inmates in the county jails. I knew that God wanted me to bridge the gap and use CCV's resources and people to connect with those kids. I was able to enter on a one-day visitor pass and was promptly told that my record prohibited me from returning.

But God's delays are not God's denials. Working from the outside, God blessed me with a team of committed brothers and sisters to lead an outreach team into the boys and girls facilities. Within six years, we grew the juvenile ministry to over fifteen volunteers, ministering through church services, mentoring and events such as soccer clinics, pizza parties, puppet shows and holiday concerts. Annual turkey donations ensure that kids detained in the juvenile homes experience a real Thanksgiving each year.

Despite God's continued blessing on the juvenile ministry, my heart still ached to get within those walls and personally impact the youth. I continued trusting God, believing that in Him, nothing is impossible.

Sure enough, in July of 2011 the Arizona State Juvenile Corrections Director announced his retirement. As a first order of business upon taking office, his replacement introduced new legislation that would open the doors for a select few ex-felons to be considered for badge access to the juvenile facilities. In November 2012, the bill was signed into law by Governor Jan Brewer. However, given my legal jacket with the state of Arizona, I did not qualify. But the staff and leaders of Arizona Department of Juvenile Corrections were so impressed with my commitment to these kids that they made a way for me to enter the facilities.

December 1, 2012, was the first day I entered Adobe Mountain in over six years. My passion and enthusiasm for reaching these young boys and girls made such an impact on the juvenile correctional leadership that for the first time in state correctional history, they asked an ex-felon to join the Directors Religious Council Committee. This allowed me to meet regularly with key juvenile corrections decision makers, allowing RNA to have a major impact on how to connect with these kids in life-changing ways.

God delivers.

I'm not throwing these numbers and statistics out to impress you. I want you to see that God has a plan for your life, and He is in the business of deliverance. You need to look at your situation not as a time of punishment or misfortune. We chose the name 'Rescued Not Arrested' because we believe that God never stops seeking to rescue us from our broken paths. God knew what was around the next corner for me when I was racing out of control on a highway of drugs and violence. Had he not stopped me with that barrier wall and gotten my attention in the rancid stink of a county jail cell, I would still have been in the thick of the drug cartel when the Feds infiltrated the organization—and would have certainly been put away for the rest of my life.

It would have ended in either a life sentence of incarceration—or death after facing the wrong end of a gun or a drug deal gone bad one too many times. Those were the only two choices on my broken path. And I am certain they are the only choices on yours as well if you continue to refuse to hear God's call.

Even if you are reading this and you are not incarcerated or living a life of crime but are living in disobedience to God, you are not only missing out on His richest blessings and a personal relationship with a Lord who's absolutely crazy about you, but your path is the same as those who are incarcerated. The only difference is God allowed the jail cell to be the instrument of their correction. What is He on the brink of using to get your attention?

If it is sexual disobedience, you're heading for a disease that can kill you. If it is alcohol or drug disobedience, a wrong twist of the steering wheel or a missed red light is all it's going to take to cause permanent disfigurement or death to yourself—or an innocent victim. If you are contemplating divorce, the tearing apart of a union-of-one brought together by God is worth a thousand deaths.

Stop listening to Satan's lies. See God's rescue.

He's reaching, desperately reaching for you now.

Wherever you are, God wants to bring you home to Him and plant your feet firmly on the path He has ordained for you. A path to freedom. A path with purpose—planned for your life before one day ever came to be (Psalm 139:16). God is a jealous God (Exodus 25:5). He does not want you to have any other gods before Him (sex, drugs, money). And He will allow the pain to come into your life because He wants to bring you to a place where He can show you how all things are possible through Him—and how He can and will abide in His eternal promise to work all things for the good of those who love Him (Romans 8:28).

God breaks. God calls. God refines.

And trust me—God *always* delivers.

Unfortunately, most do not make it past the broken part of God's path to deliverance. It's heartbreaking to realize that most people do not even make it one quarter of the way to ultimate freedom from chains that bind them. They continue to rely on the god that bound them in the first place, and, as is the case with following any false god, the consequences are disastrous.

My path has crossed many of the characters of my past as my ministry has grown. Simen pushed his case on to trial and he beat the rap. As the state of Arizona was assembling the jury for his trial, he visited a plastic surgeon and had his face altered just enough so that the witnesses could not make a positive ID on him. He walked, a free man, but although his surgeon was able to change his features enough to set him free, the gifted doc could not change his heart. He eventually went down heavy on a federal drug beef several years later.

Sally D's choices landed him homeless and dealing on the streets for survival. I didn't recognize him the day I responded to his tank order—his cry for help from his jail cell—and went to visit him in the 4th Avenue Jail. It wasn't until halfway through my visit with him that I saw a flicker of recognition in his sorrowful, pleading eyes.

"I know you, don't I?" I said.

"Yeah. It's me, man. Sally D. I was your DJ once. You put a gun to my head."

"Now I want to put a Bible in your hand."

"Man, I was *it* back then, wasn't I? What happened to me?"

He'd built a jacket so thick that he finally got sent up on a ten-year stretch for his final beef—a petty theft of a bong pipe from a downtown smoke shop.

Tony Rizzo cleaned up his act, but he hasn't yet discovered the peace that comes from Christ's ability to completely erase your past. Not long ago on a family ski trip I saw Tony ahead of me in the lift line.

As a joke, I walked up behind him and stuck my fingers in his back and said, "This is it, Tony." His face flushed white and he nearly turned the snow around us yellow.

He didn't understand what I meant when I called him brother and told him all was forgiven. Yeah, he's leading a clean life, but he continues looking back, fearing the day someone comes up behind him, this time with a real gun.

And despite my efforts with Arnulfo, he continued through his revolving door with the prison gates, getting sent up regularly on everything from domestic disputes with his latest shack-up to beefs involving burglary. He couldn't seem to shake thinking he was the king of the Blockbuster knock off. He's fallen off the radar screen for now. I'm sure our paths will cross again one day. Hopefully I'll see him in an ADOC hole somewhere and not in some county cemetery. As long as he's still alive, there's hope for God's rescue.

"As a dog returns to its vomit, so a fool returns to his folly" (Proverbs 26:11).

Like the day the doctor had to re-break my leg and fix it the right way, how many times have we returned to our own vomit—ignoring the master surgeon and relying on our own healing—only to have God break us again in order to heal us according to His plan? Every time He has to re-break us, it causes more pain and healing than He'd intended. But He is a selfish God—selfish for you. He is eternal and wants to spend eternity with you, and He will do whatever it takes to bring you back to Him. Because once those doors slam shut at the end of time it will be too late. God does not want for a single one of his children to be eternally lost and in the tormenting grips of the enemy.

God is crazy about you.

If you are reading this and you have never yielded your life to Jesus Christ, don't you think it's time to listen to His call? Don't you think it's time to use the circumstances—the chains that bind you now—to be set free by His perfect love? By the blood shed for you?

If you believe that you are a Christian—if you'd said those words of acceptance of Christ and yet you still feel the conviction of sin in your life—is it time to finally ask yourself the hard question, "'Am I a Christian in name only?"—am I a "labeled Christian."

I was a labeled Christian from birth to age twenty-five, professing to be a Christian because I was born in a Christian country. It took complete wreckage and death before I realized the destructiveness of living such a lie. You may be like I was, professing to be a Christian because of your heritage or perhaps based on an emotional moment in the past where you raised your hand at an altar call and repeated a "sinner's prayer." You've been walking with the label of Christian, but have you really committed your life to understanding the truth of God's word? Or have you continued living a sinful life without intentionally committing obedience to God?

Generations ago sinners' prayers and altar calls were effective because of our solid Biblical foundation and commitment to God's truth. However, as generations passed we have fallen further and further away from God and our tolerance for sin has increased. Even within the church, the erosion in obedience to God's word has allowed for degrees of sin to become acceptable.

It is rapidly becoming increasingly evident that the world is impacting the church—rather than the church impacting the world. But God's mercies are new every morning (Lamentations 3:23). He is faithful in bringing the lost back to Him.

So where are you today? Has God brought you to a place where you have lost everything? To where you see no hope? To where the intensity of the darkness surrounding you is beyond what you can bear? If so, realize that this is not God's judgment—this is God's call.

He has allowed darkness to enter your life to wipe the slate clean in order to begin writing His story in your life, starting today. Return to Him and receive His instruction. Job 22:22—23 promises: "Accept instruction from His mouth and lay up His words in your heart. If you return to the Almighty, you will be restored."

God breaks. God calls. God refines.

God delivers.

Your Damascus moment has come bringing the dawn of a new beginning. Choose to respond and reap the harvest of the dawn of a new day—of a bright future living in the eternal light of Jesus Christ.

Your Damascus moment has come at dawn.

You do not need to stay in the chains and allow yourself to stay under the arrest of your circumstances.

My friend—you are rescued—not arrested.

The End

TESTIMONIALS

Saying that thousands of lives per month are reached through the Rescued Not Arrested ministry short changes God because attempting to count God's infinite blessings and abilities to restore lost lives is simply impossible. I think that's part of the reason why God became so angry with David for taking a census and counting the Israelites (2 Samuel 24:1-3). It's almost as if God was telling David, "Do your job and leave the counting up to me. You cannot fathom the lives that I am reaching today. I am building a mighty army by restoring broken lives." That's because David saw his people throughout Israel for the day and the battle at hand for the now. God saw His people throughout the World for tomorrow—and for the eternal battle ahead. He saw your life; He saw my life; He saw every broken life that He was ready to set free from the bondage and chains of a broken world. The chains of addiction; the shackles of hate; the agonies of the broken heart. God's restoration is eternal and with meaning. He is giving broken lives purpose, giving them new citizenship—residents of Heaven—and enlisting them in His mighty army, marching to victory against Satan and his rebellious army, and rescuing the lost—bringing them back home to Himself.

But God uses testimonies to train, inspire, and overcome the Evil one. God promises in Revelations 12:11, "They triumphed over him by the blood of the Lamb and by the word of their testimony; they did not love their lives so much as to shrink from death" (New International Version). Below are a mere handful of the countless testimonies that are coming about as the Rescued Not Arrested ministry continues reaching the lost behind bars, including my own. As the writer of Roger's testimony, I faced an insurmountable challenge that I had not expected—but one that Christ used to reveal the depths of His eternal love for me and to clarify the incredible mission He has for me as a loyal soldier in His army of righteousness. It is my prayer, fellow Brother or Sister, that Roger's story and these testimonies inspire you to turn your life completely over to Jesus Christ and allow Him to unlock the chains that are binding you today so that you are free to experience all that He has in store for you. It's an incredible journey.

With the eternal love of Jesus Christ,
--H. Joseph Gammage

The Author's Unexpected Testimony of Recovery and Restoration in Writing Roger's Story

I was blessed to discover my God-given writing talent at an early age. Before the age of sixteen I had written my first full-length novel. It was a crime novel, steeped in gang violence, a subject that for some reason fascinated me as a young boy. When I heard my calling into ministry, God used my writing talents to write skits and productions for Children's ministry. But my true passion continued to be writing about crime. My mystery-suspense novels were far from Christian-based— rooted in the values of a crooked and fallen world. Little did I know that the day I had met a twelve-time felon by the name of Roger Munchian how God was about to turn my talents for writing crime fiction from entertaining the world to serving His eternal Kingdom.

While in ministry with our home church, CCV, my wife at the time and I had joined a CCV neighborhood group, the group to which Roger belonged. A week rarely went by when Roger would not share his testimony as a former drug lord living a fast and reckless life. I was inspired by how God used a speeding car, a sharp highway curve, and an 85 mph impact with a barrier wall to slow him down—and to get his attention. It was the kind of swashbuckling intrigue that I loved to write about. Wow, of all the hundreds of crime-filled pages I had written, of all the hundreds-of-thousands of thuggish words I had penned—Roger's life-story was one that I could not make up. The real life Roger had lived was one way beyond even this crime writer's wildest imagination.

When our paths crossed, Roger was just starting in his prison ministry. He was mentoring just a few inmates a week at the Maricopa County jails and had no volunteers. But when his testimony was published in *Prison Living Magazine* and circulated throughout the County system, hundreds of requests a week were pouring in for mentoring. During one neighborhood group meeting, he shared a vision that if God could reach hundreds of incarcerated lives through one magazine article circulating in the prison system—think of what He could do with a full-length story. God nudged me to approach him. This was a powerful testimony. Certainly he had dozens of authors vying to write his story. When I nervously asked him if he had a writer on the project, he said no. Then he told me that one woman had started writing his story, but abandoned the project after her marriage came under attack by the Enemy. He gave me a copy of the unfinished manuscript and told me that if this was something that I wanted to take on, to let him know.

On vacation, my wife and I went on a SCUBA diving trip down to the Turks and Caicos and I took the half-written manuscript with me to read. Dear Brother or Sister, I never had a more powerful vision what God wanted me to do as I had during that trip. See, I had run a very successful Executive Search business for over 17 years, but at the time we were on the cusp of the 2009 Financial Meltdown. We owned two homes—upside down on both, and investment property up in Northern Arizona that had plummeted in value. Deep down, I knew that my business was done. But I felt a rush of peace after getting the vision, God telling me, "I've blessed your career and your business all these years, and you've remained faithful in the gift of writing I gave you. This is what I want you doing now. Trust me. I will provide."

My wife, sadly, did not get the memo on that. When I took on the project, I did not realize that in writing Roger's story—my own story was about to become a testimony as well.

So this is where my story really begins.

In Matthew 14:22-32 Jesus sent the disciples ahead of Him across the Sea of Galilee—on their first mission trip, so to speak, without him physically there with them. They obeyed, and immediately came under Satan's attack with a ferocious storm. I believe that's what happened to me. After I started the project, the storm hit: we lost both of our homes and my business flat-lined. But I pressed on, and not only did God have me writing Roger's testimony, He also called me into prison ministry. I became a badged clergy volunteer for the Maricopa County Sheriff's office in Arizona, and my faith, knowledge, and walk with Christ grew deeper by mentoring inmates in the dark places of the Maricopa County jail system. After over fifteen years in Children's ministry, the truth of Hebrews 5:12-14 was revealed to me: "In fact, though by this time you ought to be teachers, you need someone to teach you the elementary truths of God's word all over again. You need milk, not solid food! Anyone who lives on milk, being still an infant, is not acquainted with the teaching about righteousness. But solid food is for the mature, who by constant use have trained themselves to distinguish good from evil" (New International). Fifteen years of ministry and I was still drinking the milk like an infant in Christ. God convicted me that if I was going to be reaching the lost in dark places like the county jails, I needed to learn to eat the solid food of the truth in Jesus Christ.

But the storm intensified. My wife decided to leave the marriage. Forced to move out, everything I owned, except what I could fit in a 5x8 storage unit and in the back of my truck, was hauled off by a St. Vincent DePaul truck. Just as Satan wanted to stop the Disciples ministry, he wanted to stop mine—and he pretty much succeeded. When Satan attacked the disciples with the storm, Peter at least had the guts to jump out of the boat and run to Jesus. I chose to cower in the boat and fled to the bottle. Looking at single parenthood, financial bankruptcy, and an uncertain future, I found comfort in alcohol and a reckless life-style that I thought I could keep secret. On the outside I was a devoted father, loyal employee, and a dedicated minister. Inside, I was crushed and dying, self-medicating with alcohol and out carousing in unhealthy, reckless relationships that I thought could fix my shattered heart and fill the excruciating void that divorce leaves deep in the soul. I remember leaving the barstool one evening to attend a prison ministry meeting, stuffing my mouth full of breath mints and peppermint candies, fooling myself, thinking I could mask the smell of booze. Roger was not fooled. The next day when he called me out on my behavior, I thought he would be furious with me. Instead, he simply said:

"Joe, I love you, brother. I am worried about you."

"I am dead inside, Roger. I am sorry I let you down. I am so, so dead inside."

"You did not let me down, Joe. I am here to talk if you need me."

This is the genuine heart of Roger Munchian—full of the kind of unconditional love and compassion that can only come from an unwavering walk with Christ.

I did take Roger up on his offer to talk. However, it was simply to tell him that I was stepping down from the prison ministry. But I did not want to quit writing his story. Something deep down inside me—deep below the deadness and decay I felt in my heart and soul—did not want to give up on the book, and I did not want Roger to find another author to pick up yet another failed attempt to write his story. Yet even though I told him I was still working on the book—I really wasn't. I'd type a few sentences here and there between hangovers and self-pity, but it really wasn't going anywhere.

But God never gave up on me. Pealing my hung-over eyes open one morning, I watched Joyce Meyers preaching the message about the Bethesda pool in John 5:8 where Jesus looked at the invalid and said, "Get up! Pick up your mat and walk." God telling me to "Get up! You're acting like this thing has crippled you. Get up—pick up your troubles and get to work."

I picked up my mat, but the toxin of booze did not let me get very far. I eventually showed up at Roger's home ready to tell him that I was calling it quits. But before I could get the words out, he opened up Acts 22:10 where Paul had just been knocked flat on his back. Paul asked Jesus "What shall I do?" Jesus simply answered, "Get up, Paul." Jesus again telling me, "GET UP!"

This time I got up. When I told Roger that I wanted to get back into prison ministry, I thought I would have to go through the process of getting my volunteer badge renewed. To my surprise, Roger told me that he never cancelled my badge.

He said, "I knew you would be coming back."

Typical Roger. He had faith in me even though I had given up on myself.

Finding a flash of hope, I started forcing myself to get up early every morning and pushed forward with the book. My appointment with God was the insane hours of 4:30 to 6:00 every morning. Each morning I woke up without a clue what I was going to write. Revitalized only with the smell of coffee and a shot from God's Word, I sat down at the keyboard and let the Holy Spirit take over. To my amazement, the words poured across my screen. Morning after morning God filled the pages with words of His choosing, not mine. I have never experienced such a presence of the Holy Spirit. After several incredible months of this—day after day of feeling God's workmanship through my fingertips tapping the keyboard—I wrote the two most cherished words of any author: "The End".

The book was finished, but my own journey to sobriety was only beginning. Every day is a new day of victory in Jesus Christ over alcohol. As with anyone with an addiction, it is a not an easy struggle, but as long as I take up my mat daily, He gives me the strength to make it through—reminding me that He has rescued me from the chains of my own making. He has also delivered me from my desire to seek reckless relationships—delivered me and rescued me before I got arrested or faced the destruction that was the certain destination of the secret road I was traveling. Only He knew where that dark and lonely road was headed— and He chose to rescue me. I will stay rescued as long as I stay grateful, seek first His Kingdom, and keep my feet firmly planted on the path that He ordained for me. His path. Not my path. His will. Not my will. As God promises in Proverbs 16:9, "In their hearts humans plan their course, but the Lord establishes their steps" (New International Version).

I've seen God do incredible things serving in jail ministry. I've seen the bulkiest, tattoo-covered men who have seen nothing but blood and murder all their lives completely break down, shedding tears they have not likely shed since the doctor first smacked them on the behind at birth. I've seen prison gang leaders turn from the iron-fisted leadership of violence and brute intimidation to leading jail pods of hundreds of chained men in prayer. I got to listen to a young inmate, barely in his twenties, telling me, "I can face the next twenty-eight years in prison. But what I can't face is eternity in Hell, and there's nothing I can do about it. I am going to Hell for what I have done." I got to see palpable fear and excruciation in his eyes dissipate to peace and joy when I told him, "Hell is not for you! You belong to Jesus Christ—He paid the price of His blood for you to be with Him. There is *nothing* you have done that cannot be forgiven by His blood." I got to see the complete transformation—to literally feel the shroud of evil lift from him—as he accepted Christ that day. I will never forget the joy on his face, the new bounce in his step as he danced back to his cell, Bible in his hand, a new citizen of Christ's Kingdom.

Rescued—not arrested.

Outside I watch the evening news and see a broken and lost world. Behind the razor wire and cold cinderblock walls of the jails—I see true revival!

Most importantly, I have seen my own life turn around. This ministry is reaching people on both sides of the prison walls. I am looking forward to seeing what Jesus Christ has next for me on this incredible journey, and I am looking forward to hearing from you, dear Brother or Sister in Christ. You can always reach me through www. rescuednotarrested.org or at www.hjosephgammage.com. I am eager to learn how our Lord and savior Jesus Christ has touched your life and has begun a permanent and eternal restoration that can only come from the one true Master.

--H. Joseph Gammage, Broken and Renewed by
the Loving Hands of Christ

Former Nazi Skinhead now Leads Prayer Circles Behind Prison Walls

I cannot remember where I chose to become full of hate that I only recognized my identity as a Nazi Skinhead. To be honest I don't even remember what made me so angry with everything, but for the first half of my life I was a ranking Skinhead who was always in and out of prison.

In 2009 I was again on my way to prison, ready to allow the hate to continue to consume me. Then in came my Brother Roger. We were in the middle of a hunger strike in the Maricopa County Jail. I was bored

271

and had seen Roger's testimony in the *Prison Living Magazine*. I sent him a postcard and had not expected to get any response or something asking for money for prayers. What I received from Roger is something money can't buy and only through God could my "arrest" become "rescued."

Roger came to visit me a week or so later and he was able to do something *no* one has ever been able to do for me in my entire life. Roger showed me a God that loves me, will always be there for me, and offers a friendship that never dies. Roger has never given up on me and has taught this angry, punk Skinhead how to love.

To see me, this tattooed-from-head-to-toe "Nazi", leading the prayer circle every night, teaching others about God's love is only because of what God has done in my heart. Roger Munchian and Rescued not Arrested loved me enough to see beyond my exterior painted with hate and introduce me to that God.

--Garrett Deetz, former Nazi Skinhead—
now loyal Disciple of Christ

Mother of a Young Offender Finds Hope as Her Son Finds Christ Behind Bars

During the most frightening and overwhelming times right after my son's arrest, Roger Munchian visited him in County Jail. I had found Roger's name and phone number on our church website. He was listed under prison ministry.

Not knowing who to turn to and who to trust, a Godly man was most reassuring to a worried Mom. Roger introduced my son to the Gospel and gave him hope for a future no matter what happened to him. This was something I had always wanted for my son, but never expected it to happen while he was behind bars. Roger had an easy-going way of making my son feel valued and accepted while slowly presenting him with the truth and comfort of God's word.

As my son grew more interested in the Bible, Roger spent time one-on-one mentoring him and helping him to gain an eternal perspective on his life. Church services were held at the jail, and my son, along with some of his cell mates, began attending. Word spread quickly of this minister who accepted them unconditionally and did not seem to care about the charges they were facing. All were equal in his eyes and they learned that Jesus sees them all as sinners needing a Savior.

Small Bible studies began sprouting up among the guys and my son actually took the initiative to lead one. As the seeds were planted, I saw a change in my son and he began to accept his situation along with any consequences he faced.

A very stressful situation was turned into an opportunity for tremendous growth and maturing in his walk with the Lord. My son accepted Jesus as his personal savior!

Roger continues to keep in touch with my son as he serves out his sentence in prison. Another volunteer from Rescued not Arrested has been writing to my son during this time and writes to hundreds more faithfully. Roger has been an invaluable support to me also. He is there whenever I need to call on him for any type of help or encouragement. I well up with tears when I hear of the amazing things that are evolving through Rescued not Arrested. Not only are offenders being rescued from a life of darkness, some are returning to the jails after release to minister and help with baptisms.

Roger's dedication and commitment has allowed RNA to grow from a tiny, one man outreach into a very powerful influence in our jails and prisons. He has been obedient to God's call on his life and inspires so many to follow and serve, and trust God for the results.

--Nancy A. Morrow, Faithful Mother,
Grateful For the Unceasing Love of Christ

Through Tragic Loss and Incarceration—the Prison Yard is now his Mission Field

In January 2011 I had been arrested and put in jail, not realizing that I was soon to be rescued. Naturally, like many other people, I felt that I was beyond saving. I had many opportunities in the past to change my life...

but I didn't. In county jail there were a few different denominational services offered and in addition there was the service that Roger offered. As many times as the jail would offer, I would attend this "spirit filled" service. It was so inspiring. The jail limited how many of us could attend. When they didn't open my cell door, I was disappointed. This is something that I really looked forward to. Emphasis was placed on seeking the truth, developing and building a relationship with Jesus, and reading scripture in context. Learning truly where salvation comes from and all that Jesus did for us, "the Gospel of God's grace."

I continued my personal Bible studies and would see Roger at the services. It wasn't until over a year later that I started meeting with Roger personally through his one-on-one mentoring. This was so much better. I felt so good after our meetings and would normally share with others what had been shared. With his help, my root continued to grow as I continued my Bible studies. I had also enrolled in the correspondence Bible study course that he recommended.

In jail, we have many negative and depressing surroundings which I had to continue to fight and lean on the Word of God for my strength. The Devil is there and ready to try and uproot you if you will allow him. My greatest trial was on February 16, 2013 when my brother came to see me through the video monitor to tell me that my wife of over thirty-four years had passed away. Through my tears, I was praying with questions of why? I thought of Ezekiel's wife being taken from him in Ezekiel 25:15-18. I immediately began thanking the Lord for all the years that we did have together. I was not going to allow the Devil to bring guilt into the picture. What I did not know is that before my brother came to see me, he remembered me mentioning Roger's name. He didn't know his last name, but quickly found him on his prison ministry website, www.rescuednotarrested.org. He had already called Roger and explained what had happened. Roger made a special trip down to the jail on that very weekend that I had received the news to see how I was doing and to help strengthen me with scripture. He did not do this out of obligation. It was truly from the heart that he came. This meant so much to me that he was there to help me through such a terrible time. Like I said, it's not out of obligation, it's him doing "God's will".

Roger and his ministry truly made a difference in so many people's lives. He puts a Bible in everyone's hands who asks. Just like Jesus said in Matthew 7:7-8 "Ask and it will be given to you; seek and you will find; knock and the door will be opened to you. For everyone who asks receives; the one who seeks finds; and the one who knocks, the door will be opened. Roger also operates on this scripture. He has inspired me to develop and lead different Bible studies and to help others grow in their walk with Christ.

After spending 3 years in county jail, I was sentenced to fifteen-years in prison. I am writing this from behind the prison walls. Including my county jail time, the state has chosen to punish me with eighteen years of incarceration for my crimes. But Christ has chosen to forgive me, to completely forget my past, and to bless me with an eternity of freedom from the chains of man—and of my own making.

After the news of my wife's passing, I knew that I had lost everything on the outside. There is nothing out there for me now. This prison is now my mission field as I continue to share "the good news". Despite the thick walls and razor wire, I am truly free in Christ—and I get to show other prisoners here how they can find that freedom for themselves. I can't think of a more important mission. Christ has chosen to use my brokenness to set the lost and hopeless free.

I continue to stay in touch with Roger and Rescued Not Arrested and include his ministry in my prayers. Roger, thank you for doing God's will and helping us all to be rescued through Jesus our Lord. The Lord is truly number one in my life and I pray that you will allow the team at Rescued not Arrested to help guide you in the truth. Roger shared with me about how important our testimony is by referencing Revelation 12:11 "They triumphed over him by the blood of the Lamb and by the word of their testimony; they did not love their lives so much as to shrink from death." May God bless you in abundance through the knowledge of God and of Jesus our Lord.

--Dan Wharton, Christ's Missionary to the Lost behind Bars

School Teacher and Coach Learns that He is God's Child—not a Modern-Day Leper

I will never forget that day in September of 2006. The principal of Liberty Elementary School walked into my classroom followed by a slew of Buckeye police officers. They told me I was under arrest, and the next thing I knew I was being processed through intake in the Maricopa County Jail. Locked inside a cinderblock holding tank feeling alone and like nothing more than a number, I was not aware that on the outside my name was hitting the news—all the major Phoenix area news outlets clamoring to get the scoop on the elementary physical education teacher turned sexual predator.

I bonded out of jail and spent the next nine months of working my way through the legal system. My sentencing date came and I went from being Josh Jacobson, Liberty Elementary School District teacher and soccer coach, to "Sex Offender". The Arizona Republic clearly defined me in the August 22, 2007 headline: "Former Teacher to be Sentenced for Sex Abuse". Wow. Making headlines in the AZ Republic; every major local news outlet vying for my interview; my name on the lips of the public. I had always dreamed of one day being a major celebrity—but not this way.

The world heard "Sex Offender". All I heard was *Former* Teacher." My life's passion of educating our youth and teaching the fundamentals of my life-blood—soccer—was gone forever.

I was not a celebrity—but now a member of today's equivalent of the leper in Jesus' time—a sex offender.

Yes, I had made some bad choices. Up to the point of being arrested I thought that I was a good person, never using illegal drugs, rarely drank alcohol, always treating people kindly. I knew of God and believed in God, which led me to believe that with all of those things I was most likely headed to Heaven. I mean, I was better than most people, right? Well, God answered that question loud and clear when my cell door slammed shut: NO. Behind bars was where the path of my own choosing had led me. But God had a very different plan in store for my life.

In October of 2007 I signed a plea deal and was sentenced to nine months in Maricopa county jail with lifetime probation. Putting on my

Maricopa County Jail stripes, I realized that I could either make this next nine months the most miserable time of my life, or use the time to do something positive with my life. I had no idea that making that choice put me on a path to meeting Jesus Christ face to face.

On New Year's Eve 2007 I called my girlfriend, Maria, which I did every night. This time she said someone from the CCV was going to come and visit me and that she wasn't sure when. When she said CCV I knew what she was talking about because while I was out on bond my roommate at the time had invited us to go there a couple of times. I also played in CCV's coed soccer. Not knowing what or who to expect, I thought it would be a few days. I was wrong. The very next morning on New Year's Day I was taken out of the pod for a visit, which was weird since we only got visits on Wednesday between noon and 2. But I went and met Roger from the CCV prison ministry. This was my first real face to face time with Jesus Christ. We talked about my up-bringing and about my beliefs. I told him that I believed in God, which to me meant that I was in good with the Big Guy. At which time he showed what the Bible says in James 2:19 "You believe that there is one God. Good! Even the demons believe and shudder." He also shared his testimony with me, which was amazing to see the hand of Jesus working to change someone's life that dramatically. I went back to the pod that day with a lot of questions and some deep self-examination of my life and choices. I prayed to Jesus and asked for forgiveness and accepted Him as my Lord and Savior that night. My life plan made a 180 degree turn that night—and I will never turn back.

Roger continued to minister to me for the rest of my sentence. He didn't stop there. When I was released from jail, and I knew that my new-found freedom opened up a lot of choices that I could make and limitless paths I could take—most of them bad if I was not plugged into Godly people. Roger connected me to a Bible study group and to church so that I could keep my feet firmly planted on His path for me and live out one of my favorite life verses, John 15:5: "I am the vine; you are the branches. If you remain in me, and I also in you, you will bear much fruit; apart from me you can do nothing" (New International Version).

I am now married to my beautiful wife Maria, and we have two beautiful children—true gifts from God. Yes, I will be a registered Sex

Offender for the rest of my life. We use the term "modern-day leper" because our offenses are the only crimes that require us to forever wear a label of shame—leaving us shunned—even most churches turning us away. I praise God that CCV is not one of those churches. My family has been welcomed as loved members of that congregation and I am a co-leader of the same men's group that accepts all men in despite the choices of their past. I give all glory to Jesus.

I can't even imagine where my life would be without Jesus and the people that He has brought into my life. It took a nine-month jail sentence for me to become the man that God wanted me to be. Every day I do my best to understand His plan for my life and to live it out, especially in recognizing that my plan only leads me into chains. It is not easy being a Christian, I have to be intentional every day to pray and get into the Bible, but there is more peace now with my new perspective of this life being temporary and also because my life is not my own.

Thank you to those that minister in the Devil's land of jail and prison. And I want to give a big thank you to Roger Munchian and his God given passion and vision.

In Christ, Joshua Jacobsen, Redeemed Disciple of Christ

Atheist Husband's New-Found Faith Reaches His Family from Behind Bars

My husband Brian was arrested December 28, 2012. During intake in the Maricopa County jail, he was handed a Bible, which is unusual. From my understanding, a Bible is something that needs to be requested through a tank order once an inmate is processed through to their housing. Since it was "contraband", receiving a Bible that day was a miracle in itself. Either way, Brian was an atheist, so receiving a Bible at the lowest point of his life only angered him more. But jail intake is a long and seemingly endless process. Moving from tank to tank awaiting his time in front of the judge, he finally peeled open the pages and started to read. That is when God began working on his heart.

He hung onto the Bible and kept it with him in his cell once he was placed into Lower Buckeye Jail. A few weeks later he was told about "this guy" who had an interesting story of how God had gotten his attention. Skeptical, he put in a tank order to have "the guy" come see him. A few days later, he met Roger Munchian through the mesh wire of his jail pod's visitation room. Roger shared his "interesting story" with him, but, more importantly, Roger shared the love and mercy that was free to him through Jesus Christ. Eventually, Brian became a believer and accepted Jesus as his personal savior.

Brian's turn was genuine and not a jailhouse prayer. He was able to make bail and continued his new walk with Christ on the outside. He became a Christ-centered leader in our home, and led me to seek Christ as well. I always believed in God, but didn't think that I deserved His love. Brian's commitment to Christ showed me how wrong I was.

Our family started attending CCV, and as a couple we joined Roger's neighborhood group. Brian also started attending Roger's Wednesday night men's Bible study. Roger approached me one day and shared with me that he saw a need for a similar Wednesday night group for women and asked if I would be interested in leading it. I didn't think I was qualified being so young in the faith, but I stayed obedient to God and have been leading the group ever since.

Brian's faith not only reached me, but also his sister Kelly. On May 19th, 2013, Roger baptized the three of us at CCV. Shortly after, Brian was sentenced to one year in County jail. He recognized it as not being sentenced—but stationed. God stationed him in the darkness of the jails to reach His lost. He became a Bible study leader in his pod and used his time of incarceration to grow closer to God and teach the truth of the saving grace and deep love of Jesus Christ.

I continue leading the Women's Wednesday night Bible study and have joined Rescued Not Arrested to mentor other wives, daughters and mothers who are facing similar challenges that I faced. I help them with the comfort and hope I received through the love and grace only Christ can offer. I am also actively involved in serving at CCV. Life is still challenging, but knowing the Lord is walking beside us and guiding our way has lifted the Devil off our shoulders and allowed us to show our true strengths. What an amazing change God brings about! It's one of peace and trust. We thank God every day for our very breaths and praise Him for everything in our lives. It's not easy but it sure is rewarding knowing that God the Father is with us in every way and is always in control.

Praise God and thank you Rescued Not Arrested and CCV.

--Tina and Brian McInerney, Loyal Servants to His Kingdom

Diagnosed with Life-Threatening Disease Behind Bars—Inmate Finds Eternal Life

I started going to services with Roger while at Maricopa County's 4th Avenue jail. This was my first time ever in jail, so it was quite stressful for me and my family.

I started going because I had heard Roger was from CCV, the church I attended on the outside. It was so easy to relate to his style of teaching because he had been in my shoes. He knew what I was going through. Although I attended church, I was not saved and had not accepted Christ as my savior yet. That happened because of Roger's spiritual mentoring.

A few months after accepting Jesus Christ as my personal savior, I was diagnosed with Hairy Cell Leukemia. They put me in complete isolation in the jail infirmary. They stripped me of all of my personal possessions and locked me away in a glassed-in infirmary cell. Roger came to see me and tried to get a Bible to me, but they would not let him. He argued with them and would not give up. He knew that I needed to have the Word of God in that isolation cell with me. Finally, they told him the only way they could allow for a Bible in my cell was if it was brand new and wrapped. Roger left and returned promptly with a brand new, wrapped Bible that he was able to get into my hands. I could only imagine the looks on their faces when Roger walked back in holding that new Bible.

Roger prayed with me and I was totally at peace with whether I lived or died because I knew I was going to be with Jesus and I give it all to Him. And for that I will always be in debt to Roger for getting me to that point in my life through his ministry.

--Darren Stanley, Eternal Citizen of Heaven

From Suicidal Thoughts to Living for God's Kingdom

October 2010. I was feeling far from rescued sitting in that tiny, cold second-floor chapel in Maricopa County's 4 Avenue jail. The pastor leading the service had us turn to Colossians 1:13-14. He explained my life of sin had led to my predicament. "God has rescued you!" he said. "He is giving you an opportunity to turn from your sinful life, to a new life of hope and purpose in Christ Jesus!"

Facing a potential twenty-eight years in prison without hope and feeling suicidal, I gave my life to Christ and looked forward to those weekly services and one-on-ones with my pastor, Roger Munchian. I know he shuns titles and prefers to be called "brother". Still, I consider him the shepherd God sent to lead me through two years of county jail wilderness.

Roger spoke to my heart, like he was reading my mail. It was obvious, even before hearing his testimony, that he shared from experience and knew exactly what I was going through. I remember messages of hope and purpose, of life service not lip service. Also true repentance leads to true life change. Doing your best and trusting God with the rest. Roger's ministry made sure we all had study Bibles. He and his faithful volunteers, week in and out, taught us how to study and apply God's word to our lives. Matthew 6:33-34 was taught often. Seek first His kingdom and His righteousness, learn to hope and think eternally. All the worries that a pre-sentenced inmate dwells on, the upcoming court dates, the past life of failures and sin, the "could'a, should'a, would'as", Roger gave scripture like these in Matthew to show us the way.

It's awesome to see how God is using Roger and his ministry team to reach the "least of these", even the worst of the worst that most jail ministries and churches neglect. I am so eternally grateful to my Lord and savior Jesus Christ for putting a faithful man of God like Roger in my life. I am excited to read his book and see the path that led us to meeting in that cold, second-story chapel, and even more excited to one day, Lord willing, join Roger's ministry team.

--Kirk Holloway, Shepherded by Christ—Living for His Kingdom

Chains of Addiction Broken by the Love and Grace of Jesus Christ

Rescued Not Arrested has had such a huge impact on my life. I am one of many success stories that have been born from this wonderful ministry. My journey with the ministry began in 2008. I was addicted to heroin and my addiction landed me in jail.

After my parents bailed me out and we all came to the startling realization of the severity of the charges I was facing, we ran straight to the church. Our church home, CCV, directed us to the prison ministry and that was when I first met Roger. I was terrified, so afraid of the mess I had made for myself. I had no idea what to expect and was so ashamed and frightened.

Roger met with my family and assured us that everything was going to be okay—trust in God's perfect plan. Roger was by my side for the next nine months as I fought my case. He accompanied me to various court dates and even spoke to the judge on my behalf. After all was said and done, I was sentenced to prison—my biggest fears becoming reality. But still, Roger reminded me, "Remember, Sister Jenny, God has a plan for you."

Out of a one-year sentence, I only had to spend four months and 23 days. Praise God! I used my time to grow closer to the Lord and to share my experience, strength, and hope with those around me. In that time, I was provided a bible and study materials to aid in my growth and knowledge of the Lord.

After my release, I had a rough few years. I finally ended up checking into rehab and by the grace of God, I found myself once again. Over all of the years and through all of my struggles it was amazing to me how so many things changed, but I always knew Roger was rooting for me, letting me know that his ministry was growing and he needed a soldier in God's army like me to do big things for the ministry.

I am proud to say that I am now serving as head of the women's mail mentoring program with Rescued Not Arrested and applied for my volunteer badge to go back into the jails and mentor women inmates one on one. The opportunities that I have because of this ministry never cease to amaze me. I share my testimony often and take every chance I can to help others know that there is hope.

I was rescued, not arrested. It has been a crazy journey, but one that I would not trade for anything in the world. The journey was twisted and crazy—but it led me to the loving arms of Jesus Christ. I am a grateful recovering addict and I desire nothing more than to help those who still suffer. This ministry helped save me and now it is my duty to help others. Thank you, Roger, and thank you to all who are involved in this life-changing ministry.

--Jenny, Saved by Grace Through Faith

The Author

Photo taken by Ovadia Milan

H. Joseph Gammage received his MBA from Grand Canyon University in 2012 and spent more than 15 years writing and producing dramas for Children's Ministry while raising a family and building a career in the Executive Search business. Inspired by his research in writing Rescued Not Arrested, he followed God's direction into prison ministry where he mentors inmates in county jails. Joe is currently seeking God's direction in adapting other true-life testimonials into life-changing stories. A father of two, Joe resides in Phoenix, Arizona where he attends Christ Church of the Valley (CCV).

9 780692 144374